A People of
MISSION

A History of General Conference Mennonite Overseas Missions

James C. Juhnke

Faith and Life Press
Newton, Kansas

Library of Congress Number 78-74809
International Standard Book Number 0-87303-019-2
Printed in the United States of America
Copyright © 1979 by Faith and Life Press
718B Main Street, Newton, Kansas 67114

Design by John Hiebert
Printing by Mennonite Press, Inc.

MENNONITE HISTORICAL SERIES

FROM THE STEPPES TO THE PRAIRIES
Cornelius Krahn, Editor

PLOCKHOY FROM ZURIK-ZEE
*The Study of a Dutch Reformer
in Puritan England and Colonial America*
Leland Harder and Marvin Harder

EXILED BY THE CZAR
Cornelius Jansen and the Great Mennonite Migration, 1874
Gustav E. Reimer and G. R. Gaeddert

JAKOB HUTER
Leben, Frommigkeit, Briefe
Hans Fischer

A CENTURY OF WITNESS
The General Conference Mennonite Church
Cornelius Krahn and John F. Schmidt, Editors

PRAIRIE PIONEER
The Christian Krehbiel Story
Christian Krehbiel

MENNONITE COUNTRY BOY
The Early Years of C. Henry Smith
C. Henry Smith

A LEGACY OF FAITH
The Heritage of Menno Simons
Cornelius J. Dyck, Editor

FAITH IN FERMENT
A History of the Central District Conference
Samuel Floyd Pannabecker

A PEOPLE OF TWO KINGDOMS
The Political Acculturation of the Kansas Mennonites
James C. Juhnke

OPEN DOORS
A History of The General Conference Mennonite Church
Samuel Floyd Pannabecker

A PEOPLE OF MISSION
A History of General Conference Mennonite Overseas Missions
James C. Juhnke

Foreword

The vision which provided the impulse to found the General Conference Mennonite Church was a desire for unity and a call to mission. At Wadsworth, Ohio, in 1872, the first Board of Missions was formed. Samuel S. and Susannah Hirschler Haury were the first "foreign" missionaries sent by that board to serve among the Oklahoma Native Americans. It was not until the turn of the century that the General Conference engaged in overseas missions. P. A. and Elizabeth Dickman Penner of Mountain Lake, Minnesota, were commissioned and sent to India in 1900.

Early General Conference world missions was a cooperative venture among a relatively small group of churches in the eastern and central states. Mission concern rapidly spread across the United States and Canada. Although the vision of foreign missions did not stem primarily from Anabaptist foundations, an evangelical fervor gripped many church leaders during the first and second decades of the nineteenth century. From scattered Mennonite communities in North America, the General Conference people broke out of their cultural and religious isolationism to become part of the greatest Christian missionary movement in history.

During my childhood and youth, I heard the missionary story in the First Mennonite Church, Berne, Indiana. My earliest recollection is Martha Burkhalter, missionary to India, dressed in a colorful sari, teaching Hindi songs to the children. The sometimes controversial S. F. Sprunger had been pastor of this church, serving also as member of the early General Conference mission board. His personal involvement as a board member led him to emphasize the need and call of foreign missions to his congregation. World mission emphasis was similarly highlighted by succeeding pastors. Missionary commissionings, mission messages, and missionary slides, presented by many sent overseas from the Berne congregation, made a deep impression on me. Some of my initial impressions, however, were negative.

The missionary vision was rekindled for me in a non-Mennonite college, Taylor University. Through playing basketball in Asia and Latin America in the early fifties, I had an opportunity to see missions and missionaries firsthand. Through these experiences God led me to prepare for the Christian ministry. Six years as a missionary in Colombia, South America, gave me a personal experience with and exposure to both the myths and realities of foreign missions. Although the realities of overseas missions sometimes dampen enthusiasm, missions has been the key in my understanding of the purpose and nature of the Christian church.

A People of Mission is a story which describes a pilgrimage of a conference of churches engaged in overseas missions for almost eighty years. I feel close to this story because it puts my involvement in historical perspective. This history gives a fresh interpretation of the motivations, moods, and methods which inspired a particular Mennonite people to send missionaries to Africa, Asia, and Latin America. The author has consciously written a mission history with people at the center of a movement that has shaped the image of the General Conference in this century.

James C. Juhnke portrays missionaries as neither saints nor sinners, but as committed Christians who believe in obeying the Great Commission. Missionaries are human beings—flesh-and-blood people who struggle, fail, and succeed often against great odds. The author clarifies many of the myths and misconceptions which have grown up around foreign missions. He criticizes various aspects of the Mennonite mission movement for failing to perceive the times clearly. There is something in *A People of Mission* to offend and please everyone connected with General Conference world missions.

Each country in which the Commission on Overseas Mission is presently involved is treated by the author. Of special note are the chapters on India, China, and Zaire (Congo)—the first three countries to which the General Conference sent missionaries. The whole historic panorama of twentieth-century missions—imperialism, dependence, independence, the birth and growth of the church—is described in these chapters. The book relives the events and retells the experiences of a people living and acting out the Great Commission. A small struggling ethnic church, inspired by a missionary vision, sends its missionary apostles to share Jesus Christ and establish His church in strange and unknown places. I sense something of the same dynamic when reading the Acts of the Apostles.

A People of Mission is history, but it is more than history. It is a tribute to the thousands of God's people who since 1900 have participated in making the Great Commission the heartbeat of the General Conference Mennonite Church. At a recent retreat of the General Board, one church leader said, "A general mission emphasis, which has remained very strong, to my mind has been one of the keys to the 'success' of the GCMC. Without it, I believe there would no longer be a GCMC."

The value of this volume is not only for this generation of Mennonites but for the next generations who carry the responsibility to be "a people of mission" in the twenty-first century.

Howard J. Habegger
Executive Secretary
Commission on Overseas Mission

1 January 1979
Newton, Kansas

Preface

Every generation must write its history anew, not only to claim the heritage of the past but also to reinterpret that heritage in the light of demands in the changing present. This historical essay on the course of General Conference Mennonite missionary movement has been written to celebrate and to reevaluate the achievements of that movement.

There is at present a good deal of ferment in Mennonite circles, and in Christian churches generally, on the meaning of missionary endeavor. This book, while not directly addressing issues of missions theology or strategy, is written from a background of growing conviction that missions based on Anabaptist-Mennonite beliefs are, or ought to be, in some measure distinct from conventional Protestant models. Mennonites have much to contribute to, as well as to learn from, the current missions dialogue.

This story represents a small fragment of Mennonite experience and a tinier fragment of the larger church in the world. While a representative fragment may reveal something of the quality and meaning of the whole, it is also important to recognize what has been excluded from the fragment. Three disclaimers are in order. First, this book is not a comprehensive chronicle but rather an interpretive survey. Many people, institutions, and events in General Conference missions history have not been mentioned in the text, but this is no reflection on their importance or significance. The purpose was not to strive for completeness, but rather to portray missions history in the light of concerns which are uppermost in our minds at this moment in time.

Second, this book represents a North American point of view. It does make some effort to take into account the meanings of mission work for receiving peoples and to highlight the emergence of national churches as the goal of missions. But people in other lands and cultures will have to write their own histories if we are to understand what it has meant and what it means to be a Mennonite in India, Zaire, Colombia, Japan, and elsewhere.

Finally, the focus upon overseas missions in this book tends to force an unnatural separation between overseas missions and missions within North America. The work with Native Americans in particular is slighted by this artificial division, and is treated only briefly in an introductory section in this book. By the same token, the Conference of Mennonites in Canada gets somewhat shortchanged in this telling, since their involvement in what is here defined as overseas missions comes relatively late in the story. A history of General Conference Mennonite home missions work is presently being researched and written.

I want to thank the many people who helped me during the year of research and writing which was available for this project. The work was commissioned and supported by the General Conference Commission on Overseas Mission. Bethel College provided a sabbatical year. Howard Habegger, Robert Kreider, and Muriel Thiessen Stackley served as an advisory committee to help brainstorm the conception of the project and to faithfully read and comment upon drafts of the chapters as they emerged from the typewriter. Dozens of additional people helped by sharing information from their memories and archives, by hosting my wife, Anna, and me on our international travel, by submitting to persistent interrogation, and in many other ways. I am grateful to all who have made this such an enjoyable and enriching year. I look forward to continued help in filling the gaps, correcting the errors, and reaching for insights in the ongoing quest to understand and to celebrate our missionary peoplehood under God.

James C. Juhnke
North Newton, Kansas
September 1978

Contents

Mennonite Indian School, Cantonment, Oklahoma, 1909

1 Prologue

Roots of Mennonite Overseas Missions

An Age of Heroism

"What is it," asked Mennonite missionary Peter A. Penner of his leprosy patients in Champa on the plains of India, "that crawls on all fours in the morning, on two at noon, and on three at night?" [1] It was the riddle of the Sphinx, posed by the ancient Greeks half a millennium before Christ. The answer is man. Man crawls on hands and knees as an infant, walks upright on two legs as an adult, and bends over with a cane in old age. Penner gave the leprosy patients one night to think about the riddle. When he told them the answer the next day, they marveled at his wisdom.

P. A. Penner was a man who walked on two legs. From the time he arrived in India right at the turn of the twentieth century (December 1900) until his retirement in Newton, Kansas, four decades later, he guided the Mennonite missionary effort from uncertain infancy into vigorous maturity. His was the heroic age of Mennonite missions. In those pioneering days mission "stations" stood on the edge of jungles full of dangerous wild animals, and missionaries risked life and limb fording rivers to preach the gospel to natives who had neither heard of Jesus nor seen a bicycle. It was the colonialist era. Missionaries built strong, imposing houses, churches, and hospitals. P. A. Penner, together with others of his generation in India, Africa, and China, planted institutions built to last.

But it was only a part of the task of this heroic generation to establish a missionary enterprise and bring it to maturity. The deeper purpose of the *mission* was to plant and to build the *church*. The preaching of the gospel and witness to Christ's love must bring forth a new community of believers. The missionary wisdom of those days set the high goal of native churches which were self-governing, self-supporting, and self-propagating. It was quite possible to have a thriving *missions* enterprise, with successfully functioning orphanages, schools, and hospitals, and at the same time to have an anemic national *church,* lacking in leadership, confidence, and resources.

When P. A. Penner died at mid-century, the Mennonite *mission* in India was in the flower of an extended maturity. At the same time, the Mennonite *church* in India was struggling to emerge from an extended infancy. While the mission was striding forward on two legs, the church was crawling on hands and knees. The church in India bore the marks of low-caste social origin. No measure of missionary nurture—or of missionary withdrawal—could erase these marks. But the times were changing.

A new generation of missionaries in the years after World War II had to come to terms with a radically different world in India as well as in other mission fields. Colonialism was dead and dying. The new frontier was in the jungle of tangled relationships between mission and church. The mission must decrease and the church must increase. Missionaries now had to overcome the very habits which had earlier worked to build a thriving mission program—the voice of authoritative command, the use of available funds from a wealthy constituency, the temptation to call more workers to staff growing mission institutions. If the national church was to grow, the missionaries would somehow have to withdraw from doing that which they knew how to do best.

It was not easy for the North American church to adjust to the new age of anticolonial nationalism and to the bewildering demands for a "moratorium" on missions. Much had changed, both at home and on the field. The mysteries of infancy, adulthood, and old age seemed so unkind to missionary enterprise. It was easy to think back to simpler days when P. A. Penner enjoyed asking riddles of a band of admiring leprosy patients.

Twice-Born

Mennonite missions is a twice-born movement. It was born the first time in the sixteenth century in the missionary consciousness of the Anabaptist left wing of the Protestant Reformation. Within a single century this early missionary thrust burned itself out in fires of persecution, dispersion, and sanctuary. It was born a second time in the nineteenth century when Mennonites latched onto a great worldwide Protestant missionary movement which had grown out of eighteenth-century Pietism and a subsequent evangelical awakening. The relationship between these first and second births is of critical importance for the understanding of the history of General Conference Mennonite overseas missions in the twentieth century.[2]

The first birth occurred in the 1500s. Anabaptists—neither Protestant nor Catholic—emerged holding a doctrine of the church as a voluntary body of disciplined believers who seriously endeavored to follow God's will and to reconstitute the early church as revealed in the Bible. Their view of Christian discipleship included mutual economic responsibility and refusal to participate in warfare. They were a missionary people. They set apart apostles and charged them with the responsibility to go out and to call others to regeneration and new life in Christ.

This first Anabaptist-Mennonite missionary movement did not survive, in part because the main-line Protestant Reformers rooted it out with the sword. Luther, Calvin, and Zwingli saw Anabaptists as heretics and subversives. The sixteenth-century establishment mind could not conceive of a state made up of different denominations of Christians, much less a stable state in which the majority might choose not to be Christian at all. The Anabaptist emphasis upon voluntary choice and upon practical discipleship seemed to contradict the Reformers' views of God's sovereignty and man's depravity. And so these Reformers—who themselves lacked a missionary consciousness— allied themselves with government power to banish and to kill the heretics. By the tens and the hundreds Anabaptists were hunted down, imprisoned, and slaughtered. The persecution was successful in scattering the Anabaptists into isolated and rural areas where they lost their missionary zeal and became content to practice their own increasingly legalistic way of life.[3]

In its second birth, on the other hand, Mennonite missions emerged in alliance with Protestantism. A great reversal had taken place in the three centuries after the Reformation. Anabaptists, who had been the only people of the Reformation to generate an effective missionary movement, gradually lost the memory of their missions-oriented beginnings. They took on the characteristics of an ethnic group, albeit one which held onto such doctrines as New Testament discipleship, a two-kingdom dualism of church and world, refusal of military service, and sharing among the community. Meanwhile the Reformation churches, which had had no missions consciousness in the sixteenth century, slowly awakened to a missionary movement which in the nineteenth century became one of the major forces of world history. Nineteenth-century Mennonites, whose Anabaptist forebears had had the missionary spirit beaten out of them by Protestant persecutors, now came to drink at Protestant wells for the renewal of the missionary spirit. The modern Mennonite missionary movement, then, did not take shape as a kind of recovery of the Anabaptist vision. It rather was fashioned by Mennonites who had been awakened to the missionary task through contacts with missions-minded Protestants.

Beginnings in Europe and Russia

Nearly eighty years before Peter A. and Elizabeth Dickman Penner and John F. and Susie Hirschler Kroeker established the first General

Conference Mennonite overseas mission stations in India, Mennonites in Europe were supporting Christian mission work in India. William Henry Angas, an English Baptist preacher, helped organize a Mennonite-dominated missions society in Holland in 1821 for the purpose of supporting English Baptist mission work in Serampore, India. Three years later Angas toured among Mennonite congregations in Prussia, Poland, Bavaria, Switzerland, and France to stir up the missions spirit.[4] In West Prussia, Friedrich W. Lange, a Mennonite boarding school teacher at Rodlofferhufen (1826-35), subscribed to missions periodicals published by mission societies at Barmen, Basel, and Herrnhut, and read the missions reports to his students and their parents.[5] He put a missions collection box at the door of the school. Lange later moved to the new Gnadenfeld colony in South Russia, where he became an elder and helped promote missions as a top priority of church congregation concern. Conservatives in Mennonite congregations resisted the missionary thrust as an innovation from the outside—something alien to the tradition, something allied with the dangerous influence of Pietistic enthusiasm. But increasing numbers of congregations found the movement a source of new life and introduced missions festivals and special services at Easter, Pentecost, and Christmas to raise funds for missions and foster the missionary spirit.

The scattered Mennonite missionary interests found a new focus in 1847 when the Dutch reorganized their aid society for Baptist missions into a Dutch Mennonite Missionary Association. Pieter Jansz became the first missionary of the association, going to Java in 1851. Heinrich Dirks of the Gnadenfeld church of South Russia went out under the Dutch board and founded a new mission station in Sumatra in 1871. Contributions for the Dutch work came from Mennonites all over Europe, but the support from Russian Mennonites eventually came to predominate to the point that this mission became "a Russian building with a Dutch facade." In some years the Gnadenfeld church alone gave more money for the mission than all Dutch churches combined.[6]

European Roots for "New" Mennonites

The first Mennonite missions thrust in America was a movement which grew out of these European roots. The origin of the General Conference Mennonite Church can be traced formally to the reforming branch of an 1847 schism among Pennsylvania Mennonites whose American roots were over a century old. The "New" Mennonites of the schism, led by John H. Oberholtzer, hoped to awaken the church through Sunday schools, education, publications, reformed church organizational procedures, and emancipation from some of the traditional rules regarding dress. Mission work among "the heathen," however, was at the margin, rather than at the center, of Oberholtzer's concern.[7]

It was recent Mennonite immigrants from South Germany who called the meeting at West Point, Iowa, the second day of Pentecost in 1860, that resulted in the organization of the General Conference. Daniel Hege, an immigrant Mennonite teacher who had been educated in Switzerland, set forth the missions imperative in the 1861 meeting of the conference:

> If we as Mennonites are not to increase our guilt by longer neglecting the duty of missions as commanded by the Lord . . . we must, not singly, but as a denomination, make missions the work of the Lord. . . . If we would undertake our mission duty, we first need Christian educational institutions.[8]

The first generation of Mennonite missionaries in North America got their training in a seminary founded at Wadsworth, Ohio, in 1868, by this union of "New" Mennonites (with centers in Pennsylvania, Ohio, and Ontario) and immigrant Mennonites (with strength in Iowa, Illinois, and Indiana). No proper superintendent to lead this school could be found among the uneducated and isolated American Mennonites, so the conference turned to Europe and invited Carl Justus van der Smissen of Friedrichstadt, Germany, to head the enterprise. Van der Smissen was a Mennonite pietist who had studied for three years at the mission school in Basel and had been a vigorous supporter of the Dutch Mennonite mission in Amsterdam. He was fifty-seven years old when he came to America, but he had visions for the future. He dreamed of an international Mennonite mission organization growing out of the Dutch mission work but eventually involving American financial support, missionary personnel, and participation in mission board administration and policy. Van der Smissen sent his first Wadsworth-educated protege, Samuel S. Haury of the South German immigrant group, to advanced study at the missions school in Barmen in Germany. Preliminary contacts were made for Haury's placement under the Amsterdam board.

When Samuel S. and Susannah Hirschler Haury founded the first North American Mennonite mission to the "heathen," however, it was under the General Conference Mennonite mission board, and it was on the North American continent among the Arapaho tribe in what was then called Indian Territory. The General Conference wanted to direct its own mission work. The Amsterdam board, for its part, would not have been willing to give up any part of policy control of its own work. Van der Smissen's dream was further eroded when the Wadsworth school closed in 1878 due to lack of support from a geographically and ethnically diverse constituency. But this founder of the American Mennonite mission endeavor had the satisfaction of seeing his students—S. S. Haury, D. B. Hirschler, H. R. Voth, and others—build an expanding mission work among the Arapaho, Cheyenne, and Hopi tribes of Native Americans.

A Skeptical Constituency

This new missionary movement was not born of easy congregational consensus. Young men educated at Wadsworth were fired with a new vision that fairly exploded upon the conservative consciousness of Mennonite churches of their day. The missions spirit was allied with everything that seemed proud and modern: the desire for Bible learning which would go beyond what the preachers at home could teach; the eagerness to go to the ends of the earth to rout the devil in heathen strongholds; the willingness to abandon the styles of the forebears in language and dress.

The return of Samuel F. Sprunger to his home congregation in Berne, Indiana, after a year and a half of study in Wadsworth, may not have been untypical:

> He carried a Bible under his arm, something most extraordinary, and he was utterly changed in appearance. No longer did he wear his homemade coat with a standup collar. His coat was too long and it didn't have the right cut. He wore a stiff white collar and a white shirt with a black stripe. And he wore a supposedly silver watch chain, a very thin thing about ten inches long that had cost him fifty cents. That really was enough excitement for one day, but more was to follow. He was asked to give the testimony that day, and as we have said before, the one who gave it always remained seated. But not Sammie, he shocked the audience by standing. The congregation kept silent, it was a breathless moment. Then he astonished them again, for he no longer spoke in his mother tongue! . . . (T)he old patriarchs of the church thought it sheer pride.[9]

The generation gap opened by such youthful proponents of prayer meetings, Sunday schools, and missions was accentuated by their insistence that the church of their parents was filled with dry bones. Missionary candidate S. S. Haury wrote that among Mennonites "nonessentials and insignificant things are emphasized and held fast, and the main thing, the foundation essence of Christianity—the new birth and the spread of the kingdom of God—is lost from attention and forgotten, indeed not even argued and struggled over."[10]

The new Wadsworth people represented the wave of the future for a General Conference Mennonite Church which put progress in Christian missions and education at the top of the agenda for coming decades. But it is worth noting that conservative Mennonite critics were not without justification in their warnings against the worldly pride, the *Hochmut*, which seemed implicit in the style of this new missionary generation. The Mennonite genius for a separated and simple life had scriptural warrant as surely as did the Great Commission. The *Martyrs Mirror*, which stood second only to the Bible as the shaper of Mennonite identity, reminded the congregations of days past when so-called Christians persecuted the church with fire and sword. Was there not great danger in becoming unequally yoked with worldly Protestants who knew not the ways of Mennonite discipleship and nonresistance? Was not this missions movement—and the modern religious enthusiasm that came with it—simply a lure to seduce Mennonites away from their historic commitments and identity? What was to be gained by joining this latest Protestant bandwagon?

Such questions, posed in a variety of forms and situations, informed the dialogue among American Mennonite leaders, congregations, and groups of congregations in the last third of the nineteenth century. Tangled in the argument was the difference between "New" Mennonites and "Old" Mennonites, going back to the 1847 schism.[11] Most Mennonite congregations in America chose not to join the new General Conference, which saw itself as a unity movement for the eventual unification of all Mennonites of North America in one common cause.

Waves of Immigrants

The "Old" Mennonites paid a high price for their aloofness from the General Conference and the missions cause to which that conference was pointing its energies. In the 1870s there occurred a massive migration of Mennonites from South Russia to the open land on the prairie frontiers of Kansas, Nebraska, Dakota, and Manitoba. Nearly all of these immigrants opted to join the General Conference, even though the "Old" Mennonites had provided generous support in the immigration process. John F. Funk of Elkhart, Indiana, a progressive leader in the awakening movement among the "Old" Mennonites, worked tirelessly for the Russian Mennonite immigrants as treasurer of the Mennonite Board of Guardians. Funk developed more contacts with the many immigrant groups, and performed more services in their behalf, than any other single person.

Why, then, did the immigrants from Russia join the General Conference? Heinrich H. Richert, elder of the largest immigrant congregation—Alexanderwohl—played a key role in this decision. Richert was one of the strong missions supporters among the immigrants. He was a close friend and correspondent of Heinrich Dirks, Russian Mennonite missionary in Sumatra. Already in 1876, not long after settlement in central Kansas, Richert attended a meeting in Halstead, Kansas, of the Western District of the General Conference (a district which then included congregations all the way from Halstead, Kansas, to western New York State!).[12] That meeting led to Richert's election to the mission board of the General Conference and to Alexanderwohl's joining of that conference. Richert's nephew, Heinrich R. Voth, had been interested in a missionary career already before

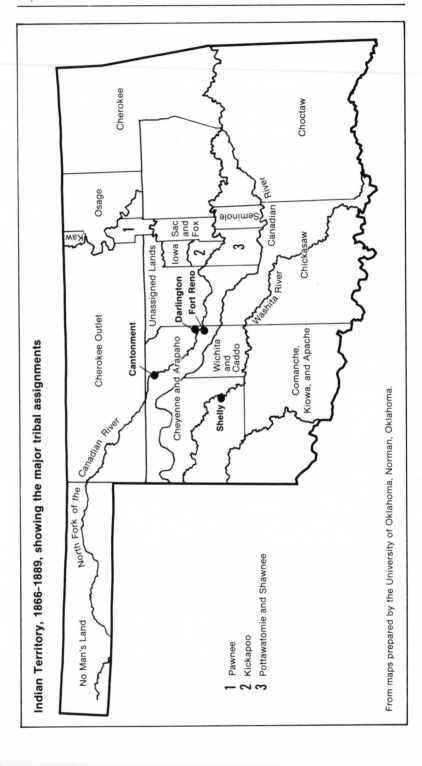

Indian Territory, 1866-1889, showing the major tribal assignments

No Man's Land

North Fork of the

Canadian River

Cherokee Outlet

Kaw

Osage

Cherokee

1

Unassigned Lands

Iowa

Sac and Fox

Cantonment

Darlington

Fort Reno

2

Seminole

3

Canadian River

Choctaw

Cheyenne and Arapaho

Wichita and Caddo

Shelly

Washita River

Chickasaw

Comanche, Kiowa, and Apache

1 Pawnee
2 Kickapoo
3 Pottawatomie and Shawnee

From maps prepared by the University of Oklahoma, Norman, Oklahoma.

immigration. Shortly after arriving in Kansas, Voth wrote to John F. Funk in Elkhart asking if American Mennonites had a mission program. Funk responded in the negative and directed Voth to the Dutch board in Amsterdam. Voth then turned to the General Conference and was quickly accepted as a missions candidate. He went on to study under Van der Smissen at Wadsworth and to become a missionary to the Cheyenne and Hopi tribes in Indian Territory and Arizona. Richert, Voth, and the Alexanderwohlers paved the way for others. The Russian Mennonite immigrants, already quickened to the missions spirit in the old country, came into the General Conference on the strength of an education and missions effort already in place. Eventually the Russian immigrants became the dominant group in the General Conference. Their numbers increased with a new wave of immigration after World War I, mostly to Canada. The General Conference Mennonite center of gravity shifted westward and northward in the paths of the immigrants. Bethel College at North Newton, Kansas, and Bluffton College in western Ohio succeeded the Wadsworth seminary as Mennonite schools. Newton became the headquarters of the General Conference Mennonite Church. Winnipeg, Manitoba, grew to contain the largest urban concentration of Mennonites in the world.

Whoso Goeth with the Wolves

General Conference Mennonites began their first "foreign" missions among next-door neighbors—the Cheyenne and Arapaho tribes in Indian Territory (now Oklahoma). It was something of an accident that the first work was neither overseas nor thousands of miles distant. S. S. Haury, the mission founder, had first applied for work in Indonesia. Later he had checked out possibilities in Alaska. But in 1880 he and his wife established the first mission work 150 miles (240 kilometers) south of the frontier Kansas Mennonite settlements.

In cultural distance, however, the Arapaho tribes near Darlington were light-years removed from any Mennonite home base. When Haury got beyond Caldwell, Kansas, which he described as a "godless and freebooter-infested border town," he entered into the strange world of "heathenism." To be sure, Haury was well aware that there were "heathen" among the "so-called Christians" of the civilized world, some of whom were responsible for the brutal persecution of Native Americans in days past. To be sure, Haury had written that the heathen were claimed and loved by God, and that their pagan religious practices were a kind of response to God's claim upon them. But when Haury first saw in person the Arapaho sun dance with its physical tortures and its awful drumming (done in a "truly heathen manner"), he was led to exclaim against ". . . this heathen superstition, in which this people is held and guided by Satan."[13] The sense that the Native Americans were somehow in the grip of the devil actually grew stronger in the first decades of mission work in Indian Territory.

The two decades of work among Native Americans before the turn of the century formed something of a prelude to General Conference overseas mission work. There was much to be learned from the prelude. But the lessons which seem obvious in retrospect from the late twentieth century are not necessarily the lessons which were learned and applied seventy-five years ago. Five characteristics of this mission stand out as noteworthy:

1. *A wholistic approach.* The early Mennonite mission to Native Americans was quite secure and unselfconscious in its total ministry to the needs of people for food, shelter, health, education, and spiritual nurture. It seemed obvious to this generation that to bring the Christian gospel meant to bring the "benefits" of Christendom. The debate between fundamentalists and modernists which split body from soul and social service from evangelism was to come in the future. The age of "prioritization" would come even later. These early missionaries had a more wholistic agenda than their children and grandchildren would have.

Certain things were obviously necessary if Christian communities were to be established among the Cheyenne and Arapaho. The buffalo were gone. Native Americans would have to be taught the rudiments of agriculture for a new means of livelihood. Free movement on the land was ending. Tribes would have to learn to live in permanent settlements and in healthful houses. In all respects, the missionaries offered to the Native Americans a new way of life which promised the benefits of civilized, Western technology to a people whose old way of life had been destroyed before their very eyes.

In those first decades there was no such thing as a missionary who was assigned solely to engage in evangelism. The missionaries were teachers, linguists, medical doctors, and administrators. They were supported by a large core of young Mennonite volunteers who worked in a great variety of roles—as farmers, gardeners, seamstresses, cooks, matrons, teachers. The close proximity of the mission field meant that it was easy to recruit and send short-term young workers, to send food and clothing to meet emergency relief needs, and even to bring young Native Americans to Mennonite farms and schools, where they could learn new ways outside of the influences of their tribal environment. From 1880 to 1900, over seventy-five Mennonites worked in some capacity on the mission field, and many others had opportunity to make brief visits to the mission stations.[14] The General Confence was not a large body of churches in those days. It grew from a total of thirty-two congregations in 1881 to sixty-six congregations in 1900.

2. *A confident community.* Missionaries of the 1880s and 1890s were sure of themselves. They had no doubts about the essential goodness of

the culture and the rural communities from which they had come. They saw their task as the need to duplicate among the Cheyenne, Arapaho, and Hopi tribes the social, economic, and religious arrangements of their home communities. There should emerge in Indian Territory a group of hard-working, God-fearing yeoman farmers who knew the values of discipline, cleanliness, thrift, and piety. Missionaries such as S. S. Haury, H. R. Voth, and M. M. Horsch never questioned the appropriateness of imposing their culture in its entirety upon the Native American people. They were too confident of the wholesomeness and goodness of their own culture to see the pagan flaws in their own social and political structures.

The mission was strongly influenced by nineteenth-century ideas of progress. Mennonite missionaries believed themselves to be participating in a worldwide crusade of human advancement. S. S. Haury praised the role of missions in suppressing cannibalism, child sacrifice, widow burning, slavery, and the slave trade.[15] Missionary candidate M. M. Horsch, in an 1892 graduation address at the Halstead (Mennonite) seminary, extolled the modern civilization which bore

> . . . the promise of a brighter day, when there will be not only the Greek ideal of a sound mind in a sound body, but also a soul animated with divine love that shall go out into kindred souls, uniting in the bonds of Christian love all races and nationalities, even to the outermost bounds of the world.[16]

The missionaries believed that the ideal of human progress was incorporated not only in their own rural Mennonite communities and in the international missionary movement which Mennonites were now joining, but also in the enlightened policies of the American government for the Native Americans. Indian policy seemed to be in the hands of benevolent reformers, who were eager to make up for past atrocities. Custer's Last Stand was in 1876, four years before the Mennonites began their work in Indian Territory. The Plains Indian Wars were over. Now government and church would cooperate in a program of enlightened uplift for these tribes which had suffered so much in the past. Indeed, right-thinking Americans knew that this was a debt which white people owed to the Native Americans.

3. *Fascination with Native American culture.* Some missionaries who officially rejected tribal culture found themselves unofficially fascinated—even entranced—by the subtleties of tribal languages, the vitality of traditional ceremonies, and the richness of Native American oral tradition. D. B. Hirschler, brother-in-law of S. S. Haury and graduate of the Wadsworth seminary, spent hours in conversations with the Cheyenne leaders, gathering evidence that the Cheyenne Indians were descendants of lost Israelites who had made their way across Asia and the Bering Strait centuries ago. H. R. Voth, after founding the new

mission station among the Hopi in Arizona in 1892, gained access to their secret ceremonies, where he took detailed notes on everything he saw. Voth's collection of photographs and artifacts won a considerable reputation for him among American ethnologists but damaged his reputation among the Hopi, who felt that he betrayed their confidence. Missionary Rodolphe Petter, a skilled linguist recruited from Switzerland, was the first person to reduce the Cheyenne language to written form and to produce a Cheyenne translation of the Bible.

It cannot be said, then, that the early missionaries were cultural illiterates who had no appreciation for the language and life-style of the Native Americans. At one level, to be sure, missionaries looked forward to the destruction of tribal life and its "heathen" practices. At another level, in somewhat contradictory fashion, the missionaries, with their busy chronicling, collecting, and translating, helped to preserve remnants of a tribal culture that otherwise would have disappeared more rapidly.

4. *Alliance with the oppressor.* The United States government in 1882 offered to the Mennonites free of charge the military post of Cantonment, 65 miles (104 kilometers) northwest up the North Canadian River from the first mission station at Darlington. Should the offer be accepted? In the light of the long Anabaptist-Mennonite history of troubled church-state relations, one might expect the mission board to reject the government offer. How could Mennonites operate from a place which had served the devastating purposes of the United States Army? Would not such an identification frustrate the very purposes of the mission?

The mission board had no such doubts. They not only gratefully accepted the abandoned post with its twenty-five stockade-type houses and two brick buildings, but they also reported to the General Conference that this marvelous gift had been "allotted to us by God."[17] They saw here resources suddenly available to create a model Christian colony of Native American converts. That colony never materialized. What did develop was an image of the Mennonites as allies of the land-hungry and bloodthirsty whites who seemed bent on destroying the Native Americans. Cheyenne Chief Red Moon explained the problem to missionary Rodolphe Petter:

> I love the good white people, but the Washington people are wolves, they tore our people apart, they tear our land, they change their paths [contracts] with us every year, they coil themselves like serpents . . . and whoso goeth with the wolves is a wolf himself, so says the great Medicine Chief in Heaven does he not?[18]

The military post, now a mission station, was used for military protection even after the Mennonites took over. In 1884 some cowboys who had killed a Cheyenne fled to it just ahead of a band of vengeful tribesmen. Missionary Haury mediated between the cowboys and the Cheyenne until a military force was summoned from Fort Reno and took the cowboys into custody. The Cheyenne were pacified with the gift of some two hundred horses which had belonged to the cowboys. Haury testified at the trial in Wichita, Kansas, and was dismayed when the cowboys were fully acquitted. The Native Americans had to return the horses. In telling about the incident, Haury expressed his clear sympathy with the cause of the brutalized Cheyenne. But the very context of his missionary work made it virtually impossible for him to make his sympathies effective in practical terms. [19]

The Mennonites were once again identified with the oppressors through their cooperation in the government policy under the Dawes Act to give away the Native American reservation land to white settlers. Missionary H. J. Kliewer actively recruited Mennonites to join the Oklahoma boomers who flooded into former reservation territory in a series of land invasions in 1889 and after. By the time of Oklahoma statehood in 1907, there were thirty-seven white Mennonite congregations in the territory, seventeen of which were affiliated with the General Conference. The missionaries, convinced that solid Mennonite congregations would make good neighbors for the local tribes, apparently never protested that this gigantic land grab was unfair to the Native Americans, nor worried that Mennonite participation in the enterprise might be problematic for the reputation of the Mennonite mission.

5. *The meager harvest.* If the measure of a successful mission program is the emergence of a viable indigenous church, the first two decades of Mennonite mission to Native Americans must be judged a near failure. There had been a magnificent mobilization of this youthful denomination's energies. Eight mission stations were founded; dozens of the best and brightest of Mennonite youth had dedicated themselves to missions service; a strong link was forged between missions and the booming Mennonite enterprise in higher education. [20] But there was virtually no Native American church. The total number of baptisms could be counted on the fingers of four missionaries' hands, and that small number had been reduced by backsliding and death. Three feeble congregations had been organized in 1897-99, but the prospects for Native American leadership were unthinkably remote. The Mennonite schools at Darlington and Cantonment, as well as the contract school at Halstead, were closed down when the government withdrew support in the late 1890s. And so it would continue until the Mennonite mission to Arapaho, Cheyenne, and Hopi tribes closed after nearly a century of persistent, prayerful, sacrificial missionary labor. There was never to be a great ingathering of souls, nor the development of strong native leaders in strong native congregations.

Could it have been otherwise? Under what circumstances would it have been possible for these three tribes to hear the Christian gospel as good news? The Mennonites surely had much to offer—education, medical aid, agricultural expertise, and the Word of a God of love. But the best of the Mennonite offering was bound up with the worst of the American frontier offering—military destruction of the tribes in brutal warfare, slaughtering of buffalo herds, forcing of the tribes onto reservations, distribution of promised Native American land to white settlers, and systematic efforts to undermine tribal social and political organization.

The missionaries were well aware of the past and present sufferings of the people they had come to serve. But Mennonites were people of their times. They felt in their bones that this was an age of progress, and that missionary work was in the vanguard. They could not develop a thorough critique of government Indian policy because they were so grateful for the many ways government assisted with resources for the establishment of their agricultural and educational work on the mission. The Mennonites were a religious, ethnic minority group which was emerging from centuries of isolation and introversion. Mission work was a primary event in this awakening. As such, the missionary endeavor proved more meaningful for the Mennonite progressive spirit than for the liberation of downtrodden Native Americans. The Mennonites tragically had no answer for the wisdom of Cheyenne Little Wolf who told missionary M. M. Horsch:

> God gives to everyone that which he needs. To the white man he gave houses, money and cattle. The white man works and knows how to make money to buy his necessary provisions. To the Indian God gave bows and arrows and ponies. He also gave him buffalos, deer, bears, turkeys, fishes and other animals which he could hunt and thereby procure his subsistence. But the white man was not satisfied with the things which God gave him, he came and took away that which belonged to the Indian. Now the Indian must adopt the white man's road, and that is very hard. When I think over this it seems to me the white man did not do what God wanted him to do.

Horsch reported that he didn't know enough of the Cheyenne language to give Little Wolf a proper answer. So he read to them the twenty-eighth chapter of Deuteronomy.[21]

Girls leaving for vacation from Funk Memorial School in Janjgir, 1943

Photo by Augusta Schmidt

2 India, 1900-1947

A Mighty Rain

In the spring of 1898, while the United States Congress was debating President McKinley's request for a declaration of war against Spain, General Conference Mennonites read in their church paper about new currents in Mennonite missions. Rodolphe Petter, missionary to the Cheyenne Native Americans wrote,

> The little stream that supported our mission until now appeared sometimes to want to dry up, but it never was completely exhausted. Now it has rained mightily somewhere and the little stream has become an uncontrollable river! Indeed, it has left its old bed and strides out toward India![1]

A new movement was afoot. An irresistible tide was carrying Mennonites toward new mission work in India. It did not occur to Petter that the mighty rains of this movement might be related to the aggressive American national climate of opinion which carried the country into a war to liberate the oppressed Cubans. On the page opposite to Petter's article, a Mennonite editorial noted with approval that the Quakers had petitioned McKinley for a peaceable arbitrated settlement with Spain.

Petter suggested three other possible sources for the new missions thrust. First he asked, *"Is it the longing of the heart to do more for the heathen than we have done so far?"* The raising of Mennonite consciousness to concern about the needs of India was due in large part to the initiative of an enterprising Mennonite world traveler named George Lambert.[2] Lambert circled the globe in 1894-95, including six weeks in India, and published a travelogue which praised missions work. When India was hit by severe famine in 1896-97, Lambert led in the organization of a Home and Foreign Relief Committee in the "Old" Mennonite Elkhart group, to mobilize Mennonite resources for India relief and missions. After an 1897 trip to India to distribute supplies and funds thus collected, Lambert wrote another book, *India, The Horror Stricken Empire,* "in the hope that it may be a means of opening the door to more earnest missionary effort in this great, benighted country."[3] General Conference Mennonite papers published Lambert's reports and letters, as well as news about the India famine from other sources, such as Alice Yoder of Lititz, Pennsylvania, a Mennonite who had gone to India under the Christian Alliance in 1895 or 1896. The urgent needs of suffering "heathen," and the awareness of a capacity to meet those needs, had never been more prominent in the Mennonite mind.

Petter's second suggested source for the new interest in missions to India was the following: *"Is it a heartfelt longing for unity and for brotherly love in the divided Mennonite household?"* The General Conference had been formed in 1860 with the dream of unifying all Mennonites in a common mission. When most Mennonite congregations refused to join, General Conference leaders nursed the hope that with the passage of time, resistance to the progressive causes of education and missions would slowly break down, and all Mennonites could join hands in common endeavor. Now after two decades of General Conference involvement in missions, it seemed that the progressive group of "Old" Mennonites, gathered around the leadership of John F. Funk in Elkhart, Indiana, were ready for a cooperative missionary enterprise. Members of the General Conference Foreign Mission Board met with members of the Elkhart Home and Foreign Relief Committee in April and August of 1898 in efforts to find a basis for joint endeavor. The efforts failed. The people, it was said, were not ready for such close cooperation. So the two major Mennonite groups, General Conference (GC) and Mennonite Church (MC), went to India at about the same time with separately administered mission programs which would eventually result in separate Mennonite churches in India. (The Mennonite Brethren of North America began mission work near Hyderabad in 1899.) Back in the spring of 1898, however, the prospect of new unity in the divided Mennonite household was a noteworthy cause of General Conference enthusiasm for mission work in India. The missionaries of the GC and MC groups got along much better than did their separated sending congregations in North America.

Finally, Petter wondered if the new push toward India did not arise from *"the backlash from a fruitless and meaningless work among the Reds?"* Petter was hardly ready to abandon his beloved work with the Cheyenne people, but he somehow had to deal with the fact that this work was not producing the desired results. Would India yield a greater harvest of souls? Petter doubted it. He warned the General Conference not to rush into a new program beyond available resources. General Conference mission board secretary A. B. Shelly did actually entertain, and conditionally reject, the possibility that India's prospects were so much brighter that the established mission stations in North America should be relinquished and replaced by a more promising work overseas.[4] In any case, Shelly counseled, it was wise to be orderly in evaluation and planning, and to do the work through established conference channels. The mission board, weary from years of trouble shooting in the Native American mission, now had to scramble to stay ahead of an expansionist-minded constituency. When the first Mennonite missionaries were sent to India, the mission board did not bother to have them tour the mission work in Indian Territory; the lessons learned from the first two decades had been mostly negative lessons.

The pressure for expansion came most insistently from the Northern District of the General Conference, and particularly from Mountain Lake, Minnesota. The northern churches had never been as closely involved with the mission work to Native Americans as had been the churches from Pennsylvania to Kansas. Mennonites in Mountain Lake now put together a match of man and money which was too attractive for the mission board to turn down. The man was young Peter A. Penner, son of a Main Street businessman. Penner had experienced a profound Christian conversion in 1894 under the preaching of J. B. Baer, traveling home minister of the conference. Yielding to Christ had not come easy for this energetic and willful young man. On the night of his conversion he walked out of the evangelistic meeting and struggled with God in the tall grass behind the church. When he got up and returned to kneel at the altar, he was a changed person, ready to serve where God would call.

The money for the project was put together by David Ewert, a prominent businessman. Ewert went around to local individuals, societies, and churches to collect commitments totaling $400 annually for five years to support a missionary couple. Then he called Penner into his office, closed the door, showed him the pledges, and said, "Brother Pete, are you willing to go to India on the strength of this pledge?" Pete was willing. The official call from the mission board to go to India was in his hands within a few months.[5]

Subject to Change

"My views regarding India," wrote P. A. Penner after a year of work there, "are like the price of sugar, subject to change."[6] Penner's cheerful tentativeness was well suited for the months of uneasy adjustment and difficult decision which followed his arrival in India on Sunday, 9 December 1900. There were four people in this pioneering group: Penner and his new bride, Elizabeth Dickman, and John F. Kroeker

General Conference Mennonite Mission Area in India

with his new bride, Susie Hirschler. It was an international group. John was a Russian citizen who had studied for mission work at Bethel College. Susie was from Germany. Peter was a naturalized American, born in Russia and acquainted with Mennonites there since a visit in 1889. Only Elizabeth had been born in America. They spoke with each other and wrote their private diaries in the German language. In the course of time, their language, like many other things—including the price of sugar—was subject to change.[7]

Some decisions of that momentous first year, however, were not easily revocable. Above all, they acquired land for new mission stations at the villages of Champa and Janjgir on the Chhattisgarh plain of India's Central Province. In choosing this location they were aided by other mission organizations which had decades of experience in India, as well as by the Mennonite Church (MC) missionaries who had established a mission station at Dhamtari in the Chhattisgarh region. J. A. Ressler of the Dhamtari mission welcomed the Penners and Kroekers to make a temporary home on the MC compound, and accompanied the young men on the search for a location which the General Conference had suggested should be near the MC work. Ferdinand Hahn of the German Lutheran Gossner mission in Bihar, who had been in correspondence with A. B. Shelly (mission board secretary), helped in the decision. Penner and Kroeker also consulted other mission groups, which eventually were to become colleagues and partners with them in regional missionary cooperation—the American Evangelical Mission at Raipur and the Disciples of Christ at Bilaspur.

The New Home

What good could come out of Champa and Janjgir? Were these remote villages more than the leftovers from a century of modern missionary occupation since the arrival of British Baptist William Carey in Calcutta in 1793? In some ways, Penner's newly adopted village of Champa could remind him of his hometown of Mountain Lake, Minnesota. Both were on rural plains areas, where one could appreciate a wide horizon, big sky, and brilliant stars. Both lay on major rail lines and depended upon rail access for contacts with the outside world. Champa was a sooty 400-mile (640-kilometer) rail ride from Calcutta on the route to Bombay. Mountain Lake was midway between St. Paul and Sioux City. Both were destined to remain small towns, bypassed and overwhelmed by booming urban centers in a new industrialized world.

But a child of Mountain Lake was bound to be more impressed with the differences. Champa was on the Hasdeo River, swollen each year with the monsoon rains so essential to the rice crop upon which these people were utterly dependent. Unlike the egalitarian American frontier, Champa was afflicted with a semifeudal economic system in which a few land-owning families accumulated great wealth while most of the people were condemned to grinding poverty. Above all, there was the caste system. The lives of the people in Champa and Janjgir—as in the rest of Hindu society—were circumscribed at every point by caste definition. Their intrinsic worth, their privileges, and their duties depended upon the caste into which they were born. A highly refined sense of pollution and purification kept caste-bound people in their places. Social contact with people lower in the caste hierarchy—or involvement in degrading tasks such as sweeping filth or disposing of dead animals—was considered highly polluting. Anyone who touched an "untouchable" must be ritually purified.[8]

The predominant caste in the GC mission area was the Chamar, a leatherworker caste spread throughout North and Central India. The Chamars were associated with the most polluting of activities—skinning and eating the meat of dead animals. Caught in a trap of poverty and demoralization, the Chamars were expected to be immoral liars, thieves, and fornicators. A popular saying held that "a chamar must tell forty lies before breakfast in order to insure digestion."[9] In the nineteenth century there emerged among the Chamars a religious prophet, Ghasi Das, who led a reform movement within Hinduism to raise the moral life, religious quality, and caste status of these people. They were to worship the one god of the "true name" *satnam*—hence their designation, Satnamis. They were to give up meat and liquor. The thousands who joined the new religion may have improved their lives, but they could not break the tyranny of caste. Their caste superiors continued to consider them to be untouchables and to insist that the Satnamis ate the flesh of dead animals.[10]

It was among the lowest of the untouchables—the Chamars and the Satnamis—that the early Mennonite missionaries came to concentrate their work. This strategy was a product of situation and circumstance rather than of any clearly thought-out theology of missions. There were opportunities for contacts with upper castes, including the Braham, priestly caste which stood at the apex of the system. J. F. Kroeker did report some success in establishing personal rapport with higher caste Hindus, but there were no conversions. Penner saw the Brahmans as hopelessly arrogant and pedantic. The Chamars, for all their wretched poverty, disease, and immorality, were at least willing to listen. "I must mention at least one very praiseworthy fact about him [the Chamar]," wrote Penner. "He is a man that listens. . . . I believe it is almost as great an accomplishment to LISTEN in one language than to SPEAK three."[11]

Acquisition of Land

The process by which Penner and Kroeker acquired land for mission stations in Champa and Janjgir is instructive regarding their relationship to both the British colonial rulers of India and to the local

Indian authorities. The British governed India by a number of patterns depending upon local conditions. Where there was a native state ruled by a local landowner-king who could maintain reasonably effective order and who was willing to abide by the laws of the British colonial government, the British preferred to keep the local ruler in power and to establish only indirect colonial rule. These native state rulers were granted varying degrees of autonomy. In some cases, including tribal districts in the northern Chhattisgarh, the British acquiesced to local rulers' demands that Christian missionaries not be allowed to establish work in the native state. Where there was no cooperative and effective local ruler, the British established direct control. The possibility of establishing new Christian mission work depended upon the receptivity of both the British and the Indian public officials, the relationship between the two, and calculation of how helpful or disruptive Christian mission work might be to the local social and political order.

Dhamtari, where the MC Mennonites established their mission work, was under direct British control. Champa and Janjgir, however, were within a locally controlled "native state" district of about 180 square miles (460 square kilometers) including sixty-six villages. To acquire land in this district for mission stations, Penner and Kroeker had to deal with the local landowner-king, who held all the land in the district in a kind of feudal relationship, and from whom land could be rented but not bought. The king, they soon learned, was not interested in renting land to the newcomers. The missionaries went to the minor government officials for help, but they refused to intercede with the king. Finally the missionaries took their case directly to the British Chief Commissioner, "a man of authority" whose "word has weight." The commissioner's weighty letter to the king resulted in the king's offer of three possible sites, all of which the missionaries rejected as unsuitable. One site was too stony; two were too swampy. The missionaries appealed once again to the British Chief Commissioner, who once again leaned upon the king, this time with sufficient force to shake loose an excellent 8-acre (3.2-hectare) site near the Hasdeo River about 1½ miles (2½ kilometers) from Champa village and railway station. The lease was for thirty years for about seven dollars per year. By much the same process, Kroeker received a 9-acre (3.6-hectare) unwooded tract for a mission station on the edge of Janjgir, seven miles (about eleven kilometers) west of Champa and three miles (about five kilometers) from the rail line. There would be two mission stations, with one family at each place.

Land for homes and for mission institutions was an absolute prerequisite for the work. Penner painted the struggle for land in cosmic terms: "Not only did a severe storm arise but a formal battle ensued in which God and his cause was on the one side and the devil and his representatives, the heathen, were on the other side."[12] There was a trap in Penner's dualism. He had put the British Chief Commissioner, wielder of British imperial control in India, on the side of "God and his cause." The alliance of missionaries with the British, who were to rule India until 1947, would not always be an unqualified asset for mission work. Nor would it always be appropriate to see local Indian rulers as representatives of the devil.

Penner's rhetoric notwithstanding, there were some critical contrasts between the ways Mennonite missionaries related to local authority in India and in earlier mission work in Oklahoma. Negotiations for land in Champa and Janjgir were clouded with colonial coercion, but they retained negotiations with local authorities. In Oklahoma negotiations for land bypassed the Native American tribes and were conducted with the American government alone. The local king in Champa retained formal political authority, and missionaries paid formal respects on proper occasions such as the marriage of the king's daughter. Nor did Mennonite missionaries build their mission station on an ex-military installation of British Empire, as would have been an equivalent of the mission station at Cantonment. Above all, the chief economic enemies of the people in India were internal problems—famine and maldistribution of resources. This was vastly different for Native Americans, whose economic enemies were external. The buffalo and the land were fully destroyed and taken over by white people, with whom the missionaries were identified. It would be much more possible in India than in Oklahoma for missionaries to proclaim a salvation in Christ which had practical and concrete meaning for their hearers' liberation in the world in which they lived. By the spring of 1902, P. A. Penner could report:

> . . . the king of Champa slew a fine tiger about half a mile from our location. He gave us the skin. The king's . . . relations to us seem to become more and more friendly. We have no reason to complain. Above all, we are so grateful that the heathen seem to open their hearts. They confide in us a great deal, and visit us gladly. [13]

Missionaries and Local Religion

Unlike H. R. Voth, with his Hopi researches and collections, and Rodolphe Petter, with his Cheyenne linguistic and ethnographic publications, none of the Mennonite missionaries in India ever became notable authorities on Hindu religion and custom. They did recognize the value in being well informed. "I am studying as much as my work will allow me," Penner wrote in 1905, "so as to get an insight into the religion of India. Only by doing this can we hope to help India." [14] But Penner's study of Hinduism, no matter how hard he may have tried to be objective or sympathetic, was tinged with a measure of condescension. In his thinking, Penner was never willing to allow for a clear separation between the "high religion" of Hinduism, on one hand, with its exalted ethical teachings, benevolent gods, and inspired ancient scriptures, and on the other hand, the "low religion" of Hinduism, with its capricious local deities, crisis rituals, and lack of scriptures or institutionalized church. Hinduism, wrote Penner, was "a conglomeration of philosophical systems, pantheism, fatalism, ceremonies and ceremonial washings, and downright common idolatry."[15] If Hinduism of the great tradition was supposed to be so exalted, Penner wondered, why did it result in such appalling superstition and degradation among the common people?

The Champa missionary compound happened to be just two miles (about three kilometers) from a popular local shrine to the great god Shiva at the village of Pithampore. Penner and Kroeker went to Pithampore in March 1902 to see the observance *holi,* a festival of purging and renewal prior to the beginning of the new lunar year. The festival was rich in phallic symbolism, role reversals (men dressed as women), and sexual licentiousness; it convinced the youthful missionaries of the utter evil of this religion.[16] Penner and Kroeker requested admittance to the big shrine (and were at first refused, then admitted) to see the people bringing offerings and being sprinkled with holy water. "Many of these poor deluded people evidently have a consciousness of sin," reported Penner, "but others give an offering out of habit." This first time they simply observed and held their peace. Next time it would be different: "Bro. Kroeker and I said to ourselves that this year the priests would not be hindered by us in their deviltry, but if it please God, opposition shall begin for them on next Holi. We will pitch our tent in that village and preach Christ, who truly and freely gives the water of life."[17]

The missionary conversations with Brahman priests apparently typically turned into occasion for argumentative sparring and irreverent insults. The Brahmans were fond of making obscene comments about the parenthood of God and the Virgin Mary, while Penner tried to turn the conversation to the question of sin and salvation. "That invariably touches a sore spot in the Brahman, inasmuch as he knows he is a big sinner and yet wants to be regarded as a saint. I am aided in my discussions by a little knowledge of the deviltry of this caste."[18] Penner delighted to shame the Brahmans by telling about "the gross sins of the Hindoo deities. . . . A mere touch upon them before a Brahman shuts him up like a jackknife."[19]

The most troublesome challenge to the Christian missionary argument came from adherents to the Arya Somaj society, a Hindu reform movement which seemed to borrow some characteristics of Christianity while bitterly opposing the Christian missionaries. The Arya Somajists rejected idol worship, held to the Vedas as revealed scripture, and professed belief in one God. They attacked missions for taking advantage of famine conditions and the homelessness of orphans to gain an entering wedge into Hindu society and to bribe the poor and ignorant into acceptance of Christ.[20] But the missionaries never accepted the possibility that geniune reform was possible within Hinduism. Penner knew personally that the immoral living of the Arya Somajists was adequate proof that the movement was dead and irrelevant.

Relationships with Local People

The missionaries had sustained an intimate contact with the local people at one point. They employed native servants. Labor was cheap. Missionaries had limited budgets by North American standards, but in the early days of mission compound buildings, Kroeker employed about five hundred national laborers in Janjgir.[21] With so many demands on missionary time, it made sense to employ local people for cooking, cleaning, gardening, building, transporting, and other tasks. But it seemed nearly impossible to find servants who were honest, trustworthy, and hardworking. The missionary reports are filled with laments about servants who complained about salary, pretended to misunderstand instructions, stole from the mission, and absconded at the slightest excuse. Penner admitted that wages were extremely low. The mission paid women servants the equivalent of three cents for ten hours work. The same women would get only two cents working for an Indian employer,[22] but the "high" wages on the mission compound did not make them happy. "Nothing makes our life here in India more bitter than the servants," confided P. A. Penner to his diary.[23]

The dynamics of the missionaries' relationships with the local people had far-reaching significance for the achievement of missionary goals. The early converts were to be employees of the mission. A church was to grow out of that relationship. The strength of the church would depend upon the ability of missionaries and local people to transcend the traditional roles thrust upon them by their histories and by their social order. The Indian people would have to overcome the degraded self-image and habits of subservience which afflicted their lives at the bottom end of the caste system. The missionaries would have to overcome the arrogance and impatience which came so naturally to representatives of a highly developed, educated, industrialized, imperialist Western world. Penner said it was absolutely essential for missionaries to act with authority. He told one newly arrived missionary,

> The Indians expect us to have the servant-master attitude. The British officials have it. The village-owners have it. The police officials have it in the villages. I have been here seventeen years. I have used all the methods. Some results are good and some results are not good. You use your own methods as long as you want to. But if you want their respect you have to teach with authority, you have to act with authority, you have to forgive with authority, you have to show tolerance and love with authority.[24]

It would have been quite impossible, both psychologically and practically, for missionaries seventy-five years ago not to have appeared as figures of great authority. Their manner of speaking, their physical bearing and appearance, the kind of dwellings they lived in—all testified to Western self-confidence and status.

The missionary house was called a *bungalow*, but it was not the small cottage implied by the American popular usage of that term. *Bungalow* was a word derived from Hindi which literally meant "belonging to Bengal." It originally referred to a thatched house, but for Mennonite missionaries it came to mean a large structure built of red bricks and with a red tile roof that reached down over wide, sweeping verandas. From the outside view, the missionary bungalows appeared to be two-story dwellings, with windows located in the walls above the veranda roof. There was, however, just one story with an 18.5-foot (5.6-meter) high ceiling in the central rooms. The central concern of bungalow design was to combat the severe summer heat, which could rise to 110° or 120° F. (43°-49° C.) in the summer. From the ceiling hung a large ruglike fan which could be moved by a servant on the veranda who pulled a cord through the wall. Missionary dwellings were in their own way as impressive and imposing as the lavish houses of the local Indian elite—the landowner kings.

The bungalows, then, which so dramatically set the missionaries apart from the low caste people, served purposes of both physical and psychological survival. Penner wrote that missionaries with experience in India "predicted our death in case we do not build high houses."[25] The fear of death was not misplaced. Penner buried his wife and his second daughter in India during his first term in Champa. Susie Kroeker nearly died of pneumonia in the first year. Even so, there remained some embarrassment that missionaries lived in grander houses than did their relatives in South Russia and North America. The bungalow dedicated at the new mission station near Mauhadih in 1912 was so fancy that photographs of it were not allowed to appear in Mennonite church papers at home. The coming of electricity and electric fans made the high ceilings unnecessary, while the coming of anticolonialism and national independence made the disparity in life-style between mission and church a potential source of conflict. With the departure of missionaries in the 1970s, some of these bungalows would become white elephants, empty and deserted reminders of a day when the relationships between missionaries and nationals were vastly different.

Soup, Soap, and Salvation

Like the Mennonite missionaries who worked with Native Americans beginning in 1880, the Penners and Kroekers and those who joined them in India in succeeding years were confident about the virtues of their own culture and society. They were the advance guard of civilization. Their challenge was to demonstrate Christ's love by ministering to the physical and spiritual needs of the people in the context of a new

Christian community which would be an alternative to traditional Hindu society. The missionaries offered a counterculture to India. The center of the counterculture was the mission station. The center of the mission station was the bungalow. Around the bungalows there grew up clinics, orphanages, boarding schools, homes for people with leprosy, hospitals, churches, gardens, and dwellings for new Christian converts and for mission station employees.

The growth of the mission stations justified the confidence of the progressive founders and put to shame the timidity of conservative doubters of Mennonite ability to sustain the work with volunteers and money. After the first five spartan years, nine new workers arrived between 1906 and 1909. In this group were the founders of two new mission stations at Mauhadih (1911) and Korba (1915), on the banks of the Hasdeo River about thirty-five miles (fifty-six kilometers) upstream and downstream from Champa. P. J. and Agnes Harder Wiens, builders of the Mauhadih station, had come from Sagradovka and Molotschna in South Russia, respectively, and received pledges of support from churches there. C. H. and Lulu Johnson Suckau, founders of the Korba station (he from First Mennonite in Newton, Kansas), had accompanied P. A. Penner to India at the completion of Penner's first furlough in 1909. Also in that group was P. A. Penner's new bride, Martha Richert, daughter of Heinrich H. Richert of Alexanderwohl congregation in Kansas.

In the first decade of work in India, the missionaries wasted no words in discussion or debate about the relative priority which should be placed on physical or spiritual ministries in the mission program. No one was tempted to focus exclusively upon evangelism. No one imagined that medical or social services were so important that workers in these activities could be excused from going on evangelistic tours. The missionaries were all generalists. They had to supervise construction projects, oversee a corps of employees in house and garden, diagnose ailments and prescribe medicines, develop school curricula, serve as legal advisors, and much more. Professional specialization was a luxury the early mission could not afford.

The natural wholeness of the missionary program of those days was a product of the mission's confidence in its own counterculture and the mission's conviction that conversion to Christianity involved total confrontation with the non-Christian way of life. In the early years of the mission, most of the converts to Christianity were literally and forcibly evicted from their villages by fellow villagers. Most of them came to the mission compound for personal safety and livelihood. Although this removal from the villages had the negative effect of alienating Christian converts from their native culture—and to some degree delaying the indigenization of the new church—there was the advantage that Christianity was seen from the beginning to involve the whole person, both body and soul.

The organic unity of the early mission approach is evident in the case of transition from the initial relief work to mission work. Mennonite attention was first drawn to India by the awareness of *hungry* people. The problem was famine. David Goerz of Halstead, Kansas, was the organizer of fund raising by the General Conference Emergency Relief Commission, counterpart to the Elkhart-based Home and Foreign Relief Committee. Goerz traveled to India in 1899 to distribute the commission's money and foodstuffs in famine areas. The account of the Emergency Relief Commission was turned over to the General Conference mission when it became established in India. Penner later expressed the highest regard for Goerz, "that noble man to whom I owe so much. . . ."[26] The use of relief monies to start a mission did not raise theological or practical problems for this generation. It was all the Lord's work.

Part of the early mission focused on help for orphans who had lost home and family in the famine years. The missionaries cast lots to decide that the Kroekers at Janjgir should take in orphan boys and the Penners would have the girls at Champa. This allocation proved unfortunate when Elizabeth Penner died. P. A. Penner was left alone in Champa and reported "the heathen slander tongue is already very busy with me, altho there is no reason for it."[27] Tongues were wagging about another India missionary, one Dr. Sanderson, who had ruined thirteen orphan girls. It was urgent for P. A. Penner to return to America on furlough and find a wife to accompany him to India.

What should be done with mission station orphans when they came of age? It was clearly insufficient to send young Christians out into a hostile Hindu society and expect them to survive. They needed an economic stake. For the first such young man, Kroeker purchased a wagon and a yoke of oxen with which he could find employment. The young man began working at Champa. Kroeker proposed for the future to give each orphan $20 upon his departure from the mission, $15 of which he was to pay back. The money would be sufficient for him to rent a piece of land for cultivation.[28] A more comprehensive strategy given some considera- tion (and eventually rejected) was a plan to purchase a whole village as had been done by the MC Mennonites at Dhamtari, who acquired the 830-acre (332-hectare) village of Balodgahan in 1906.[29] P. A. Penner set a very high price for the proposed GC project. First, he said, there must be additional missionaries to carry on the work at Champa and Janjgir. A village should be paid for entirely at once so that no debts would be accumulated. The new missionary for the village should have completed agricultural school, because the orphans knew very little about farming and the opportunity should be grasped to introduce new scientific methods. If these conditions could be met (and it did appear that a potential Mennonite donor, one Gerhard Vogt, was interested), Penner was in favor of this kind of expansion because the "field is large and we have many many thousands of people here who have never heard the name of Jesus."[30]

Penner's rationale was an example of the community-oriented wholeness which undergirded the unarticulated missionary philosophy of those early days. He asked for an agriculturist who would teach orphans and others the techniques of modern farming because there were so many "who have never heard the name of Jesus"! The assumption in his thinking was that for Indian people to hear the name of Jesus, they would need to see the Jesus way of living incorporated in a new community. In the Christian community, people would keep their homes clean and healthy, use new methods of growing grain, and receive a proper disciplined education. They would have a new identity, liberated from the ravages of the caste system. They would worship God in a church building with pointed steeple and Gothic-arched windows. "We believe in the three S's," wrote P. A. Penner, "soup, soap, and salvation."[31]

The Planting of Three Churches

The language of Mennonite mission work, like Protestant missions generally, was steeped in biblical imagery. The country or region work was the "field." The missionaries were "laborers" in the field. Early converts were the "firstfruits" of the labor. The object of mission was to "plant" the church on the field. Rural Mennonites felt the force of this language in their bones.

The Mennonite mission was a single mission. The missionaries expected to plant one church. As it turned out, they planted three different churches in the first three decades. The three churches held together in a fledgling alliance known as the Church Conference, founded in 1922. Each of three churches had its own social makeup, its own problems, and its own potential.[32] The differences between these churches, as well as the common bonds which united them into a single conference, need to be understood in order to comprehend the history and current situation of the Mennonite church in India.

1. *Church of compassion.* The first church was the Bethesda church at Champa for persons suffering from Hansen's disease (leprosy). It had its inauspicious origins at lunchtime on 27 April 1902, when P. A. and Elizabeth Penner shared their meal of rice and curry with two begging victims of leprosy. These two were followed by others, and soon a little squatters' village sprouted on the bank of the Hasdeo a half mile (.8 kilometer) from the Champa bungalow.[33] Penner was not altogether pleased with the situation which was resulting from his unreflective benevolence. When the group reached about twenty or twenty-five, he tried to get rid of the whole lot of them by promising their travel allowance to an existing asylum at Baitalpur. They refused to leave.

Penner said that the work with leprosy patients was something he first tried to avoid. He believed it was thrust upon the mission by the Lord Jesus Christ.

To take up leprosy work required dramatic confrontation with one's own fears and revulsions, as well as with superstitions of Hindu society. People suffering from Hansen's disease were dirty, degraded, and disfigured. They were stigmatized with the name "leper." (No one calls a person with tuberculosis a "tuber"!) They were socially ostracized from family and caste, but they were not segregated in a manner to keep the disease from spreading. Somehow P. A. Penner overcame his fears and made service to leprosy patients his life's work. He personally dressed their wounds, gave them food, and prepared their bodies for burial when they died. He invited his Hindu friends—who refused such activities because it would involve breaking of caste—to share this freedom in Christ.

The Bethesda Leper Home (later called Bethesda Leprosy Hospital) which Penner built in Champa was funded and owned by the Mission to Lepers in India and the East, with headquarters in Edinburgh and London. Some of the operating expenses were paid by the government in India. The Mennonites had full charge of the superintendency and operation of the internal affairs. As the home grew, primary schools were started both for children within the home as well as for "untainted" children who were segregated from their parents and kept outside the home. The institution was a total welfare society, with complete care provided for patients who were unable to pay. A work program in garden, farm, and building projects provided activities to divert patients' attention from their physical and social condition. The number of patients in the home grew from about a hundred in 1909 to more than six hundred in the late 1930s. By 1941 the records showed that about thirty-three hundred persons had been admitted.

The first Mennonite Christian convert in India was a person with Hansen's disease who was baptized in July 1904 and died soon afterward. Eight patients accepted baptism the following year and observed the first Lord's Supper in the Bethesda Home. By 1914 over a hundred Christians had been baptized. In the long run, slightly over one-half of the persons admitted to the home were baptized.

What did baptism of a person with Hansen's disease mean for the individual and for the life of the emerging Mennonite church in India? These were utterly dependent people. They were mostly of low-caste origin, but they came from a great variety of caste, religious, and geographical backgrounds. They were a more heterogeneous church than any other to grow out of missions in India. Their ties to their social and religious setting were not broken earlier by the calamity they had in common. They were people apart, separated both from their origins and from the Christian congregations on mission compounds.

Membership in the Bethesda church peaked at nearly five hundred in the 1940s but declined to less than half that number thereafter. New medicines and new policies combined to liberate patients from dependency on the Bethesda Home. In the 1950s it became possible to cure, or at least to arrest, Hansen's disease cases through use of new sulfa drugs. At the same time, the government stopped providing funds for noninfectious cases. The length of individual residence in the home was reduced while the total number of residents went down.[34] The possibility of government restriction on religious activities in the home had long loomed in the background. In the late 1970s there was serious discussion of whether baptisms should be allowed at all in this church because it was a government-supported institution.

Although the Bethesda Leper Home was an institution designed for effective expression of Christian compassion, it was quite limited in its potential for long-range church building. There were ways in which this work contributed to church development. P. A. (superintendent until 1941) and Martha Richert Penner provided capable leadership and continuity for the overall mission evangelical and church-building efforts. Some of the "untainted" children, as well as some of the patients discharged as "arrested cases," became members of Mennonite churches (and other Christian churches) outside the Bethesda Home. One dramatic conversion story is that of Harihar Mahapatra, a man of Brahman background who had been groomed for the Hindu priesthood. Brought to despair and near death from his growing disease, from the debilitating Hindu "cures," and from his addiction to opium, Mahapatra arrived at the door of Bethesda. Here he was brought to health by the miraculous power of the new miracle drugs, by the surgical skill of missionary doctor Arthur Thiessen, and by the spiritual ministry of missionary Kenneth Bauman. He married an orphan girl from the mission compound and studied for the Christian ministry at Yavatmal seminary. Today he is a pastor in the Mennonite church.[35] His upper caste background and his knowledge of traditional Hindu religion enable him to witness to upper caste Hindus on equal terms. While Mahapatra is an exception to the history of a Bethesda Leper Home which has produced few members or leaders to the greater Mennonite church in India, his story illustrates the variety of results from this ministry of compassion.

2. *Church of compounds.* A second kind of church to emerge from General Conference Mennonite mission work in India centered around the activity of the mission stations. The members of these churches, especially in the early decades, lived on or near the mission compounds and usually were employed in mission work. Like the Hansen's disease patients, they were overwhelmingly of lower caste background and from a variety of castes. They were also economically dependent upon the mission, but their dependence was less decisive. Mission compound

Christians could take advantage of educational opportunities to achieve personal freedom and independence, both for themselves and for their children. Churches of the mission compound type emerged with the establishment of each new mission station. Congregations were formally organized at Champa and Janjgir in 1912, at Korba in 1915, and at Mauhadih in 1916. Champa was the station with greatest class and prestige. Champa had good railway access, a beautiful location, a home for Hansen's disease patients, and a hospital—all of which served as institutional magnets for money and jobs. Above all, Champa had continuity of leadership with P. A. and Martha Penner, and with Drs. Harvey and Ella Garber Bauman in the hospital.

The Janjgir station carried on a strong educational program, including a boys boarding school growing out of early orphan work, a girls school founded by Annie C. Funk in 1908, and a pastors training school which flourished in the 1930s. The Janjgir work was less deeply rooted, however, and had less continuity in mission station leadership. J. F. and Susie Kroeker returned to Russia in 1909,[36] and Annie Funk perished in the famous *Titanic* disaster of 1912.

The Mauhadih station had a thriving program for some twenty-five years and was noted especially by its school for boys. But in 1937 a disastrous flood at the confluence of the Hasdeo and Mahanadi rivers led to its retrenchment and to eventual abandonment.

The Korba station, which had earlier appeared to be a more "jungly" outpost, turned out to be located in a region rich with mineral deposits. After independence, the government of India moved to develop Korba as a major industrial center.

In these four places the mission strategy was basically similar. The early hope was that the entire "field" could be Christianized. The missionaries were eager to take the gospel to the people. An early method was the evangelistic "tour" during which they traveled with a retinue of servants, drivers, and native evangelists from village to village, preaching the gospel to those who would listen. In eighteen January days in 1905, for example, J. F. Kroeker preached in ninety-two villages.[37] Such tours put missionaries in some cantact, however superficial, with their wider social and physical environment. For many villagers, the touring mission band provided the very first contact with the Christian gospel, their first view of a bicycle, and their first encounter with the magic of stereopticon slides. Missionaries identified sites for new stations on such tours. It became clear, however, that successful evangelism required more sustained contact with the people.

To move beyond the "once-over-lightly" touring system, the missionaries established a series of outstations in selected villages which showed some promise of receptivity to the gospel. The first outstations from Champa and Janjgir were established in 1910. Native Indian evangelists, recruited from older established Christian mission programs, served as evangelists and teachers. "India must receive the Gospel through Indians," wrote P. A. Penner.[38] Mission-established primary schools (grades 1-4) in the villages followed the curriculum prescribed by the Indian government, but also included Bible teaching and Christian songs. The mission in India, so much farther removed from the home churches than the mission to Native Americans, found itself more quickly depending upon native people for the basic evangelistic work; it simply was too expensive to send more missionaries. By 1904 the missionary salary was up to $900 per year, while a national evangelist could be employed for around $100 per year.[39] The first Indian evangelist in Janjgir was Rufus Asna, whose father was a minister and evangelist in the Lutheran mission. In Champa the first Indian evangelist was Joseph Banwar.

As the Mennonite church community began to grow, the missionaries planned celebrative occasions to inspire the new converts and to develop their self-confidence in their Christian identity and witness. One way to show the strength of numbers was to pack up the entire mission and church community and go on a pilgrimage. On the day after Christmas in 1912, for example, the Champa mission community of fifty-two persons—missionaries, converts, and servants—set out for a twenty-five-mile (forty-kilometer) walk south to the new mission station at Mauhadih. They had three oxcarts: one for mothers and children, and two for the tent and supplies. As they traveled through villages along the way, they burst into songs of praise to God, which proclaimed the strength and joy of their alternative community to the onlooking wondering villagers. A similar delegation of forty-eight pilgrims from Janjgir came on the same route. At Mauhadih they held a week of camp meetings, with missionary messages and much singing every day.

Public Christian festivals in India were an essential counterpart to local celebrations and fairs of a Hinduism which was largely defined by the ritual acts of the adherent—by what was done rather than what was believed. A Christian *mela* ("festival") was needed to counter the Hindu *melas*. The Mennonites joined together with other Protestant missions in the Chhattisgarh region (Lutherans, Methodists, Disciples, Pentecostals, Mennonites from Dhamtari) to sponsor a weeklong celebration to demonstrate "that we are not such a feeble folk and that our cause is a great cause, allied to great powers, and its triumph assured."[40] The Chhattisgarh Christian *mela,* first held in March 1908, included prayer and praise meetings, industrial and music competition, scriptural examinations, and outdoor exercises. At this Madkughat *mela,* which became an annual or semiannual affair, missionaries could compare notes and find ecumenical fellowship.

The young church in India was in great need of self-confidence. Growth was slow and painful. The first converts outside the groups of orphans and Hansen's disease patients, Chandu and his wife, Potaitin, were baptized in Champa on 9 January 1910. Chandu had been employed as a driver, and Potaitin as a housekeeper, for the mission for many years. Chandu became a Christian after the way was shown to him clearly in two dreams.[41] From this couple forward, the new Christians came along singly or in very small groups. None of the outstations were successful in developing congregations which could survive on their own. Villagers who became Christians were severely ostracized by family and friends. A new Christian might face not only verbal and physical abuse but withdrawal of communal privileges such as the right to draw water at the village well. Such persons threw themselves on the mercy of the mission for employment, residence, and social acceptance. They moved to the mission compound and became part of the Christian community there.

By the end of 1912 the tiny mission compound congregations at Champa and Janjgir, together with the Bethesda congregation, were formally organized into "the General Conference Mennonite Church for India."[42] The name inadvertently told an uncomfortable truth: This was a church *for* India, but not yet *of* India. On the afternoon of 31 December 1912, P. A. Penner read the rules in public for the new Christians, "explaining, where necessary, some points on which we Mennonites lay stress." Unfortunately, no copy of these rules is extant, but we may be sure that they included the substance of a missionary resolution from 1909 which discouraged "the use of superfluous ornaments as being signs of heathenism."[43] The General Conference missionaries may have been influenced to form a church by the example of the MC missionaries at Dhamtari, who organized a church conference in January 1912. J. S. Shoemaker, secretary of the MC Board of Missions, had attended the World Missionary Conference at Edinburgh, where the case for self-supporting and self-propagating churches was vigorously stated.[44]

Visions of a self-supporting indigenous church would have been wildly optimistic for Mennonite missionaries in 1912, or, as it turned out, even two or three decades later. When the Mennonite mission celebrated its twenty-fifth anniversary, there were only 115 Christian families in the four mission station churches at Champa, Janjgir, Korba, and Mauhadih. Of this group, 85 percent depended upon the mission for salaries or support. Less than a quarter of the members owned their own houses, land, or cattle.[45] It was a poor church, drawn from the outcastes, separated onto the mission station, and dependent in the long run upon mission institutions financed from North America. Only the vigor of developing mission institutions could mask the great distance to the goal of the triumph of Christianity in this part of India.

The long-range viability of these mission compound churches depended upon education. Through education the new Christians and their children might acquire the skills to move into positions of administration and take over mission schools and hospitals themselves. Through education they would be able to compete in the job market of a gradually changing India which would need white-collar workers in modern-sector government, schools, and industry. Through education they could compensate for the loss of wider social acceptance which came with conversion. So they threw themselves into the educational enterprise with a passion. Education meant liberation.

Primary schools were started first at Champa and Janjgir and then in villages beyond. By 1925 there were fifteen mission primary schools; by 1948 there were twenty-eight. A girls school grew at Janjgir from the pioneering work of Annie Funk. In 1915 the school was expanded and renamed The Funk Memorial School. In a society which traditionally withheld education from women, hundreds of girls received their education here. An accounting in 1950 reported that among the former pupils of Funk Memorial School were "six headmistresses, sixty-four nurses, twenty-four primary teachers, fourteen middle school teachers, three doctors, and forty-two Bible women."[46] The school was finally closed in 1960, but the fruits of the girls' schoolwork were still being counted in the 1970s when a Hindu family in the village Bara Pipar converted to Christianity through the influence of the mother who had attended Funk Memorial School in Janjgir some twenty-one years earlier, and who had kept her faith alive through two decades of marriage to a Hindu husband.[47]

A boys middle school grew out of the primary school established at the Mauhadih station in 1912. From 1917 to 1937 it became "a fully established flourishing upper middle school with a normal training department attached to it."[48] Missionary John Thiessen, director of this school for many years, reported that the curriculum shifted in 1932 from the traditional academic pattern to include industrial education in specific trades for each student. The school industrial activities included weaving, spinning, tailoring, bookkeeping, printing, papermaking, animal husbandry, horticulture, and farming.[49] After the great flood at Mauhadih ruined this school and station in 1937, the school was transferred to Jagdeeshpur, where it expanded into a high school in 1944. The Janzen Memorial High School at Jagdeeshpur became the primary channel for the education of church leaders, and its faculty and staff became important leadership for the General Conference Mennonite Church in India.

The importance of education in lives of mission compound Christians was underlined in a caste and occupation survey of the Champa Mennonite community in 1970.[50] The Champa Mennonites identified themselves as coming from eighteen different castes and three tribal groups. Over three-fourths were of low-caste origin. The Chamar caste had the largest number. Of the entire group, not a single person was in the occupation prescribed by caste for parents or grandparents. The occupations shifted sharply from unskilled laborer in the grandparent's generation toward clerks and administrators in the present generation. Meanwhile, the educational attainment of the new generations underwent a dramatic increase. Education for Christians of low-caste origin allowed them to compete with high-caste people for jobs and wealth in the modern economy. Education has also freed many to seek positions in the job market in urban areas far beyond the villages where Mennonite mission stations and churches are located.

The future of the mission compound churches at Champa, Janjgir, Mauhadih, and Korba depended upon the ability of the Christians to rise above their original status as uprooted and dependent people. Would their loyalty to Christ and to the church remain strong from one generation to the next, as they gradually achieved social, economic, and psychological independence? Would they be strong enough to take responsibility for mission educational and medical institutions when it came time for missionaries to withdraw? Would they avoid the dangers of becoming a new Christian white-collar caste within the traditional Hindu system, content to defer to their caste superiors and unwilling to touch or associate with occupations and people of lower caste identity? The challenge of faithful Christian discipleship in an Indian context was as awesome and formidable for twentieth-century Christians based in mission compound churches, as it was for pioneer missionaries who faced a strange and different world on the plains of central India.

3. *Church of caste.* A third kind of church emerged on the southern part of the General Conference Mennonite field, in the Phuljhar area to the south of Mauhadih and the Mahanadi River. Here Mennonites reaped what Baptists planted. Here there were Christians of the farmer-weaver Gara caste, holding to the faith before Mennonite missionaries arrived, and pleading for the continuing nurture of a Christian mission program. Unlike the heterogeneous mission compound churches to the north, all the members of this church belonged to a single caste. Unlike the uprooted Christians at Champa, Janjgir, Korba, and Mauhadih, these Gara Christians remained in their own villages and did not depend upon the mission for their economic livelihood. They came into the church in family groups rather than as individuals. In the parlance of North American missiology, they would be known as "people's movement" Christians. The term "people's movement" was misleading, however, for most of the people in the Phuljhar region remained Hindus. The Gara church was a tiny minority of less than 5 percent in a society which saw their Christian ways as alien and threatening.

The Phuljhar kingdom was a native state in what is now the southeast section of Central Province (Madhya Pradesh). The first approach to this area was made around the turn of the century by the English Baptist mission, with its stations in Sambalpur and Balangir in Orissa Province. P. E. Heberlet of the English Baptist Mission began preaching among the untouchables, contrary to the general policy of that mission and the wishes of his assisting Indian evangelists. The gospel was received by members of the lowly weaver caste, a people who lived by weaving cloth, small farming, and beating drums for marriage feasts. They were said to eat the flesh of dead animals and to have a bad reputation with the police. The movement among this caste expanded rapidly, but the Baptists had neither the available resources nor the philosophy of missions nurture to follow up the movement and to organize strong churches.[51]

Mennonites made contact with the outer reaches of this movement through missionary touring. P. A. Penner and P. J. Wiens toured in the Phuljhar kingdom as early as 1912.[52] The contact which led to the founding of Mennonite mission work in Phuljhar came at the end of tour by Ezra and Elizabeth Geiger Steiner in 1916. On market day in the village of Pirda, where the Steiners presented the life of Jesus by stereopticon pictures, a weaver named Gopal begged the missionaries to extend their tour to his home village of Sukhri. In Sukhri lived a small group of isolated Christians who had moved here some years earlier from the English Baptist field to the southeast. Gopal and his friends pleaded for missionary help. "Is it necessary for our children to grow up in ignorance, darkness, and sin as did we?" they asked. "Is there no other way? Cannot you come and help us?"[53]

The mission established an outstation at Sukhri one year later, January 1917, under the direction of Indian evangelist Isa Das, who earlier had been recruited from the Disciples of Christ mission at Bilaspur. The ministry of evangelist Das, together with his gifted wife, Mathuria "Bai," flourished.[54] On 20 May 1917, missionary P. J. Wiens of Mauhadih station was in Sukhri to baptize twenty-nine persons, bless eighteen children, and serve communion to forty believers.[55] Missionaries did the baptisms. But evangelist Das was responsible for the ingathering of 1917-23. Wrote one missionary, "It was his touring by foot far and wide which galvanized that movement and brought the people by the scores and the hundreds to be baptized."[56]

The English Baptist Mission had charge of Christian mission work in the Phuljhar area according to comity agreements among the Protestant mission groups. In 1920 they agreed to have Mennonites work in part of the area; in 1938 that was expanded to all of Phuljhar. There was not full agreement about the 1920 arrangement, however. Baptist missionary J. W. Jarry, who felt that Mennonites were encroaching on Baptist territory, drafted a "statement of alleged breach of comity" and made a vigorous personal protest to Mennonite missionaries Samuel T. and Metta Habegger Moyer.[57] Other Baptist missionaries apparently had no objection to the Mennonite advance, especially in the 1930s when economic depression had reduced Baptist mission resources.

The sequence of *church* and *mission* in this new southern area was all-important. Elsewhere the mission began first and gathered converts around the activities at the mission stations. In the Phuljhar kingdom the church began first, and the mission station's task was to nurture and extend a movement already in process.

Although the Mennonite mission station came to Phuljhar by invitation, the early Gara Christians were quite powerless to help in the process of finding land. The Garas were outcastes. Their quest for liberation through Christian conversion and education found little sympathy among Indian authorities. Those in political power saw the missionaries as intruders who threatened to upset the prevailing social and religious order. S. T. and Metta Moyer, the missionaries assigned to begin this station, faced the same kinds of official delays, evasions, and outright opposition that the Penners and Kroekers contended with twenty-three years earlier. Moyer finally got the help of a friendly British district commissioner to secure a plot of unallocated reserved forest land, where they built what is now known as Jagdeeshpur. The first buildings were constructed in the face of a storm of local opposition. A team of bricklayers sent from Champa abandoned their jobs after local opponents pelted their tents with clods and pieces of broken brick.[58] But the hardy missionaries persisted. By June 1926 the Moyers moved into a newly constructed bungalow. On 12 February 1927, one month before departing for their first furlough in America, the Moyers proudly presided over the dedication of a mission station where the work of education, medical care, Sunday schools, and evangelism was in full swing.

S. T. Moyer was a man of many gifts and interests. From his father, a medical doctor in Lansdale, Pennsylvania (who had attended the Wadsworth seminary), Samuel got an interest in health services. He studied agriculture several years at Pennsylvania State College. At the new Mennonite seminary in Bluffton, Ohio, Samuel and his wife-to-be, YWCA president Metta Habegger of Berne, Indiana, were charged with the missionary vision. The Moyers' gifts came to focus in their second term in India—spanning the 1930s—when they were freed from mission station administration responsibilities and assigned to full-time evangelistic work in the Phuljhar area villages.

The new vision was timely: The great worldwide economic depression had brought a decline of church giving for missions, forcing cutbacks in mission programs and reduction of missionaries' and evangelists' salaries. The decline of foreign funds Moyers saw not as a setback but as an opportunity to move the Indian church rapidly toward full self-support. They introduced a new pattern of evangelism oriented to more intensive encounter with villagers in their homes, rather than one- or two-day public preaching in village squares on extensive tours. In 1931 they reported on the first results of the new method as "laying spiritual dynamite."[59] They selected nine villages and compiled a list of 250 names of potentially interested people. Working in five evangelism groups, they met in individual homes for Bible stories, singing, and, in some cases, the medical services of Dr. Herbert Dester from the Jagdeeshpur mission station. After a month of work there were twenty-four persons who confessed Christ publicly. This resulted in a public outcry and persecution against the new believers. S. T. Moyer reported, "Hinduism in all these nine villages is very shaken and now defends itself."

Moyer identified three sources of the new thrust of the 1930s: "Mott gave the principle, Ingram the power, and Pickett the method for work in India."[60] The first was John R. Mott, world missions crusader, who affirmed the primacy of evangelism at an all-India retreat at Nagpur. The second was George Ingram, layman from England, who inspired Moyer with an emphasis upon "the work and fullness of the Holy Spirit." The third was Bishop J. Waskom Pickett of New Delhi, who conducted an extensive survey of missionary successes and failures in India, concluding that the old mission-station-based strategy was faulty and needed to be superceded by people's movements along natural family and group lines.[61] Moyer was in close touch with India mission leaders in the Forward Movement in Evangelism. Missionary Donald McGavran, of the Disciples mission bordering the Mennonite field to the northwest, invited Moyer and his volunteer evangelists to work for a month in the Disciples mission area. McGavran later reported, "I want to thank you very much for sending the team which has been a genuine help and inspiration. You have a jewel in Purushttam [sic]. I have never heard preaching with as much conviction anywhere in India."[62] McGavran and Moyer combined to visit other missions on behalf of the Forward Movement in Evangelism.

S. T. Moyer received wider recognition for his evangelistic work through an article he wrote for the *Indian Witness,* September 1933: "The Self-Supporting Church at Basna, C. P."[63] The article critiqued the standard mission station approach which, he wrote, "robs the church of opportunity for growth and power by supplying money, by doing the witnessing, by supplying much of the service, by importing leaders." The answer was to stop putting Indians on the payroll and start challenging them to consecrated self-sacrificial service and giving. Moyer listed eight possible indigenous sources of income, including such things as "a daily offering of *one fistful of rice* for every meal for every family for every day of the year," and "a piece of cloth or fee to the Pastor at *time of marriage.*" In the place of mission-paid Indian pastors, Moyer organized a core of volunteer church helpers, modeled upon the village headman assistants (*muktiers*). These unpaid laymen *muktiers* took full responsibility for leading Sunday worship, conducting daily evening Bible teaching, instructing catechumens for baptism, and for collection of daily rice offerings, Sunday offerings, and yearly dues. Moyer reported it was too early to declare the self-support system an unqualified success; he was sure, however, that "we will never go back to the old system."

The Gara church grew in both numbers and self-support during Moyers' second term, through the end of 1937. In the following year, the Baptist mission agreed to withdraw and to give entire responsibility for the Phuljhar area to the Mennonites. The Moyers' successors were William F. and Pauline Schmidt Unruh. In 1938, Unruh baptized 223 persons in the formerly Baptist area. He organized the entire 700-square-mile (1,820-square-kilometer) area into a southern district conference (Sammelan). Representatives from the various churches gathered monthly to learn the Bible lessons for teaching in the villages, and to discuss and resolve common problems. Other missionaries, such as Jacob R. and Christina Harder Duerksen, continued the evangelistic work. The goal of self-support took longer than the Moyers had hoped, but the Gara church grew dramatically in numbers in the early 1940s, until by 1946 it nearly trebled the membership in mission compound churches to the north.

The years of growth and expansion were the 1930s until the mid-1940s, about the time of India's political independence. From 1946 to 1970 there was a general decline or leveling off in membership both in the Gara church (except for temporary increase in the late 1950s) and in the churches to the north. Moyer's early vision for a diminishing role by institutions on the mission compounds was not to be realized in his lifetime. For their third term, beginning 1939, the Moyers were assigned, against their own wishes, to the Janjgir mission station, where S. T. became the director of the Bible School. Although they were able to engage in yearly evangelistic work with their student evangelists and pastors, it is notable that the Moyers finished their missionary career working basically with mission station institutions rather than with their first love—village evangelism. S. T. became principal of Janzen Memorial High School in Jagdeeshpur during their fourth and final term.

The Jagdeeshpur station came to play an increasingly significant role in the life of the General Conference Mennonite Church in India. In its earliest years, young girls and boys wanting education had been sent from the south up to the schools in Janjgir and Mauhadih. Over the years this flow was reversed. The high school moved from Mauhadih to Jagdeeshpur in 1941. The Janjgir girls school closed its doors in 1960, and girls from the north wanting Mennonite education came to board in Jagdeeshpur. Meanwhile Dr. Herbert Dester's medical ministry at Jagdeeshpur grew from a small dispensary and village itineration into a hospital which required the employment of two doctors plus nurses.[64] The Jagdeeshpur mission station institutions, then, attracted money and personnel and became as powerful as the mission stations to the north. The most talented and best educated of a new generation of Indian Gara Christians took positions as teachers and medical workers on the station. The Gara church remained and grew strong, not primarily because of the strength of the foreign-funded mission activities, but because the rank-and-file grass roots membership of the church had a secure social and economic base in the villages.

Church Organization and the Question of Unity

Three sets of differences formed the basis of identity for the General Conference Mennonite Church in India. One was the difference between the new Christians and their dominant Hindu environment. A second was the difference between the Indian church and the Mennonite mission. The third was the difference between the southern churches of the Gara farmer-weaver caste origin and the northern churches of multicaste origin. All three of these relationships were fraught with tension and with potential for both creativity and conflict.

In their relationship to their Hindu social and religious environment, the Christians would remain a beleaguered minority. Even after Indian independence from Britain in 1947 and the official implementation of religious toleration in a secular state, the Christians were accused of belonging to an alien religion and of having converted in order to gain social and material advantage. Their emancipation from the caste system and their self-improvement through education made the Christians an upwardly mobile people in a modernizing world. But it would take many decades for them to overcome the psychological sense of inferiority which came from outcaste origins and from minority religious identity.

It was also possible for Indian Mennonite Christians to be overwhelmed in their relationship to the highly educated, well-financed, and authoritative Mennonite missionaries. From the beginning, the mission was committed to the goal of an indigenous, independent church.[65] To this end the first congregations were organized in 1912, and the Hindustani Congress of churches was established in 1922. Missionary C. H. Suckau was the first chairman of the Hindustani Congress at the outset, but he was succeeded by Indian leaders Datan Bhadra, Paul "Babu," and B. D. Stephen. The Hindustani Congress (or "Conference" as it was called after a reorganization in 1943) evolved as a separate organization from the missionary conference. There was some discussion of possible amalgamation of the church and missionary conferences in 1933,[66] but the two organizations actually became increasingly distinct in the following decades. Church and mission worked side by side in partnership. Efforts were made to make the church autonomous and self-sufficient as far as evangelism and discipline were concerned. But the mission grew ever larger and more powerful with control over the work of education, medicine, literature, and Christian nurture.

The relationship of the northern and southern churches had to adapt to the reality of increasing southern growth and influence over the years. Initially the southern area was considered as only one church congregation in the Hindustani Congress. With the 1942 reorganization, the southern group was represented as six congregations (compared to five from the north—one from each station, plus the Bethesda church for persons with Hansen's disease). With the different group identities including different languages (Chhattisgarhi in the north and Oriya in the south), the General Conference Mennonite Church in India faced challenges to unity even more severe than the North American Mennonite divisions which had resulted in separate Mennonite mission programs in India.

By the standards of both church planting and ministries of compassion and uplift, the General Conference Mennonite mission to India was more succesful than the General Conference Mennonite mission to Native Americans. Christians in India gathered each Easter sunrise for praise services in the church cemeteries. Their singing testified to new hope for life beyond this earth as well as new liberation from poverty, illiteracy, disease, and untouchability in this world. For missionaries whose grander goal was to Christianize India, however, the three to four thousand General Conference Mennonites seemed a small band compared to India's Hindu millions. In his last term in India, P. A. Penner compared the potential impact of two Indian reformers: Mohandas K. Gandhi, with his *satyagraha* philosophy, and B. R. Ambedkar of the University of Bombay. Gandhi's reforms, said Penner, had achieved practically nothing because he failed to break with the Hindu religion which undergirds the caste system. Ambedkar, himself of the untouchable classes, announced an impending break from Hinduism which Penner saw as potentially the greatest event in church affairs since Martin Luther posted ninety-five theses in 1517. Ambedkar's conversion to Christianity, Penner thought, might bring India's sixty million untouchables into the Christian faith and pose a great challenge for missionary instruction and nurture.[67] As it turned out, Dr. Ambedkar converted to Buddhism. Penner's optimism was fully warranted neither for India as a whole nor for the Mennonite church in India.

The Gospel Team at Taming Fu, China, New Years Day, 1934. In the back is Aganetha Fast.

3 China

Hard Work and a Big Cross

Wide awake one evening in Rochester, New York, missionary candidate Henry J. Brown received a vision which supported him for the rest of his life:

> While I waited before the Lord in prayer, I noticed the dark room all lit up, and high before me in the air I saw a big cross and just above it a beautiful golden crown with a number of precious stones inset. Under the crown I saw plainly the words, "Your Reward," and under the cross, "But You Must Work Hard."[1]

Things never came easily to Henry J. Brown, founder of the General Conference Mennonite mission in China. Henry worked for what he got. In an age of inner-directed and hardworking pioneers, he was among the most self-reliant of them all. "I had to fight every inch for my education," he wrote. His mother died when he was seven; his father when he was twenty. He received an inner call to foreign mission work when he was eleven years old, after hearing reports of the Dutch Mennonite mission work in Sumatra. From that call he never wavered, even though it meant working through high school in Mountain Lake, college in St. Paul, and Baptist Theological Seminary in Rochester.

Brown married a Mennonite girl from South Dakota, Maria Miller, who had received her missionary call "while plowing in the field with three big horses." Together Henry and Maria went to China, worked hard, and eventually bore the cross of expulsion from the mission field. Henry might have said of the whole Mennonite China mission story, as he said for himself, "Hard work and a big cross, that is the lot assigned me by my Master."[2]

Henry and Maria Brown had to "fight every inch" for missionary appointments under the General Conference as hard as they fought for education. The mission board turned them down at first. The reasons for the refusal are not clear. Mission board secretary A. B. Shelly said it was because there were too many candidates and insufficient funds. An invitation to attend a mission board meeting in September 1908 went astray in the mail, so the Browns found others appointed ahead of them. J. J. Balzer, president of the home mission board, accused the foreign mission board of passing over Brown because he had attended a Baptist seminary rather than the Mennonite Bethel College, where other candidates had gone.[3] When Brown took it upon himself to collect money in Mennonite churches and offer it to the foreign mission board as proof that adequate funding would be available, Shelly reprimanded him for unauthorized fund raising and made him return all the money to the original donors.[4]

With his customary purposiveness, Brown proceeded to make private arrangements to go to China, establish an independent mission work, and then invite the General Conference once again to accept him, this time with an established mission program supported privately by General Conference congregations. By the time the Brown mission came under the General Conference wing in 1914, P. H. Richert had replaced A. B. Shelly as mission board secretary.

Independent Mission Efforts

Henry and Maria Brown were not the first General Conference Mennonite missionaries in China, however. Ella C. Funk, a sister of A. E. Funk of New York, was in China under another board by 1890. Miss Funk's letters about the place of women in Chinese society were occasionally published in the *Mennonite*.[5] Henry C. and Nellie Schmidt Bartel (of Hillsboro, Kansas, and Avon, South Dakota) had gone to China in 1901 with the independent missionary leader, Horace W. Houlding. The Bartels were in voluntary service orphanage work with J. A. Sprunger's Light and Hope Society in Berne, Indiana, when Houlding came with his appeal for replacements for the over two hundred foreign missionaries killed in the Boxer Rebellion of 1900. The Houlding mission was located near Taming Fu village in the southern neck of Chihli province. In 1905 the Bartels broke with the Houlding mission and established an independent mission across the Huang Ho River at Tsao Hsien, Shantung province. The Bartel mission received support from a number of different Mennonite groups and in 1913 was incorporated as the China Mennonite Mission Society.[6] Maria Brown's cousin, J. J. Schrag of Freeman, South Dakota, went to China with the Bartel mission and served as host to the Browns for a year during their language study and search for a mission location.

The Houlding, Bartel, and Brown mission stations were about 300

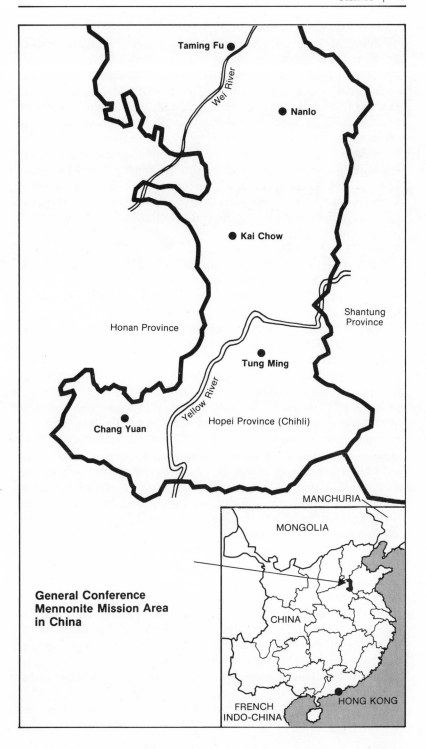

Taming Fu

Wei River

Nanlo

Kai Chow

Honan Province

Shantung Province

Tung Ming

Yellow River

Chang Yuan

Hopei Province (Chihli)

MANCHURIA

MONGOLIA

CHINA

FRENCH INDO-CHINA

HONG KONG

General Conference Mennonite Mission Area in China

miles (480 kilometers) inland at the meeting point of the three provinces of Chihli, Shantung, and Honan. The mission area straddled the famous Huang Ho (Yellow) River whose frequently flooded banks had seen several millennia of civilization before the Protestant missionaries arrived. The fertile northern China plain, enriched by silt from the flooding Huang Ho, had seen the rise and fall of highly developed dynasties and of sophisticated art and literature, long before the Germanic ancestors of the Mennonite missionaries knew of handwriting or woven cloth in northern Europe. The great traditionalist philosopher-scholar Confucius set forth the dominant social ethics of China at the same time (sixth century B.C.) that Second Isaiah responded to Israel's Babylonian exile with his vision of the power of righteous suffering and divine control over history.

A Period of Creative Chaos

The four or five decades of Mennonite missionary activity in China span a tiny period in the broad context of rising and declining civilizations. But it was an especially significant period of transition. The Manchu dynasty, which had ruled China for some three centuries and had successfully resisted Western influences until the late nineteenth century, had collapsed. In 1911 and 1912, when H. J. and Maria Brown began work in the village of Kai Chow, a revolutionary movement led by the westernized Christian Chinese patriot Sun Yat-sen, overthrew the ancient Manchu monarchy and announced a republic. The Manchus had survived two military defeats at the hands of Western powers in the mid-nineteenth century (1839-42 and 1856-60) but finally folded after late nineteenth-century imperialist penetration, defeat in war with Japan (1894-95), and humiliation after the Boxer Rebellion of 1900. What happened was no mere surface political phenomenon of coup and countercoup. The very basis of Chinese civilization was shaken to the core. The old ways of religion, of family life, of education and intellectual life, of technology and economic life—all were being transformed under the impact of Western rationality, commercial expansion, and religious reform.

The Mennonite mission, then, worked in China in a time of maximum creative chaos. The discrediting of Confucianism and the old order it supported meant unparalleled opportunity for the Christian gospel to reach alienated people hungry for new alternatives. However, the perpetual political ferment, fed by deep-seated Chinese hatred of Western arrogance and exploitation, meant that the mission worked under the threat of expulsion by whatever warlords, revolutionaries, or counterrevolutionaries happened to be in control of their region at any given time.

The contrast between China and India is instructive.[7] India absorbed the impact of the West over a longer period of time, and within the stability provided by relatively benign British colonial control. China was culturally more homogeneous than India, resisted the West at first more successfully, and finally capitulated more rapidly and thoroughly. No one government, either domestic or foreign, was able to establish firm political control in China prior to the 1950s. England, France, Germany, Japan, the United States, and other imperialist powers fought with each other and against Chinese resisters for relative advantage. In India the General Conference Mennonite missionaries never had to evacuate from the mission stations in Madya Pradesh—a remarkable record of continuity in a century ripped by world wars and colonial rebellions. In China the history of the Mennonite mission was punctuated by evacuations which had a telling effect upon mission institutions as well as upon mission-church relationships.

The social systems of India and China formed another contrast. China lacked the rigid stratification of a caste system. The entry of Christianity into this society could not be through depressed classes, equivalent to the Chamars of Chhattisgarh or the Garas of Phuljhar, who saw the new religion as a means of escape from hereditary subservience. Of poverty there was plenty in China. Landholdings were small and inadequate, especially in years of drought. But the land was more widely owned than in India. And the climate of the Huang Ho valley was conducive to cultivation of a greater variety of grains and vegetables than in the rice-dominated monsoon area of the central Indian plains. When H. J. Brown visited the Mennonite mission area in India in 1927, he noted the blight of superstition and sloth on Indian agriculture: "The Indian farmer should go to the Chinese farmer and take a lesson or two," he wrote.[8]

The Mennonite mission developed more rapidly and the Chinese church grew to challenge mission leadership more quickly than had been the case in India. The Chinese Christians seemed more aggressive, more impatient, more nationalistic than the Indians. Chinese Christians came from a broader cross section of society, including persons in prominent social and political positions, and did not have to contend with the subservient psychology of India's untouchables. Moreover, there were highly visible Christians at the head of Chinese revolutionary nationalist movements. The example of prominent so-called Christians such as Sun Yat-sen, Feng Yu-hsiang, and Chiang Kai-shek gave the Christian religion an aura of authority and legitimacy far out of proportion to the actual numbers of Chinese Christians (never more than 1 percent of the total population). In contrast, the religious identification of Indian national leaders Mohandas K. Gandhi, Jawaharlal Nehru, and Mohammed Ali Jinnah never remotely suggested the prospect of forging a common Christian and national destiny. In short, there was a brief moment of Christian opportunity in China in the years following the foundation of the republic in 1912.

The Cross Under the Crown

In these decades missionaries brought a whole range of modernizing reforms for which the victorious Communists would later take exclusive credit. Historian John K. Fairbank outlines missionary pioneering activity which helped foment creative revolution:

> . . . the spread of literacy to ordinary people, the publication of journals and pamphlets in the vernacular, education and equality for women, the abolition of arranged child-marriages, the supremacy of public duty over filial obedience and family obligations, increased agricultural productivity through the sinking of wells and improved tools, crops, and breeds, dike and road building for protection against flood and famine, public health clinics to treat common ailments and prevent disease, discussion groups to foster better conduct, student organizations to promote healthy recreation and moral guidance, and the acquisition and Sinification of Western knowledge for use in remaking Chinese life.[9]

Impressive though the list of missionary-initiated reforms may be, there remains the question of whether the missionary enterprise was so wrapped in Western dress, so identified with foreign political interests, and so unwilling to acknowledge and promote national leadership over church and mission institutions that successful indigenization of Christianity in Chinese life was inevitably doomed. A conclusive answer to this question is not at hand. But we do know that H. J. Brown in China had to face this question much more quickly and urgently than did P. A. Penner in India. The cross loomed under the crown for all China missionaries.

The history of General Conference mission work in China can be divided into three stages, each separated from the other by major evacuations from the mission field. The first sixteen years, until the evacuation in the face of civil war in 1927, were a time of solid foundation building and rapid expansion. The second stage, until the Japanese invasion in World War II, was a time of unsettlement and reorientation. In the years after the war, the work on the old field was disrupted by civil war. The last General Conference missionaries left China in 1951.

By the time of the 1927 evacuation, twenty-three missionaries had arrived on the GC field in China. The major influx came in the 1918-21 period, with an increase of funds and volunteers which seems to have resulted from the impact of World War I in North America. The field covered the six southernmost counties in Chihli (changed to Hopei in 1928) province, an area of some 4,000 square miles (10,400 square kilometers) and 2,220,000 people living in 4,500 villages. The major mission stations were at Kai Chow, with one large church built in the town and one at the main station in the southeast suburb; and at Taming Fu, where a church building with capacity to seat 1,200 people was under construction in 1927. The four other county seats—Nan-lo, Tsing-feng, Chang-yuan, and Tung-ming (the latter separated from the rest by the Huang Ho River), served as centers for schools, for regular church services, and for evangelistic and medical itineration to the villages.

The medical work at first depended upon the audacity of H. J. Brown, who performed many surgical operations that went far beyond what he had learned in two years of training. Dr. Abe M. (and Marie Wollmann) Lohrentz and nurses Elizabeth Goertz and Frieda Sprunger came in 1921 as the first professional medical workers. In 1926 they made a total of 6,451 outpatient visits. Central hospital facilities were developed at Kai Chow.

Authority and Cultural Confrontation

The quality of personal relationships between the Mennonite missionaries and the Chinese people cannot be fully known or reconstructed from our distance in time and space. The stories of pioneer China missionaries, like stories from India, picture them as figures of towering authority and courage. It was told how H. J. Brown once faced a threatening, screaming village mob which had barricaded the street and was grabbing at the buggy wheels and mule reins: "Rev. Brown jumped out of the buggy and shouted something at them which evidently told them to open the way. He was so tall and his black goatee made him an impressive figure. They slowly backed away as he walked ahead of our mules dispersing the crowd."[10]

Brown was a figure of great spiritual authority as well. One hot and dry Sunday in Kai Chow after a year of drought, the Chinese Christians gathered to pray for rain. Brown preached to them on Solomon, who had asked for wisdom rather than for material benefits. The next day it began pouring rain. According to one account, "Many Chinese said they had prayed to their gods for months and no rain had come; the missionary had prayed to his God once and it rained next day!"[11]

For some missionaries, perhaps even for Brown, the posture of authority and self-confidence must have masked feelings of fear and insecurity.[12] Adaptation to the remote and different Chinese physical and social environment was not easy. Aganetha Fast, who had wanted to go to India, reported what an awful struggle it was for her to learn to love China and the Chinese people. China was so *yellow,* she said, beginning with the dirty yellow ocean she saw upon arrival.

> As we faced inland, I saw the yellow skinned people. And after we docked, I saw the yellow soil, the yellow sky and the drab yellow mud huts. Everything was yellow! Even the very air that we breathed was yellow as was the sky, the sun, the trees, and the bushes because the fine yellow dust clung to everything.[13]

Fast's language teacher was a sixty-year-old local scholar, Leo Hsien Sheng, who wore a traditional braided queue with a black silk tassel reaching down to his heels. For breakfast he ate garlic and *chi tsai,* an onion-type vegetable which she said smelled like a skunk. At language lessons he sat just across from his uncultivated, culture-shocked missionary students and spat out Mandarin pronunciations with an exaggerated blow from his lips. "We always got the full benefit of the kind of food he had eaten for breakfast," Fast wrote.[14] She also told of her instinctive recoil from the lice-ridden children, from adults who did not bathe all winter, and from hot tea served in unwashed cups. In time, missionary Fast learned that the Chinese, on the other hand, were often nauseated by the peculiar missionary body odor and house smells. The Chinese were also facing major culture shock. The Confucianist learning of scholar Leo, together with his proud queue, belonged to a discredited and crumbling world.

It was virtually impossible for missionaries to avoid assuming their own cultural superiority. Their very reason for being in China had to do with a better way of life for these people who bound their daughters' feet, made offerings to snake gods in holy trees, and left unwanted babies to die of exposure in the fields. The grand artistic and architectural Chinese achievements, which some missionaries greatly appreciated during their visits or vacations in the cities, seemed quite remote from the backward life of the remote villages. In Kai Chow and Taming Fu the totality of missionary life was shaped by the unflattering difference between superior foreigners and inferior Chinese. Missionary mothers could be heard reprimanding their unruly children at the table: "You are behaving just like Chinese."[15]

Missionary confrontation with local Chinese custom was decisive. Christian parents were not allowed to bind the feet of their daughters no matter how much they feared raising daughters to face community prejudice. (All big-footed Chinese women were considered degraded prostitutes.) Boarding students in Mennonite schools had to abide by strict rules of discipline.

A classic confrontation of Christian missionary and local religious superstition occurred around the fate of one holy tree just outside the city wall at Kai Chow. It happened that the tree stood on property owned by the local postmaster, who was one of the most prominent members of the Mennonite church as well as a leader in the Young Men's Christian Association. Missionaries E. G. Kaufman and Sam Goering counseled with the Christian postmaster, suggesting that he cut down the tree, which was a focus of popular religiosity. The postmaster demurred. He did not want to offend the people who came to the tree to say prayers and make offerings, even though he personally agreed that the worship which went on there was worthless superstition. Eventually, the postmaster accepted an offer from the mission to buy the tree, cut it down, and use the lumber for school buildings.

Kaufman and Goering saw here an opportunity to demonstrate the power of Christ and the weakness of the forces of darkness in a marvelous way. They made a public announcement of the day and time when they, together with Christians from the Kai Chow church, would cut down the tree. A huge crowd gathered for the event. The Christians posed for the obligatory camera photo and proceeded to saw down the tree, with Kaufman and Goering taking the first cuts. Kaufman later wondered if they had not taken a foolish risk. The local crowd might well have turned into an angry and violent mob. Moreover, if anything unfortunate for the mission took place in connection with the event, it would be attributed to the offense against the snake god in the tree. As it turned out, the tree crashed down in Christian triumph. Popular superstition took one more beating, and the Mennonites had more lumber to build schools for the teaching of science and Christianity. Kaufman reported, however, that the resilient local belief system made its accommodations: One story circulated that the snake god slithered onto a plate held by a woman, and that this woman carried it to a nearby pond before the Christians could harm it. Another story told how the clever missionaries pointed a little black box at the tree, the box made a "click," and the god was captured in the box so it couldn't hurt the Christians![16]

Christian Gospel in Western Clothing

Questions about the propriety of missionaries living in large Western-style houses arose earlier in China than in India. The climate in the interior Huang Ho valley was less severe than the summer heat in India which dictated the high-ceilinged bungalows. Missionary health in China was a major concern and problem, nonetheless. H. J. and Maria Brown buried two sons in China. E. G. and Hazel Dester Kaufman and W. C. and Matilda Kliewer Voth each lost one child. E. G. Kaufman nearly died of smallpox. Missionaries argued that Western-style homes, besides being more comfortable and familiar, would be more sanitary and healthful. When W. C. Voth arrived in 1919 to oversee the building of a number of new dwellings, the question of architectural style was thoroughly discussed and settled by majority vote. Voth presented a plan for a one-story house in the Chinese courtyard style. But the majority favored a semibungalow type, such as was currently popular in California where the Voths had visited.[17] The neighboring Presbyterian and Nazarene missions had two-story houses, as did the missionaries in Peking. The Mennonites were like other Protestants in housing as well as in other matters.

Missionary homes served evangelistic purposes as surely as did the large touring tents and the village home visitation teams. The Chinese were curious about missionary life-style and eagerly accepted invitations. In one New Year season two missionary homes were opened to small groups who came in for a half-hour of gospel stories and songs, and then were let out a side door while another group crowded through the front door. In this way they shared with about five hundred people between 8:30 A.M. and 2:00 P.M. Some missionaries remained critical of the multistoried houses with their furniture ordered from Montgomery Ward. Such houses were expensive, and they were a temptation to invading Nationalist, Japanese, and Communist soldiers. They were not suited for transfer to Chinese Christians when missionaries left, in part because of inter-Chinese jealousies and in part because the houses were not well adapted to the Chinese way of living. The old Mennonite ideal of a simple life, rapidly eroding with the onset of affluence and acculturation in North America, did not become part of the missionary message.[18]

The missionaries brought a Christian gospel wrapped in Western clothing to China. They were not students of cultural anthropology. They assumed the proper way to praise God in song was with melodies, rhythms, and harmonies they had learned from childhood in their Mennonite homes and churches. They introduced into Kai Chow, Taming Fu, and the surrounding villages their Western forms of church architecture, order of worship, rituals for marriage and burial, and disciplines for Chinese employees within mission institutions. The mission had great power and authority to impose its own forms of the Christian faith and life upon the rural people in China's interior.

Freedom and Compromise

But it would not be accurate to see the missionaries as unthinking autocrats, their message as simple imposition, and their Chinese followers as passive sponges who soaked up whatever the missionaries presented. The Chinese had considerable latitude in choosing which aspects of mission services and witness they would accept or reject. They could come to the mission hospital, pay the price of listening to the songs and messages of the Christians in the waiting room, receive the doctor's advice or medicines, and return home to reflect on what part of the experience, if any, had been worthwhile. They could sing lustily when Chinese tunes were used and weakly for Western tunes. The Chinese quickly learned that one did not have to convert to Christianity to receive medical care or to attend the Mennonite schools. The missionaries wanted people to join their churches not by force, but by their own free will.

Chinese who decided to join the church found themselves in an institution firmly controlled by the missionaries. But here again there were limits to missionary control, and a considerable gray area existed where there was room for disagreement, dialogue, and even disobedience within the church. Missionaries had no canned answer, for example, for matters relating to Chinese veneration of the ancestors. The Mennonites honored their dead with stone or marble grave markers and paid respects in the church graveyard. This was not considered worship or idolatry. But what did it mean when a Chinese Christian continued the traditional family New Year's ceremony of bringing out the ancestral tablets and burning incense, and insisted that this was not worshiping but simply paying proper respect? The Mennonite missionaries were not agreed on the matter, and their disagreement created room for Chinese freedom in the matter. H. J. Brown took a hard line. On one occasion, it was said, he went to the home of a church deacon who was "worshiping" the family ancestral tablets, denounced the ceremony, and threw the tablets on the floor. E. G. Kaufman disagreed with Brown. The ceremony, Kaufman said, should not be considered worship.[19] The offending deacon was not powerless; he threatened withdrawal from the church. He also had a son who was a university student who could make an articulate defense of his father's behavior.

A compromise between Chinese and Western tradition was sometimes possible—for example, when missionaries disagreed about marriage ritual. The Mennonite mission board, in response to a 1914 inquiry from H. J. Brown about policy regarding marriage and polygamy, instructed him to "follow the practice of other more experienced missions." In particular they referred him to the written policies of the Moravian and Basel mission societies. These regulations forbade Christians from entering polygamous marriages but did not absolutely require persons in polygamous marriages who became Christians to give up those marriages.[20] It was not possible, of course, for a mission board in North America, or even a mission station in China, to determine a policy which would answer all questions regarding marriage practice and ritual. Brown performed all the Christian weddings in the early years of the mission, using a pattern derived from other Protestant missions.

Not all the Christians were satisfied with the marriage ritual, however. Three of E. G. Kaufman's students who wanted Christian marriages came to Kaufman with their problem. They wanted marriage ceremonies which would conform more closely to Chinese custom. They found it particularly offensive for the marriage partners to hold hands in public and for the preacher to hold his hand over their joined hands in pronouncing the blessing. Kaufman worked out a new pattern together with them. The preacher would put his hands on the heads of the couple, rather than on their united hands. They would bow to their parents and to each other, but not to heaven. Instead of mixing brandy from two cups to symbolize unity, as in traditional Chinese marriage, they would use tea. Kaufman was afraid that the senior missionaries would veto these plans if he consulted with them, so he went ahead on his own and married the three students and their brides one day in a village home.[21]

When Kaufman's innovations and virtual insubordination became known in the mission, a storm of controversy ensued. For a time Kaufman feared "they might send me home yet." The marriage ceremony conflict was resolved by the appointment of a committee of three Chinese Christians and three missionaries, which drafted a "Policy on Engagement, Marriages, and Burial." The policy, adopted in the 1924 meeting of the Executive Committee and the Workers' Conference, consisted of twenty-two statements, including the following:

> (a) Marriage of either boy or girl shall not take place before the age of eighteen. (b) There shall be liberty as to the marriage garb worn. (c) All customs which are in contradiction to Christian teachings (such as idol worship, and k'o-t'ow to heaven and earth) are forbidden, and noisy serenading is not to be connected with weddings. (d) The ceremony is conducted by an ordained minister of the Gospel.[22]

Autonomy and Shared Authority

The committee's work on marriage and burial policy in the early 1920s was part of a larger ferment by Chinese church leaders for greater autonomy and authority over their own affairs. There had been a decade of fairly rapid growth since H. J. Brown had baptized his first class of eight Christians at Kai Chow in 1913. By 1923 there were ten church congregations.[23] Eight college graduates and many high school graduates worked in mission institutions.[24] These potential leaders were eager to have a larger role in church affairs, in administrating mission institutions, and in shaping the structure of the mission constitution. Events in this process moved much more rapidly than in the Mennonite India mission. The mandate of the six-person committee on marriage and burial policy was expanded to include the question of church-mission relationships. Then in 1923 a special committee on constitutional revision was created, and an interim procedure for Chinese church representation in mission decision making was adopted. The temporary plan was

> that any Christian community of fifty church members, calling their own preacher, shall receive a total grant, from the Mission, of nine-tenths of the salary of the preacher (according to the Mission wage scale), and be given the power to send a delegate with full voting privileges to our annual meetings. This arrangement is to be valid for one year.[25]

This "temporary" arrangement was extended for over a decade. The Chinese Christians and the missionaries were unable to come to an agreement regarding shared authority under a new constitution. The constitution revision committee made reports and recommendations which were vigorously debated in annual meetings but which could not be finally accepted because the Chinese demanded more authority than the missionaries were willing to give. The basic plan was to create a missionary-Chinese council which would act as executive committee for the entire work of the mission. There would be equal Chinese and missionary representation on the evangelistic, medical, and educational committees, with some exceptions. The plan foundered on the question of money, and specifically the matter of whether a Chinese national would be allowed to hold the position of mission treasurer. The missionaries refused to allow provision for a Chinese treasurer. The Chinese refused to agree to a constitution which in principle excluded them from this position. By the end of 1927 the distraught Mennonite mission-church community in China was at an impasse and had to refer the issue to a higher authority—the foreign mission board in North America.

Growing Nationalism

Meanwhile political events in China overtook the mission. The Great War (1914-1918) fostered a strong nationalist movement throughout China. Students educated in Protestant mission schools were in the vanguard of the movement. Their nationalistic fervor was roused first by Japanese wartime aggression and expansion into China (the famous "Twenty-One Demands") and by the failure of the 1919 Versailles Peace Treaty to protect the Chinese national right of self-determination.[26] The students organized nationwide protests and boycotts of Japanese goods. E. G. Kaufman felt the sting of the protests in Kai Chow when his students demanded that he stop selling Japanese-made pencils, and that he return the money to students who had bought such pencils from him earlier. Kaufman wrote of being awakened in the middle of the night by students who had received political news and who "felt they could not wait until morning to discuss the possibilities and dangers confronting their nation and wanted to know what they might do far off in an interior town to help the great cause along."[27]

In 1927 General Chiang Kai-shek moved his armies northward to defeat the Communists and the warlords who had taken over from the defunct republic. In the spring of that year, at the time of the "Shanghai massacres" in which Chiang's Kuomintang forces routed the Communists, the Mennonite missionaries turned over their keys to the Chinese church leaders and fled in response to urging from the American consulate. Some missionaries went to North America on furlough, some went to coastal areas, and a few returned to the field temporarily to oversee transition of the work.[28]

The warlord in the Northwest was General Feng Yu-hsiang. Feng was a "Christian" general who had been influenced by John R. Mott and who was noted for mass baptisms of his soldiers—up to 3,719 in a single day. The Mennonite mission was near the edge of territory under Feng's control, and in the crisis of 1927 his army occupied the mission schools, hospital, and some missionary homes. Missionaries Talitha Neufeld and Frieda Sprunger were alone on the station at the time and were treated with respect by the army.[29] E. G. Kaufman had very high regard for General Feng. He had been at one of the mass army baptisms in 1923 and reported that it "reminded one of Pentecost." Kaufman wrote of Feng, "The Christians of the land however have great faith in him and pray that he may be used as an instrument in God's hand to bring order out of chaos in China."[30] It was Kaufman's view, writing in 1925, that Feng had the support of the student movement as well as of the missionaries.[31] As it turned out, after six months of desperate fighting and the loss of some 150,000 men, Feng surrendered to a victorious Chiang Kai-shek. The Mennonite missionaries returned in the fall of 1928 to a China controlled by the Nationalist Kuomintang. But Nationalist control, like all authority in China, it seemed, was not secure. It was threatened by the Japanese in Manchuria and by the Communists in the interior.

Developing Church Leaders

Meanwhile the Mennonite mission board had to reach a decision regarding the impasse between the Chinese Christians and the Mennonite missionaries in the mission constitution dispute. After hearing the advice of missionaries on furlough, the board asked the Chinese to appoint a seven-person committee, consisting of four Chinese and three missionaries selected from a slate of five proposed by the board.[32] The new committee in its turn faced months and years of proposals, counterproposals, arguments, and compromises, until a constitution was finally adopted in Kai Chow in August 1935. It had been twelve years since the first joint committee began work on the constitution. The twelve-year failure of the mission and the church to come to conclusive agreement on a constitution governing mutual relationships and shared authority is testimony to the strained relationships between national and foreigner in China and the complexity of the Chinese social and political situation.

The antiforeign and anti-Christian student movement of the 1920s involved a setback for the mission. In January 1927 the students at Hua Mei middle and high school at Kai Chow went out on strike. To H. J. Brown's great dismay, students at the Bible school which had been founded in 1925 joined in the strike, and "a few of them seemed even worse than the rest." When the strike fever subsided, the Hua Mei students were all reinstated, but the mission closed the Bible school. Another Bible school was begun at Taming Fu under the leadership of P. J. Boehr.[33] The mission was not successful in attracting and holding educated leaders. Brown complained that they had to depend upon "second grade men" sent from other Protestant missions.[34] Most of the college-educated men who worked with the mission in the mid-1920s eventually left the Mennonites. The extensive Mennonite education program which, according to one survey published in 1922, had more children in school per church members than any other mission in North China,[35] yielded a disappointing harvest for church leadership. One missionary wrote, "Thousands of young promising people have gone through our schools, but to a large extent the church members have consisted of old illiterate women."[36]

There were some notable exceptions to the pattern of generally weak leadership. Two of the most promising Mennonite students, Stephen Wang and James C. Liu, attended American schools at Bluffton and Bethel colleges beginning in the fall of 1930. E. G. Kaufman, who became president of Bethel College instead of returning to China after his first furlough, arranged private support for Wang and Liu. Both of these men returned to take positions of leadership in the church and schools and to suffer the severe consequences which followed from Communist takeover of China. Both Wang and Liu wrote articles for the twenty-fifth anniversary publication of the mission in 1936. Wang attempted to disentangle the Christian gospel from the structures of Western Christendom in adapting to the Chinese environment. He wrote, "It is, therefore, not the Jesus of the creeds and the ceremony, not the Jesus of Christendom with its economic and military might, it is the Jesus of the Galilean ministry and the redemptive work in Jerusalem who is being discovered by and is discovering the young men and women of China today."[37]

Significant leadership roles in the Chinese church were taken by Christian women. From the earliest years, adult women converts worked as "Bible women" in village evangelism. Maria Brown paid special tribute to the work of Bible women Chia and Liu, as well as Mrs. Wang, the mother of Stephen Wang.[38]

Elizabeth Goertz, Aganetha Fast, Marie Regier, and other women missionaries found in mission work greater challenges and greater status than they would have had in church vocations at home. Goertz founded the successful Yu Jen School of Nursing in Kai Chow in 1930. Fast and Regier worked for many years in village itineration at outstations and in the countryside. Matilda Voth took special interest in infant welfare. Mothers' clubs for Christian women were organized at both Kai Chow and Taming Fu. Pauline Miller Goering organized a Women's Missionary Society in the Taming Fu church. Appalled by the suppresssion of women in Chinese society, nearly all of the women missionaries became involved in women's uplift work of one kind or another.

The most aggressive Chinese Mennonite woman leader was Li Ching Fen (known also as Mrs. Lu or "Lu Tai Tai") who was chosen moderator of the Taming Fu congregation many years before women in North America were allowed to serve in equivalent positions of church authority. Matilda Voth wrote that Mrs. Lu "was respected by men and women alike, and her independence was not resented by the men of the congregation or mission."[39]

Toward Financial Autonomy

Missionary problems in church leadership development were matched by difficulties in moving toward church self-support. A plan adopted in 1923 proposed to have local congregations pay for 10 percent of their pastor's support, and to increase their percentage an additional ten points yearly until they would achieve full self-support in a decade. With the exception of the Kai Chow east suburb church, where gifts of mission salaried employees helped the budget, none of the Chinese congregations met their commitments on the graduated scale. Missionaries linked the issue of governance to the matter of support. Was it fair for a congregation to be self-governing if it was not self-supporting? There were various reasons for this failure of self-support. Missionary W. C. Voth mentioned four:

1. Poverty. Landholdings were small and crops were ravaged by drought, flood, and grasshoppers.

2. Desire for material gain. Converts became Christians with mixed motives. They hoped to receive rather than give.

3. Misleading teachings. Evangelists taught that salvation was free and that converts would not have to buy incense for the gods and paper money for the dead.

4. Banditry and wars. Available resources were drained by political chaos.[40]

There seemed to be little prospect when Voth wrote in 1936 that this bleak picture would change for the better in the future. The Chinese Mennonite Church was quite unable or unwilling to bear the costs of local maintenance, administration, and leadership. Meanwhile the mission schools and hospitals were far too expensive in their operations to plan for institutional self-support.

At the twenty-fifth anniversary of the mission in 1936, total church membership stood at 1,175. This was almost exactly the same number at the twenty-fifth anniversary of the India mission eleven years earlier. But the mood projected in the two "jubilee celebrations" contrasted sharply. The India missionaries published a 250-page book entitled *Twenty-Five Years with God in India,* in which they predicted great Christian growth: "In the next twenty-five years we or others shall see such an ingathering as we have hardly dreamed. We are in the dawn of a new era for India."[41] The China missionaries, sobered by the depression, by warfare, and by troubled mission-church relationships, were less optimistic. Sunday school attendance and the number of "Enquirers" were down since 1930. A yearly average of about seventy new Christians was being baptized into fifteen churches in a "field" with a population of over two million. "We must work and labor while it is yet day," wrote Maria Brown. "Only too soon it will be night, when man can work no more."[42]

The Beginning of the End

World War II and the subsequent Communist triumph in China drew a curtain across the General Conference Mennonite mission work in China. The work continued with surprisingly little disruption for two years after invading Japanese troops occupied Kai Chow on 11 February 1939. There were seventeen adult missionaries plus children at the annual mission conference in late 1940, but only eight remained after the evacuation of married women and children in April 1941.[43] Others left later. Two single missionaries, Marie Regier and Elizabeth Goertz, remained and were interned in a Japanese concentration camp, Shantung Compound.[44] Three families who had gone to the Philippines also spent the duration of the war in concentration camps.

But the politically chaotic and dangerous years from 1938 to 1941 were years of religious revival and church growth. Mission-church relationships improved and anti-Western feelings diminished in the face of Japanese aggression. Church membership nearly doubled (88 percent increase) to a total of 2,273 members between 1935 and 1940. In the year of 1940 alone there was an increase of 15.6 percent. Taken by themselves, the membership statistics suggested that the church had reached a takeoff stage.

The leadership of the twin brothers S. F. and C. L. Pannabecker lent a degree of maturity and sophistication to the General Conference China mission in its latter years. C. L. came as a medical doctor to take the post of medical superintendent at the Kai Chow hospital, where the number of inpatients increased from 810 in 1938 to 1,205 in 1940. S. F., who at the time of evacuation was principal of the Bible school and editor of the missions paper *The China-Home Bond,* articulated most clearly the problems and prospects of the mission.

Shortly before his August 1941 departure from the field, S. F. Pannabecker summarized the condition of the Chinese Mennonite Church in an article, "Withdrawal and the Future."[45] He noted the Chinese church's strength in the three areas critical for survival under difficulties. There was a spiritually alive "central Christian nucleus," a strong core of available leaders, and a good overall indigenous church organization. All mission institutions, including schools, hospitals, and churches, were administered by trained Chinese. (The Pannabecker brothers were replaced by Dr. Paul Hu at the hospital and the reverend Chang Ching in the Bible school.) The first five Chinese pastors had been ordained in 1940. A new church conference had been organized in March 1940 with an elected general committee which had authority to make decisions formerly reserved for the mission conference. James Liu was the chairman of the new church conference, with Ku Tung-ching (hospital business manager) serving as secretary.

Pannabecker's optimism was guarded, but he had great hope for the future. ". . . It seems quite possible," he wrote, "that we have a setup independent of foreign operation. In general our work is in the best condition it has ever been to face future eventualities."[46] In later years Pannabecker came to see that Mennonite mission-church institutions were more fragile than was realized in 1941.[47] Financial dependence on outside sources was especially dramatic. Only one of the twenty-four Chinese church congregations in 1940 operated without mission subsidy. The foreign subsidy for the hospital in 1940 was $22,551.50. Even though subsequent events exposed the church's weakness, it is important to note in a comparative context that this Chinese Mennonite Church in 1941 was stronger and more independent than any of the General Conference mission churches of that time, including the work in Oklahoma, Arizona, Montana, India, and the Belgian Congo.

After the War

Some attempts were made to return to the field after World War II, but the war between the Nationalists and the Communists made it impossible to carry on any sustained work. The Mennonite Central Committee (MCC), an inter-Mennonite relief agency, established a unit for agricultural rehabilitation and medical services at Kaifeng, Honan province, 100 miles (260 kilometers) southwest of Kai Chow. S. F. Pannabecker served as unit director from 28 September 1945 until July 1946. James Liu worked as MCC interpreter and liaison with the Chinese community. The MCC unit left Kaifeng in December 1947 as the area came under Communist control.[48]

Mennonite missionaries demonstrated remarkable fortitude and tenacity as they lived through evacuations, concentration camps, and removal to western China in search of a field. After removal from Kaifeng the missionaries moved to Paoki in Shensi province, and thence to Chengtu in Szechwan province. The last GC missionaries to leave China were P. J. and Frieda Sprunger Boehr in 1951. The Chinese Mennonite Church had experienced revival and growth in 1946. In 1948 H. J. Brown received a letter reporting seven hundred conversions in six months.[49] With the consolidation of Communist control over the area, however, the educated Mennonite church leaders fled the area, and the church was discredited as a foreign, counterrevolutionary, imperialist institution. Missionaries gradually lost touch with their friends and fellow-believers in China. It finally became such a liability for a Chinese Christian to receive a letter from abroad that missionaries had to discontinue written correspondence. In the late 1970s former Mennonite missionaries had some evidence that there were some Chinese Christians in the mission area who were still meeting for worship and fellowship, although the days of public worship and of thriving church institutions were long past.

The Mennonite mission work in Kai Chow, Taming Fu, and vicinity was a tiny fragment of a Protestant enterprise in China which peaked at nearly 10,000 missionaries. And this Protestant force was small in numbers compared to China's 500 million people. But the relatively small size of the Mennonite mission was no shield or consolation for the great sense of disappointment and failure which flowed from the defeat of the mission and the church. What went wrong in China? Mennonite answers to that question shaped the outlines of new mission programs in Japan and Taiwan, and stimulated an assessment of Mennonite missions priorities in India.[50] Missionaries who calculated results in terms of numbers of baptisms, outpatient visits, schools started, and the like, had a difficult time to come to terms with the destruction of mission properties in the war and with the virtual collapse of the Chinese church. God had called us to this work. Didn't God keep His promises?

In Retrospect

The Christian "failure" in China was especially striking in the light of original mission intentions which Mennonites shared with other Protestants. Nathaniel B. Grubb had written in the *Mennonite* that the objective was nothing less than Chinese national salvation through Christianity. Grubb, who had studied under C. J. van der Smissen at the Wadsworth school, wrote, "The missionary in China has the responsibility of making over old China into a new China as well as caring for the soul, the minds, and the bodies of the Chinese."[51] Measured against the hope for a Christian-based national regeneration, the missionary accomplishment seemed weak and futile.

In the first decade after their exclusion, the missionaries looked forward to the day of their return. As additional years passed, it became clear that Mao Tse Tung's People's Republic of China was having remarkable success in national economic development and in socialization of Chinese peoples to an order of high public and private morality. China had found it possible to break decisively with its Confucianist and feudal past, to achieve a kind of secular national salvation, and to become a model for revolutionary development in "poor" countries—all this without reference to God, Christ, or the Christian church. The Chinese experiment raised deep questions for contemporary Christian theology, as surely as for the aging "old China hands."[52]

From one point of view the Mennonite mission work in China needed no grander justification than that of faithful Christian discipleship. It was the cup of cold water given in the name of Christ. Missionaries had saved infants with sanitary dressings for the umbilical cord, liberated girl children from foot binding, fended off starvation with relief goods in famine times, taught science and literature to hundreds of young people, and preached the gospel of a Christ who died to save people from sin and death. The Communists were by no means the first to "go to the people" with the liberating benefits of science, technology, and rationality to combat the deadening weight of popular superstition. Nor could missionaries be accused of seeking after financial gain.

To be sure, the missionaries had had their full share of human frailty and were burdened with the weight of their Western institutions. Too often they cultivated an attitude and a life-style of superiority. Too often they wrangled among themselves over theological issues or mission policy. They were preoccupied with meeting individual needs and did not sufficiently address the structural sociopolitical issues of justice and oppression. They were too slow in handing over their positions, their money, and their keys to national church leaders. Such failures were not entirely unacknowledged. Missionaries were often their own best critics. They made adjustments in policy and program—from the use of more Chinese tunes to the transfer of schools to Chinese authorities—as new conditions yielded new insights. H. J. Brown in the 1920s saw the need "to subdue western initiative so that it takes no advantage of Chinese courtesy."[53] Nevertheless, in 1941, Brown yielded to the courteous insistence of the Chinese that he take the post of church conference chairman. At the same time he was serving as acting church conference treasurer and elder of Taming Fu Village. Despite better intentions, missionary authority dominated until the missionary departure.

In the broader perspective of Anabaptist-Mennonite history, it may be wondered why the Mennonite China missionaries were so thoroughly *Protestant* in their attitudes and theology. If they had been in touch with their Anabaptist origins, they might have more clearly understood the possibility of a remnant church which endeavors to be faithful in an unregenerate world. Instead of preparing the church for suffering and martyrdom, the missionaries looked forward to a triumphant Christianizing of China at the hands of a political savior such as General Feng Yu-hsiang or General Chiang Kai-shek.[54]

The Chinese Mennonite discovery of their radical Anabaptist heritage might have evolved if given more time. James Liu gave a talk on Anabaptist history at the twenty-fifth anniversary celebration of the mission. Stephen Wang looked beyond the Jesus of Christendom to the "Jesus of the Galilean ministry and the redemptive work in Jerusalem."[55] There were resources in the models of a non-Christendom church to be found in the experiences of the first-century church and of Anabaptist Christians, which could nourish the identity of a minority church in a totalitarian society. It was one of the many tragedies of Christian missions in China that Mennonites were so much a part of Protestant Christendom that they were unable to share more completely their distinctive Anabaptist heritage.

4 Congo, 1911-1960

Doering's Grand Vision

It happened in a thoroughly patriarchal Mennonite brotherhood that the dominant figure in the early years of mission work in the Congo[1] was a woman. Her name was Alma Doering. She was baptized as an infant, daughter of German Lutheran immigrant parents in Chicago. She never was rebaptized, never became a Mennonite. Although she was always something of an outsider to the work, she was able to play a role in choosing the Congo mission field location, in recruiting missionary personnel, and in raising missions funds among Mennonites. In the broader context of early twentieth-century missionary enterprise, Doering was certainly no oddity. Strong, aggressive women were common in missions work generally in those days. Single women were in charge of forty evangelical boards of missions in 1910.[2] The Union Missionary Training Center in Brooklyn, where many early Mennonite missionaries went for preparation, was founded by a woman.[3] The missionary movement was on the cutting edge of social reform, and out on that edge were new opportunities for women.[4]

In launching the Congo mission effort, Doering made an unlikely and uneasy alliance with two small Mennonite groups—the Defenseless Mennonites and the Central Conference of Mennonites. Both of these groups had emerged around the leadership of Amish bishops who broke away from their churches over issues of religious or social change. The Defenseless Mennonites, earlier known as Egli Amish, originated in about 1864 in Adams County, Indiana. Members were in agreement with Bishop Henry Egli's criticism of formalism and emphasis upon regeneration of heart. The Central Conference, earlier known as the Stucky Mennonites, originated with an 1872 division in the North Danvers Church in Illinois, led by Bishop Joseph Stucky (1825-1902).

Stucky kept in touch with the General Conference Mennonite churches in his lifetime, but the Central Conference did not join the General Conference—merging with the Middle District of the General Conference—until 1945. Both the Defenseless Mennonites and the Central Conference established formal organizations in 1908.[5] Together they cooperated to create a joint mission work, the Congo Inland Mission (CIM), and to send missionaries to the Congo in 1911. The General Conference foreign mission board did not have its own separate work in Africa, but became increasingly involved through the CIM, especially after World War II.

Although Doering's first contact with Mennonites may have been during her study at Moody Bible Institute, by the time Congo Inland Mission was formed in 1912 she had served with Mennonites during two missionary terms in Africa. She first served under a Swedish mission in Lower Congo, working together with Mathilda Kohn, who had been sent out by the Defenseless Mennonites. Then she went for a term to British East Africa together with Lawrence and Rose Boehning Haigh under Central Conference sponsorship. Between the terms she gave a "stirring missionary address" to a Central Conference meeting near Meadows, Illinois.[6]

The weak spot in Congo Inland Mission's early work was missionary recruitment. Mennonites from the Defenseless and Central Conference groups gave money for the work, but they produced few volunteers. When the first group of CIM missionaries went out to search for a mission field in the Kasai region in 1911, Alma Doering stayed at home to intinerate among the churches and find workers. The CIM board then appointed Doering and Elizabeth Schlanzky of Germany to recruit candidates in Europe. They were successful in finding a number of persons from Sweden who went to Congo under CIM but provided their own personal support. The outbreak of the World War in 1914 interfered with Doering's activities, however, and she did not return to North America until 1919.

Doering had a grand vision for the Congo Inland Mission as an extensive international and interdenominational faith mission along lines similar to Hudson Taylor's China Inland Mission. While in Europe she set forth her missions philosophy and appeal in a number of pamphlets, such as *Ready for Service, Light in Darkness,* and *The Congo Inland Mission—Her Origin and Guiding Principles.* As a missions strategist, Doering was far more sophisticated than the untutored Mennonites back in Illinois and Indiana. Central to her "guiding principles" was the idea of a self-propagating church in the Congo. As every true Christian is a missionary, she wrote in *The Congo Inland Mission,* the newly converted Congolese must be convinced that the purpose of his existence is to bring fellowmen to Jesus. The missionaries' first task is evangelistic—to win souls to Jesus. But as soon as the firstfruits are won, the Africans must take up the evangelistic task, while the missionary becomes the shepherd and teacher who builds up the newly won lambs into a biblical congregation and teaches them God's full plan of salvation. The saved ones must be prepared for practical service in building up the body of Christ.[7] She warned against premature baptism of the Negroes, against introduction of European food and clothing, and against school education without manual labor.

Doering wrote with authority. Readers might well have assumed that she was entirely in charge of CIM and its mission policies. She included policies which had not been adopted by the CIM board. She did not mention that CIM was a Mennonite mission, nor did she address the question of infant baptism, which was to become a divisive issue on the field. Doering wrote for an audience in Germany, but the CIM board may well have been concerned with a statement written by her companion, Schlanzky, that the German missionaries would eventually be allowed to separate and start an independent mission work in the Congo.[8]

In 1923 Doering finally got to the CIM Congo mission field for which she had worked so long at a distance. She quickly moved into leadership positions. In March 1924 she was elected secretary of the field committee, chairman of the literature and censorship committee, and member of the evangelistic committee and of the statistical and annual letter committee.[9] The Mennonite framework proved to be too restrictive, however, both for Doering and for the non-Mennonite missionaries she recruited. The mission was finally torn apart in 1925 by a crisis which pitted missionaries against each other and the field against the home board. The issues included the baptism question, financial support from the board, the relationship to the Congo All-Protestant Conference, the denominational identity of the mission, and a fundamentalist-modernist dispute. The mission conference, with Alma Doering writing the minutes, passed a list of ten demands to the board, including "that the Congo Inland Mission no longer consider itself a denominational organization, and that it publicly declare itself as an interdenominational organization."[10] The offended mission board dug in its heels. They not only reaffirmed their Mennonite identity but also demanded that the missionaries apologize for presuming to change the basis of the mission.

Alma Doering's stormy relationship with CIM came to an end. She resigned from the mission, along with a substantial number of the missionaries. She moved to found a mission work of her own, the Unevangelized Tribes Mission (UTM), calling upon support she had developed earlier from churches in Grand Rapids, Michigan, and elsewhere. The UTM chose for its field a region to the south and west of the CIM area. Within a number of years the UTM established twelve mission stations and many outstations. Doering's skills in recruitment and fund raising served the UTM well, but as she grew older and less active, the mission declined. In 1952 the UTM was disbanded and given over to stronger mission organizations. CIM took over responsibility for the UTM Kamayala station which included three missionaries, an orphanage, a leprosarium, numerous primary schools, and two thousand church members.[11] Back in North America, Doering founded a vacation and retirement center for missionaries in St. Petersburg, Florida, and continued working there until her death in 1959 at age eighty-one.[12]

Mission Work on the "Dark Continent"

From the point of view of North American Mennonites, the mission work in the Congo was much like mission work in India or China. The missionaries were hardworking pioneers who sacrificed the comforts of home to preach the gospel to those who had not heard. The receivers of the word were considered "heathen" who needed liberation from the evils of superstition, slavery, and illiteracy. As in India and China, the Mennonites established their mission work in the remote rural interior. Like the Hasdeo and Huang Ho rivers in India and China, the Kasai River, flowing northward from the Angola highlands toward the mighty Congo River, played a major role in the life and work of Mennonite CIM missionaires. The CIM area was for the most part an extensive plain covered by tall savanna grass, with limited tropical forests in the river valleys.[13] Wherever in the world they worked, Mennonites seemed inevitably drawn to the inland plains.

The missionary strategy in Congo was similar to equivalent work in India and China. Missionaries based their evangelistic, educational, and medical work in central stations, and carried the work beyond with a series of outstations. The rhetoric of CIM mission work was also virtually indistinguishable from Mennonite mission work elsewhere, although images of blackness and whiteness surfaced more often in reports from work among black people on the "dark continent." Missionaries were laborers on a field white unto harvest, and they gathered the fruits of labor in the face of obstacles from the powers of darkness.

Yet the CIM mission was also different in many ways from the other GC Mennonite missions. The difference was most remarkable in the relative degree of success the CIM had in achieving its goals. To anticipate the following account somewhat, the CIM-founded church experienced continued growth from its beginning years until the 1970s. The number of Congolese CIM Mennonites surpassed the numbers of the founding Central Conference and Defenseless Mennonites in the 1930s. By the 1970s, this Congo church, with some 35,000 members, was roughly 60 percent as large as the entire North American General Conference Mennonite Church.

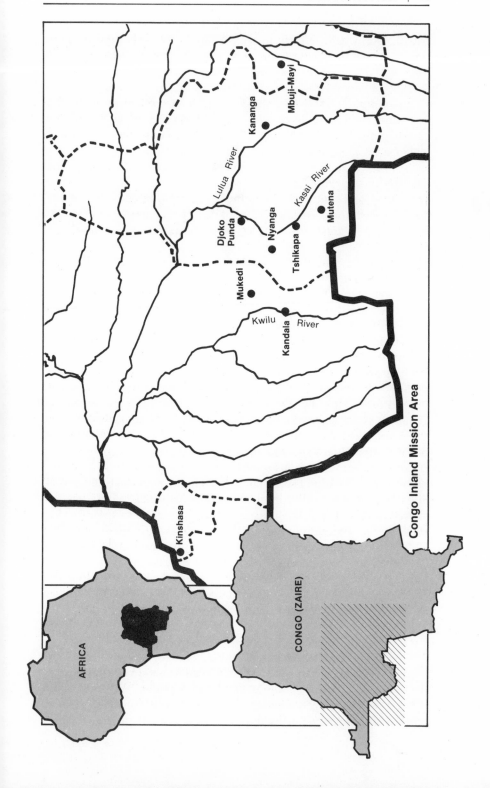

The CIM mission was relatively successful not only in terms of church growth, but also in efforts to transfer authority and control of the church to national leadership. The mission and church underwent traumatic upheaval in the independence revolution of 1960 and the Kwilu rebellion of 1964, but the outcome was an agreement to hand over all mission property and institutions to the Zaire Mennonite Church. That church remained dependent upon financial support and leadership personnel from North America but took charge of its own affairs with missionaries in a subordinate and supportive role.

CIM success in Congo was a small part of broader Christian growth not only in the great Congo basin area of central Africa, but also in West, East, and southern Africa. In the twentieth century, contrary to many expectations, Africa became largely a Christian continent. By 1970 the Christians accounted for 34 to 44 percent of the total sub-Sahara population. By the year 2000 it was projected to be up to 57 percent.[14] The young African leaders who headed independence movements and struggled to establish viable nations in the 1960s and 1970s were typically graduates of Christian mission schools. While traditional tribal religion remained influential in many areas, and the impact of Islam continued strong, Christianity, in a variety of expressions which included thousands of independent sects, came to dominate the African religious scene.

The growth of Christianity in Africa, and particularly in the Congo, cannot be attributed to enlightened or progressive colonial policies. For four centuries after the Portuguese arrival in 1482, central Africa was disrupted by the slave trade which killed millions and marked millions more with the scars of human bondage. From the 1880s to 1908 the so-called Congo Free State was the personal fiefdom of Leopold II, an international adventurer who exploited Congo's wealth in ivory and rubber through a brutal system of forced labor and through destruction of traditional tribal authority structures. By the time CIM missionaries arrived in 1911, Leopold's imperialist iniquities had been exposed, and the Congo had been turned into a Belgian colony. L. B. Haigh, founding CIM missionary, wrote in one of his first reports: "Leopoldville receives its name from the wicked King Leopold of Belgium, who died about a year ago. The land cries out with pain because of the atrocities and cruelties, carried out under his regime and at his command."[15] Haigh expected Belgian colonial rule to be an improvement.

Mennonites and Belgian Colonialists

From the beginning the Mennonite missionaries were caught in the cross fire of relationships between the Belgian colonial authorities and the native tribespeople. The most significant wealth of the Kasai, which was to fatten European pocketbooks more than to develop tribal resources, was found in the discovery of diamonds in 1907. Mining rights were vested in a company known as FORMINIERE (Societe Internationale Forestiere et Miniere du Congo) which employed many Africans who moved into the mining areas, especially at Djoko Punda and Tshikapa. The Mennonite missionaries worked not only with traditional African hunters and cultivators, but also with a dislocated people whose traditional way of life was changing under the impact of modern economic development and exploitation.

Stories from the early years bespeak an effort on the part of missionaries to distinguish themselves from the Belgian authorities. Sarah Kroeker, who worked in the Congo from 1912 to 1916, reported a crisis on the Kalamba mission station arising from the refusal of the Africans to pay taxes to the state. The white authorities came to Kalamba, captured two chiefs, killed one African in the skirmish, and imprisoned the chiefs at Luebo. The Mennonite missionaries were forced to evacuate the station because of antiwhite, anti-European hostility, although Kroeker remembered gratefully the protection of her faithful servant, Mutombo. At Luebo Mennonite Brethren (CIM) missionary Aaron Janzen visited the chief in jail and got him to agree that missionaries should be allowed to return to Kalamba and that their property should not be disturbed. [16] The Mennonites wanted the chief to testify to their good name as separate from the Belgian tax collectors.

There were also times, however, when Mennonite missionaries called upon the Belgian authorities for protection against African chiefs. Missionary Haigh recorded in his diary how pleased he was when "two state men" arrived and heard his report of "the evil doings of the chiefs." It seems that Chief Ndicansa had designs upon the wife of Mutombo, a faithful helper and evangelist for the mission. [17] It was a serious matter to use the power of the colonial government against an African chief, especially since Haigh apparently accepted the missionary strategy of winning the people through the chief. After reading of the work of Robert Moffatt in southern Africa, Haigh wrote, "I see the value of the soul of a chief as never before." [18]

The missionaries had no choice but to work in the framework provided by Belgian colonial rule. The Belgian philosophy was not to prepare the Congolese for self-rule, but to give them a rudimentary general education and technical training to take subordinate places in the colonial system. Missions were encouraged to provide a six-year primary school program, but advanced schools were forbidden until 1948. Post-secondary schools were not allowed until 1955. Congolese could not study in Belgium or elsewhere abroad. [19] Mission education reflected this colonial policy, and was not geared to rapid education and advancement of Africans to displace missionary leadership in the church.

Mennonite missionaries, nevertheless, maintained a greater degree of detachment from the Belgain authorities than was true, for example, of

Mennonites in India in relation to British authorities. The Belgians spoke French. More importantly, they were Catholic. Protestant missionaries in the Congo saw themselves as competitors and adversaries of Catholic missionaries who had the unfair advantages of preferential treatment and generous subsidies from the Catholic-oriented government. The Mennonites scorned Catholic missionary practice and strategy. The Catholics, it was said, "rule entirely by fear."[20] Mennonites considered Roman Catholic ritual as superstitious as native religion, with "holy water" simply replacing traditional fetishes. Rivalry with the Catholics proved a spur to mission expansion, as the CIM was challenged by the Scheutists in the East, Jesuits in the West, and Oblats in the North.[21] It was typical for one CIM station to report, "We have again attempted to place evangelists behind the 'purple curtain,' and have again encountered organized Catholic resistance to drive us out."[22] This Protestant-Catholic enmity helped preserve the Mennonites from unqualified identification with Belgian colonial presence and policy.

CIM missionaries had their closest Protestant contacts with the American Presbyterian Mission located just to the east of the CIM area. The Presbyterians helped the CIM select a field location, provided steamboat river transportation for Mennonite personnel and goods, and supplied the missionaries with a Tshiluba-English dictionary and grammar so they could rapidly learn the language of the Baluba and Lulua tribes. CIM missionaries had additional ecumenical contacts through membership in the Congo Protestant Council (CPC), an organization which promoted Protestant interests for the whole colony. At first the conservative missionaries were suspicious of an organization such as the CPC which was "open to all protestant missions irrespective of belief, 'fundamental' or 'radical.'"[23] But CIM cooperation with the CPC increased over the years. In 1959 CIM missionary Vernon Sprunger served as temporary interim executive secretary of the CPC, and Mennonite missionaries were chosen chairmen of the literature, educational, and nominating committees at the CPC annual meeting.[24]

An Identity Crisis

If the Congo Inland Mission experienced any success in its early years, it was in spite of, rather than because of, the pattern of relationships between the CIM board and the missionaries on the field. Until the late 1920s, the mission was troubled by policy disagreements, personnel tensions, and premature missionary resignations. John P. and Mathilda Stucky Barkman, who went to Congo in 1916, were the seventeenth and eighteenth missionaries sent by CIM. Yet they were the first to spend more than a decade on the field. At one point the dissensions among missionaires in the Congo became so disruptive that the CIM board threatened to ship all of them back to their homes!

Behind the troubles from 1911 to 1926 lay an acute identity crisis. There was no consensus on whether CIM was to be a Mennonite mission which aimed to establish a Mennonite church in the Congo. The Central Conference and Defenseless Mennonites in 1911 had chosen the name United Mennonite Board of Missions and resolved to "request" that all missionary candidates join with a Mennonite church before going to the Congo.[25] But a year later the name was changed to Congo Inland Mission, and subsequently the CIM became dependent upon the recruitment of non-Mennonite missionaries by Alma Doering. While Doering's early contribution to the CIM is unquestionable, it is also true that stable and consistent CIM development was not possible until she and her independent-minded friends resigned in 1926 and their places were taken by missionaries rooted in Mennonite understandings of baptism, church, and discipleship. In the same year when Doering left to form the Unevangelized Tribes Mission, Frank J. and Agnes Neufeld Enns from Inman, Kansas, arrived on the CIM field. Frank Enns gave the Congo Inland Mission the long-term leadership and stability that P. A. Penner and H. J. Brown provided in India and China. His service spanned forty-seven years, until 1969.

The Congo Inland Mission entered a new phase in its self-definition with the appointment of A. M. Eash, a member of the Central Conference, as mission board secretary. Eash visited the mission field in 1928-29, including in his schedule the West Africa Jubilee Missionary Conference in Kinshasa and the International Missionary Council meeting in Jerusalem. Upon returning, Eash published a new statement of CIM missions policy in the first issue of a new CIM magazine, *The Congo Missionary Messenger*.[26] The policy could be summarized simply: "In short, the missionary going to the field of the Congo Inland Mission needs to be a pioneer in bringing the message of Jesus Christ and a Christian civilization to the primitive peoples of Central Africa." The first priority was to lead Africans to "accept the Christ as their personal Savior." The second task was to build the "native Christian church" through leadership development and training in a style of life compatible with Christian standards. This would include improvement in house building, diet, medical care, child welfare, agriculture, industry, and other areas. The goal was a church "which will fully propagate, govern and finance its activities." Missionaries would have to be highly qualified for the tasks of reducing tribal languages to writing, translating the Scriptures, producing literature, and developing educational programs.

While Eash proposed to bring Christian civilization to Africa, he specifically excluded any intention "to implant western church ideas and methods in the Congo." He did not want a Mennonite denominational church to emerge in the Congo. There must be instead "a Christian Church of Africa which will know only Christ as its head." It is interesting that Eash's strong affirmation of CIM's interdenominational or ecumenical goals came so soon after Alma Doering left because CIM was not sufficiently interdenominational.

In the long run, the CIM did in fact produce a "Mennonite" church in the Congo. When the mission and church adopted a plan of "integration" in February 1960, they chose the name Eglise Evangelique Mennonite au Congo (Evangelical Mennonite Church of Congo). The name Mennonite distinguished this church from other Protestants in the Congo, but the specific meaning of that distinction needed to be clarified in coming decades. What did it mean to be Mennonite in the African context?

Although the CIM official ideology did not support the creation of a Mennonite church in the Congo, the Mennonite missionaries were undeniably influenced by the distinctive faith and practice of their home communities. In 1919 the CIM missionaries voted to institute the foot-washing service "according to the command of our Lord, beginning the first quarter after the arrival of the necessary equipment."[27] The mission practiced adult baptism by immersion, although Mennonite constituent groups were not in agreement on the form of baptism. The Mennonite doctrine of nonresistance, which was visible in the very name of the supporting "Defenseless" Mennonites, was mentioned officially in Congo for the first time in a new list of "Rules Governing Church Membership" in 1936. The meaning of *nonresistance* in Congo was not explained; the item appeared as the last in a series of prohibitions.[28] In October of 1959, as Congo was rushing headlong toward independence, the CIM board minutes recorded the strategic importance of a "Peace Witness" in the Congo "as an integral part of the gospel ministry."[29]

Mennonites and Tribal Identity

From the beginning, Mennonite missionaries, as well as the CIM board, assumed they were working among "primitive" people who lived in heathen darkness. In one moment of self-pity in 1925, the missionaries complained to the board of their tribulations in "this dark, cheerless and demon ridden land of superstition and sin."[30] A more realistic and appreciative view of African culture emerged slowly over the decades. Frank Enns was one who tried to understand and describe tribal customs. Enns's conclusion, published in the *Congo Missionary Messenger* in 1930, was that it would be unwise to "ruthlessly attack and ridicule the African's religion." "There is danger," Enns wrote, "that we uproot before we can supplant and the latter state become worse than the first." The missionary should sympathetically understand Africans and their problems. "If he [the African] is brought under conviction by the Holy Spirit he will see the folly of his own religion.[31]

Missionaries who inquired into the histories and cultures of the tribes in the Kasai area became aware of significant differences between tribal groups. The Bena Lulua and the Baluba tribes were patrilineal, with lineage traced through the father who was the clan head. Both these tribes had unified tribal structures with a chief whose authority was recognized by the clans. The Bampende, Bashilele, and Batshioko tribes, located west of the Kasai, were matrilineal, with lineage traced through the mother and with the mother's brother taking responsibility for the child. The Bena Lulua was the truly indigenous tribe east of the Kasai. The Baluba had moved in at the turn of the century after being displaced by conflicts with slave traders. The Baluba were a more mobile and aggressive group, which adapted quickly and benefitted from educational and commercial economic opportunities offered by white traders and missionaries. Tribal identities were more important than Congolese national identity for these people until well after the independence revolution of 1960. Tribalism was also a barrier or challenge to the development of the church in the Congo.

The reports and stories of the missionaries suggested that central issues in the confrontation of Christianity and the tribal people were matters related to witchcraft or to marriage and family relationships. The mission took an uncompromising stance against polygamy. Sexual offenses were by far the most frequent causes of church discipline to exclude church workers or members. Tribal culture was a functional whole. Changes in one area had repercussions in other areas as well. For example, tribal custom held that the husband must abstain from sexual relations with his wife after childbirth until she was no longer nursing the child. During this time he could be with his other wives. The monogamous Christians found it necessary to pass rules to keep husband and wife together during the nursing period. Thus the CIM field minutes of 1918 record the adoption of a rule "that native Christians should not be allowed to be separated from their wives because of childbirth, as according to native custom, but must stay together as husband and wife. Upon refusal to abide by this rule, discipline will be necessary."[32]

There was a difference, of course, between passing a rule and seeing its effective enforcement. Nor did the missionaries at the various stations always agree on policies and manners of enforcement. The missionaries were strong and rugged individualists and exercised considerable autonomy on their own stations.

Tension Between the Old and the New

Kornelia Unrau, who worked in the Congo from 1926 to 1960, told the story of a twelve-year-old girl who ran away from "an old and cruel Chief's harem" and came to attend school on the mission compound. Although the old chief had paid the traditional "bride price" for the girl, he did not protest her departure for about four years, even though he had occasions to visit the mission compound. When the girl was sixteen years old, however, the chief went to the girl's father and demanded that the bride price he had paid be returned, since the girl was now gone. The chief threatened "a curse on the whole village" if his demands were not met. The father came to get the girl, offering to the missionaries a younger daughter in exchange. The girl at first refused to go. Eventually the parents did take the girl back, but she eloped with a young Christian man before she could be returned to the old chief. For a time the young couple lived at a mining camp until the incident was forgotten. Then they returned to the mission where the young man finished the Bible study course and became an evangelist.[33]

This story illustrates the erosion of traditional tribal authority through new opportunities offered by the mission compound and the mining camp for those who wanted to escape the restrictions of traditional life. Not all the stories were equally dramatic, but every African who came to study in a mission school, or who was baptized into the church, lived with the tension between the old and the new, between the demands of the traditional community and the demands of the Christian community.

The life story of Kabangu Lubadi, recounted in a first-person narrative by missionary Levi Keidel, has numerous examples of this tension.[34] Kabangu was a CIM evangelist who suffered humiliation when his wife failed to bear children. Kabangu's tribal friends urged him to put away his wife, arguing that infertility was clear evidence that she had done something evil and was now being troubled by ancestral spirits. After great internal struggle, Kabangu decided to keep his wife. As a Christian, his relationship with his wife was a higher value than the supreme African value of fertility. His wife, he said, had done nothing evil and was not being punished. They would be content to raise nieces and nephews and to teach many children in the church.[35]

Traditional African culture was more sophisticated and more functional than the missionaries, especially in the first decades, were able to recognize. The Pende tribe, among whom missionaries at the Nyanga and Mukedi mission stations worked, had one of the most extensive and highly developed system of masks and mask rituals in all of Africa. No effort has ever been made, either by missionaries or by the African CIM Christians, to adapt elements from the Pende mask tradition in Christian worship or understanding. Missionaries misunderstood and rejected African drumming and dancing as expressions of heathenism. Traditional African tunes were not used in Christian worship until after independence.

The missionaries brought a rich tradition of Western Christian hymns and four-part harmony to Africa. The Africans responded to this musical tradition more enthusiastically than seemed to be true in India, China, or among the Native Americans. Missionary John P. Barkman, himself a gifted singer and director, had a choir of seventy-five voices at the Kalamba station. Barkman took it for proof that the Africans could be civilized when they learned to sing Christian songs "instead of their native chants." "Whenever opportunity presents itself," Barkman reported, "we take pleasure in displaying their talents before visitors such as official [*sic*] from the Belgian State, and individuals from the Forminiere Diamond Co, etc. . . . They enjoy it immensely and express amazement that such accomplishments can be made among the natives."[36] Music played a significant role in the life of the church, and one mark of its importance was the great degree to which missionaries kept control. The mission Literature and Censorship Committee had control over song selection for the annual Native Convention. In 1940, for example, the missionary Music Committee mandated that "the following songs be rendered at the 1941 convention: 'Glad Day,' 'Hallelujah for the Cross' and 'All Hail Immanuel,'" and that "the annual closing hymn of Native Convention be 'Diadem.'"[37]

Accepting Cultural Diversity

Missionaries who rejected African rhythms were able to be more open to the rich African treasure of proverbs and stories. Stories were less threatening than rhythms to Westerners, perhaps because the African tales had something more in common with Western literary tradition. In any case, African evangelists were allowed to illustrate biblical truth with African traditional stories long before the Africans were allowed to praise God with the rhythms in their bones. The *Congo Missionary Messenger* of June 1930 repeated the story of "The Snake and the Toad" told by an African evangelist. At one level the story was an explanation of why toads are found around people's houses. At another level the story was a parable of the toad (representing the Christian) being saved from the snake (Satan) by a man of mercy (Jesus) who leaves footprints for the toad to follow (discipleship).[38]

The task of translating the gospel into a cultural idiom appropriate to African culture was one which could finally be done only by Africans themselves. The world of the Christian mission compound in Africa was, to be sure, strictly controlled by the missionaries with their advanced technology, authority, and power. But the African people responded to that which they found meaningful. In some cases, the Africans simply nullified the missionaries' rules by refusing to obey. There was, for example, a long-standing mission rule that African teachers and evangelists employed by the mission were not allowed to have regular servants except for caring for small children and at the discretion of the missionary. This proved to be an unenforceable rule, and it was rescinded in 1934 with the following wry comment:

It is difficult to understand the customs of the natives in this respect, but it seems that unless the leaders among the natives have children or others to help them, then they are inferior in the eyes of the native populace, and a good for nothing. The natives have continually broken this rule, so it was considered wise to remove it.[39]

The practice of name giving was one of the more fascinating dimensions of intercultural influence and definition. To receive a new name was to authenticate the reality of a new identity. This was done in traditional society when youth emerged from circumcision camps. Christian converts took new names often at the time of baptism. Biblical names such as Thomas, Elizabeth, and David were favored, especially in the early years, but French names such as Leonhard, Marceline, and Alfonso were also used. The Africans gave African names to the missionaries, thereby giving an indigenous shape and definition to the missionary presence among them. The African missionary names often had to do with certain qualities such as "helper," "happiness," or "wisdom." Some missionaries or missionary children were named according to physical characteristics such as tall stature, after natural objects such as lakes or rivers, or simply after traditional names common in the tribe. Among the Bapende, missionaries were renamed after the birth of their first child and thereafter known as the mother and the father of that child.[40] Practices varied widely from tribe to tribe. Dr. Rudolph Unruh in the 1930s was given three different African names, so the missionary conference took official action to avoid confusion by selecting one of the three for Unruh's "native name."[41] In 1941 the missionaries moved to establish a regularized system of family names for all the tribes. The native name of the father was to be the family name; only two other names would be accepted: the native given name would be used first and the Christian given name, second.[42] The coming of independence shifted the power in name giving to the Africans. President Mobutu's authenticity campaign included the requirement that the Africans give up their Christian names and be known by their "authentic" traditional names. The African practice of naming missionaries became less regular, but such names were still given in 1977.

A Growing National Church

Nothing was more obvious in Christian missions work than the direct relationship between a vigorous and expanding mission program on the one hand and a growing and healthy national church on the other hand. Missions was a growth-oriented enterprise. More missionaries, more money, and more mission institutions, it was assumed, would result in more Christians and more churches abroad. The experience of Congo Inland Mission in the 1930s directly contradicted this assumption. During the years of the Great Depression, the mission from America underwent a radical and painful decline, while the church in the Congo experienced explosive growth!

The economic pinch of the depression forced cutbacks at all levels of mission activity. The number of CIM missionaries dropped from twenty-eight in 1925 to twenty-two in 1935. Missionary salaries were slashed, and even then the payments lagged up to three months behind schedule. The missionary support system was totally revamped so the funds would be solicited from categories of projects rather than for individual missionary support as had been done earlier. In 1936 A. M. Eash resigned as secretary and was replaced by C. E. Rediger. Added to the financial crisis was a crisis of personal mistrust and theological misunderstanding among board members and missionaries. This episode in Mennonite fundamentalist-modernist polarization reached its peak at an emotional mission board meeting in 1934 where, according to the minutes, "the Members of the Board representing the Central Conference were asked to make statements of doctren and Faith [sic]. . . ." The CIM board survived the crisis, but some of the wounds inflicted were long in healing.[43]

While gloom and depression reigned in North America, the understaffed and underpaid mission in the Congo witnessed a marvelous ingathering. CIM church membership shot up by 540 percent between 1930 and 1935, from 662 to 3,577 members.[44] Missionaries had to struggle with the question of how many of the thousands of professing Christians wanting baptism (a total of 5,681 in 1935) should actually be taken into the church. The rate of growth was by no means equal among the four stations of Djoko Punda, Kalamba, Nyanga, and Mukedi. Djoko Punda (Charlesville) grew most rapidly in the early thirties and served as the center for CIM mission work, with its industrial and teacher-training schools, a central printing press, and freight services on the Kasai River. The Mukedi station, with less than a hundred Christians in 1935, experienced a great revival in the late 1930s. Missionary Vernon Sprunger told how the Africans were desperately eager to possess the small card that was issued to the new Christians at the time of baptism and that was carefully marked each time they brought their tithe to the church. This Christian membership card had become another fetish which had greater power to ward off evil spirits than traditional fetishes.[45] In some cases church growth could be attributed to the work of a single effective African evangelist, such as Kleinboy, an outstation teacher from the Kalamba station who organized and developed a Christian village in Angola Territory in the 1920s.[46] In other cases, such as the Mukedi revival, the growth seemed related to changing currents in an entire tribe.

Other events of the middle years for CIM (the thirties and forties) deserve to be noted. In 1938 the Evangelical Mennonite Brethren group appointed official members to the CIM board, and the numbers of EMB missionaries gradually increased. Agnes Sprunger's translation of the New Testament into Kipende, a ten-year project, was completed in 1932 and published in 1935. The first fully trained medical doctor, Rudolph Unruh, arrived in 1931. The second doctor, Merle Schwartz, was delayed in getting to the Congo because the rickety Egyptian ship he and his wife, Dorothy, were traveling on in 1941 was sunk by a German raider.[47] While wartime conditions interfered with missionary travel, communication, and supplies, it is also true that World War II seemed to have a positive effect upon Mennonite financial contributions for missions and, after the war, upon the number of missionary volunteers.

A New Missionary Vision

In the 1950s the Congo Inland Mission was transformed, both at home and on the field, by Harvey Driver, an energetic layman from Ohio. Driver's impressive inter-Mennonite credentials included attendance at Eastern Mennonite High School, Virginia; Hesston and Bethel Colleges, Kansas; and Goshen College, Indiana. After some years of public school teaching in Kansas and Colorado and graduate work in anthropology at the University of Colorado, he went into a highly successful poultry business with his brother in Fulton County, Ohio. He joined the Evangelical Mennonite Church in the early 1940s, the first college graduate in that conference. He experienced personal Christian regeneration under the preaching of Reuben Short and began to turn his considerable talents, energies, and finances to support of the CIM. Driver was an unofficial counselor and sponsor of CIM secretary-treasurer C. E. Rediger from 1943 on, and served as executive secretary himself from 1951 to 1960.[48]

Driver's missionary vision was well suited for North American Mennonites who were recovering from experiences of isolation and alienation during the war which ended in 1945. Mennonites were pacifists of German-speaking background and could not identify with the great American or Canadian national wartime enterprise. The war somehow dammed up Mennonite energy and will to be of service to mankind. Driver put together the national spirit and the Christian spirit in a way which helped to burst the dam in the postwar period. Upon returning from a 1951-52 trip to Africa, he wrote: "It's wonderful to be alive in America, *the land of today*. And I want my country to be great. Great in all things. Not only in Armies, Navies, skyscrapers, science, industry and wealth, but also in things of the Spirit—in bending low as a good Samaritan over those broken in heart and spirit and helping them rise to the full dignity of reborn creatures in Christ Jesus—in pioneering with the gospel of Salvation and goodwill in lands like Congo that still know very little of either modern war or peace. It's great to be an American like that. . . ."[49]

Driver took the message to the Mennonite people in a vigorous effort to expand the CIM constituency base and to recruit more missionaries. He gave over two thousand presentations for Mennonite audiences, paying special attention to Mennonite businessmen who would understand his appeal for investment in kingdom work. Ignoring warnings from conservatives who feared association with the "liberal" General Conference, whose Board of Missions had affiliated with CIM in 1944, Driver recruited missionary candidates and missions dollars in GC churches from Pennsylvania to California. The expansion effort, which included all supporting bodies, was a great success. The CIM budget contributions more than trebled. Driver interviewed 552 prospective young missionaries. Ninety-seven new missionaries were sent out between 1945 and 1959, 26 more than the total who had served with CIM before 1945.[50]

Driver took a much more aggressive role than had his predecessors in dealing both with the CIM board and with the missionaries to regularize policies and procedures for mission work in the Congo. He commonly brought drafts of proposals to board meetings with the obvious expectation that they would be accepted. Driver considered the earlier missions piously narrow-minded and chaotically organized. He introduced standard business practices for all CIM mission stations and defined clear lines of responsibility from the stations to the field chairman to the executive secretary. That there was resistance to this tightening up is manifest in a 1952 "Memo of Understanding" from Driver to the Field Committee: "I have been told many times while among you that the C.I.M. is very democratic and that no one wishes to tell the other what should be done. I warn you that is not Democracy but Socialism and can easily lead to Anarchy in Missions. . . ."[51] It was Driver's good fortune that the field secretary for these years was missionary Frank Enns, an old-timer who saw the advantages of the new system and who could communicate well with the younger recently arrived missionaries, as well as with those who had been on the field for several decades. Another veteran, Vernon Sprunger, worked as the mission's legal representative and assisted the process of transfer of authority to the national church.

Expanding Mission Education and Stations

Belgium initiated a new policy in the postwar period for promoting education through subsidies to mission schools, including the Protestant missions. The Mennonites feared the prospect of government control which would come along with the subsidies, but they were assured that missionaries could continue to teach religious classes in the subsidized mission schools. For Driver the acceptance of government money was a triumph of practical considerations over ideology. "I find myself accepting something I do not believe in," he wrote in 1952. "I accept it because the Congolese want and deserve an education."[52] It would have been possible to refuse the government education subsidies, as the Conservative Baptist Mission and the Christian and Missionary

Alliance initially did, but this would have denied the legitimate aspirations of the Africans, who were inclined to choose between Catholicism and Protestantism on the grounds of which offered best opportunities for advancement. The Africans had a passion for learning and for material gain. The challenge, Driver said, was "to satisfy this passion and direct it to a passion for personal salvation and spiritual gain and to make it result in the establishment of Christian homes and communities."[53] Rather than separating himself from Belgian colonial developments, Driver joined the Belgian Chamber of Commerce and kept up to date on current colonial information and planning.

Belgian funds made possible rapid expansion of mission education. The subsidy grew from $30,000 in 1949 to $200,000 in 1959. In 1959 the CIM mission schools of various kinds served more than 27,000 students.[54] Despite freedom to teach religion in the schools, the expansion led to considerable secularization of mission efforts. Mission Bible schools, which earlier had been the highest mission schools leading to wage-earning employment, now suffered loss of status. The best educators in mission and church were placed in government-subsidized schools, where the level of Bible learning and the general spiritual environment left something to be desired. A new Bible Institute to train local pastors, started at Tshikapa in 1953, tried to counter the trend by strongly emphasizing character and Christian living.[55]

The CIM field also expanded in the 1950s through the addition of new territory and new mission stations. The four stations of the early years— Djoko Punda, Kalamba, Nyanga, and Mukedi—continued their work, except for the replacement of the old Kalamba station with a new one at nearby Mutena. New work was begun at four additional locations. In 1950, building for a new station began at the diamond mining center of Tshikapa. This station was strategically located for transportation and communication and was also a population center for tribes served by the CIM. Tshikapa eventually became the administrative center for the Congo Mennonite Church after independence. Another new station was founded among the Bashilele tribe at Banga, west of Djoko Punda. Unlike urban Tshikapa, Banga was in a rural area, and church growth there was less rapid. A third additional mission station, Kamayala, came to the CIM with two thousand church members, an orphanage, a leprosarium, and an extensive primary school program. Located among the Batshioko tribe near the Angolan border, this mission station was an outgrowth of Alma Doering's Unevangelized Tribes Mission. Finally, CIM took over an independent Protestant station at Kandala, which had been serving the southern Bapende. The Kandala mission station had eight hundred church members and represented a consolidation of the CIM field as a geographic unit.[56] Taking over existing missions, including active missionaries, involved sensitive negotiations. Driver was concerned that the formerly independent UTM missionaries were too dogmatic and narrow-minded about minor doctrines such as the manner of the Lord's return or the correct mode of baptism, instead of holding to the evangelical biblical "middle of the road" preferred by CIM.[57] The transition to CIM ownership and control, however, proceeded without great difficulty. At its peak, CIM had eight mission stations and 101 missionaries.[58]

Emerging Independence

At the same time that Driver was vigorously expanding the numbers of missionaries, mission stations, and mission institutions, he was also committed to the goal of independence for the emerging African church. The goal was not new. Missionary rhetoric for decades had called for a "church-centric" strategy and for the "three selfs" of self-support, self-leadership, and self-propagation. But progress toward the goal was painfully slow. One problem was that every step of institutional missions development made the total program more expensive, more complex, and more incapable of being taken over by Africans of limited financial and leadership resources. Moreover, the professional standards for church leadership escalated both in America and in the Congo over the years. Mennonites at home underwent a transition from untrained, unpaid pastors to seminary-trained, professional leadership. The application of similar standards in the Congo worked against the older mission evangelists and assistant pastors who had worked for many years with zeal and dedication, but who had limited education.

The Belgian colonial system, even in the 1950s, had never been geared to train Congolese leadership in top administrative positions. The CIM reflected this colonial situation. Theoretically Congolese leaders could move up the scale in the church from evangelist to deacon to assistant pastor to pastor. But until political independence in 1960, the Congolese CIM church leaders were unable to break the barrier to becoming full pastors. This was partly due to the realization that the term *pasteur* in French strongly implied a level of theological training which the Congolese Mennonites did not have. Mission failure to promote the assistant pastors caused a serious rift between the African church leaders and the missionaries in the early 1950s. Field chairman Frank Enns reported the crisis candidly in 1952:

> What caused seemingly an irreparable break was when we refused their (assistant pastors) request to make them pastors. We were probably too frank with them. We told them that they could not hope to receive that title. It would only be given to a new generation that would have the necessary training to entitle them to it. Since then a number of them have left the missionary carry most of the responsibility. It seems as though that took the sails out of them.[59]

The number of assistant pastors increased from seven in 1945 to twenty-seven in 1959, but there were still no full pastors. When asked in

1977 why he had not been promoted more rapidly in church leadership, one of the strongest Congolese leaders, Kazadi Matthew, replied simply, "There wasn't any vision for that kind of thing."[60] In 1957 Kazadi became the first CIM Congolese leader to visit the American churches. Driver was eager to have Kazadi tour Mennonite churches, not only for his own education but also to stir up support for the mission. "The old missionary appeals are growing stale," Driver wrote.[61]

The pressure to give Africans increasing control of their own church affairs came with a rush as the Congo swept rapidly toward political independence in the late 1950s. There was no adequate structure for Congolese participation in real decision making. Since the early years the missionaries had met for an annual conference where common issues were discussed and policies adopted. The Africans also met for an annual "native conference." Although missionaries played a major role in directing the native conferences, Africans were not invited to attend the missionary conferences until 1955 and even then did not have the right to vote. In 1956, when missionaries balked at the proposal that Africans have a voice in requesting or denying the return of missionaries on furlough, Driver wrote in a characteristically blunt letter to field chairman Enns, "I think it is no secret that most of the Congolese Church leaders have chafed considerably under the autocratic discipline of the missionaries."[62]

Turning Over the Keys

It was Driver's ambition to seize the initiative and to offer independence to the Congolese church even before they demanded it. "This psychological edge is priceless here in dealing with the Congolese," he wrote.[63] To this end the CIM in 1959 proposed a plan of complete integration of the heretofore separate entities, the CIM mission and the Congolese church. The mission and church would become a single legal body, with equality of representation on the top administrative committee, on the sixteen-member general council, and on the various committees responsible for the various areas of church activity such as education, evangelism, literature, and others. Five delegates from the North American board met with missionaries and representatives of the African church in Djoko Punda in February 1960 to sign the new agreement. The new independent organization took the name Eglise Evangelique Mennonite au Congo (Evangelical Mennonite Church of Congo), thus officially restoring the name Mennonite which had been abandoned in 1912.

The new organization was born just in time for the chaos which accompanied the achievement of political independence in June 1960. Indeed, tribal fighting broke out between the Lulua and Baluba already in late 1959. The three eastern mission stations at Charlesville, Tshikapa, and Mutena were deeply affected, as members from both tribes were in the CIM schools, churches, and other work. By July of 1960 the political situation had become so volatile that the missionaries decided to evacuate and turn the work over to the African leaders in the Evangelical Mennonite Church of the Congo. The wholesale departure of the missionaries in 1960, and partial evacuation during the Kwilu rebellion in 1964, was a painful and bitter experience for all those involved. But the pain was accompanied by gratefulness for the rapid progress that had been made in the previous few years in transfer of responsibility to African leadership.

Without ignoring the suffering and trauma undergone by the church and mission from 1960 to 1965, it is possible to see the revolutionary upheaval and the missionary evacuations as blessings in disguise for church-mission relationships. In the the mid-1950s no one among the missionaries or the Africans could imagine a situation in which CIM would sign away its separate existence in the Congo. The mission seemed as natural and as permanent a part of the landscape as the Kasai River. But the CIM, after decades of caution and hesitation, took the initiative to confront the African church leadership with the reality of their own identity. This was fundamentally the work of the CIM executive secretary, Harvey Driver, although it can also be said that Driver guided and channeled, rather than generated, the dynamics of this era.

The CIM, with its plan of mission-church integration, beat the political revolution to the punch by a matter of just a few months. The missionary evacuation, while no part of Driver's plan, continued the rapid process of church independence. Missionaries turned over the keys to African leaders. Things which otherwise would have required years of negotiation simply happened overnight. Missionaries who returned to the field after the evacuation were overjoyed to report that the church had survived their absence. They also realized that permanent changes had taken place in their relationship with a young church which had gone through an unprecedented experience of self-definition and self-survival in crisis.[64]

Peter H. and Eva Schmidt Richert, 1900

Cornelius H. and Lulu Johnson Suckau with their children, Theodore and Edna

Edmund G. and Hazel Dester Kaufman with their children, Gordon and Karolyn

Mennonite Library and Archives

88

5 Sending Church in Transition

The Progressive Spirit

The Mennonite missions movement was born in an age of confidence and of growth. The General Conference was a small body, but it almost trebled its membership in the last two decades of the nineteenth century, from 3,300 members in thirty-two congregations in 1881 to 9,650 members in sixty-five congregations in 1899.[1] H. P. Krehbiel, a young Mennonite pastor who had attended Oberlin Seminary, chronicled GC development in a confident five-hundred-page history of the General Conference in 1898. Krehbiel continued to carry the torch of Mennonite unity. The conference, he wrote, was "not a 'branch' of the Mennonite Denomination, and as an organization must in theory always consider itself as embracing all Mennonites of America."[2]

Mennonites at the turn of the century were in an expansionist mood, perhaps reflecting the spirit of a United States which had recently won Cuba and the Philippines in the Spanish-American War. Even though the GC ideal of Mennonite union slipped away as other Mennonite groups organized separately for missions and education, GC leaders welcomed the "Americanization" of all Mennonites. H. G. Allebach, former missions schoolteacher in Oklahoma Territory and associate editor of the *Mennonite,* wrote an editorial entitled "Mennonite Expansion" in 1900, in which he announced that not only were conservative Mennonite bodies being awakened, but that the world at large was about ready to accept the validity of Mennonite doctrines. "The better our principles are known," wrote Allebach, "the better they are liked."[3]

Bright young Mennonites who attended graduate school and seminary around 1900 were inspired by the ideal of human progress. J. W. Kliewer earned a Bachelor of Sacred Theology degree at Garrett

Biblical Institute in 1901 and moved to pastorates first at Wadsworth, Ohio, and then Berne, Indiana. He was to serve as president of the GC foreign missions board in 1908-35. In the spring of 1901 Kliewer articulated a kind of progressive missions manifesto in a sermon at a missions festival in Dalton, Ohio. The tenor of Kliewer's inspiration was suggested in the titles of two books he identified as sources, James S. Dennis's *Christian Missions and Social Progress,* and John R. Mott's *The Evangelization of the World in This Generation.* Kliewer identified the main hindrances to missions endeavor (including the relativism that says the religion of the heathen is best for them in their circumstances) and said that the purpose of these challenges is to call forth a heroic response. Modern transportation and communication made it possible to mobilize Christian resources to reach a world which is open to the gospel. Kliewer's militant rhetoric was almost a match for the stirring appeals of Theodore Roosevelt, then vice-president of the United States! Said Kliewer,

> Every normally endowed person has something of heroic valor in his being. He wants to be able to fight to win. Missions heroes and missions winners are possible only where there are missions difficulties and missions battles.[4]

The progressive spirit also apparently reigned at the Union Missionary Training Institute (UMTI) of Brooklyn, New York, where GC missionary candidates received advanced training until about 1910. Missionaries P. A. Penner, P. J. Wiens, C. H. Suckau, Annie Funk, and others were channeled to the UMTI by mission board secretary A. B. Shelly, and they spoke appreciatively of their training there. J. B. Epp of Whitewater, Kansas, missionary candidate to the Hopi Indians, was the valedictorian of the UMTI class of 1905. His valedictory address was entitled "The Gospel as a Means of True Civilization." Civilization, Epp said, was "the humanizing of man to the full satisfaction of his true nature. Only the Christian gospel can lead to fulfillment of true human nature. The forces which drag down human progress are those which are unnatural. To become more truly civilized (i. e., more truly humanized) ourselves and to learn of the methods and means to help others become so, was the purpose of our coming to this Institute."[5]

Undergirding the progressive optimism of this first generation of Mennonite graduate students in America were the facts of booming Mennonite social and economic development in the early twentieth century. Everywhere sprouted evidence of Mennonite prosperity. New church buildings, modern agricultural machinery, expanding publications, successful small-town businesses—all these and much more testified to healthy Mennonite growth in rural America. The Progressive Era in American history from 1900 to 1917 was a time of aggressive reform under the leadership of presidents Theodore Roosevelt and Woodrow Wilson. Mennonites shared in the euphoria of those times, not as avid American nationalists, but as a hardworking, prosperous German-American people who were happily finding a home for themselves in a world unafflicted by warfare and persecution.[6]

A handful of solid, unflappable patriarchs led the General Conference foreign mission board from its beginning in 1872 until about 1911, when A. B. Shelly resigned as executive secretary after thirty-nine years of service.[7] Mission board operations in those days reflected a social and religious Mennonite milieu with firm foundations. Shelly asked prospective candidates to send him an autobiography and letters of recommendation from the church elder and a reliable doctor. The process assumed that the elder knew the applicant and his or her family personally and that the doctor's judgment could be trusted. In the close-knit web of family relationships in Mennonite rural congregations, led by long-term lay elders, one could judge character with confidence.

Somewhere in the twentieth century, the mood of progressive optimism and self-confidence began to disintegrate. The Progressive Era gave way to an Age of Anxiety under the assault of the two world wars, worldwide depression, social upheaval, and intellectual relativism and nihilism in a variety of forms. The General Conference Mennonite Church was subjected to intense frustration and polarization around the very issues which were its reason for existence—union, education, and missions. On several occasions it appeared that a Mennonite version of the Protestant battle between modernism and fundamentalism would result in a split in the General Conference and the closing of Mennonite colleges. But the conference somehow held together, and it was the common task of overseas missions which provided a unifying rallying point for all factions in the church.

Holding the Center: Richert, Suckau, and Kaufman

1. *P. H. Richert.* The decentralized structure of the General Conference inhibited the rise of strong leadership and made the denomination vulnerable to separatist movements at the local level. Despite the absence of any one towering figure to rally loyalty and dictate policy for the church as a whole, it is possible to point to one man who, more than any other, embodied a consensus for GC Mennonites through World War II and helped keep the conference together. That man was Peter H. Richert, secretary of the board of foreign missions from 1910 to 1946. Richert's thirty-six-year mission board term, added to A. B. Shelly's thirty-nine years, represented three-fourths of a century of leadership continuity and conservative judgments on the mission board.

P. H. Richert was one of seventeen children of Heinrich Richert, the missions-minded elder of Alexanderwohl who helped bring his immigrant congregation from Russia into the General Conference in the 1870s. P. H.'s sister Martha was the second wife of P. A. Penner, a family connection which tied Richert to GC mission leadership in India. Richert grew into a benevolent patriarch who exercised a dominating influence over private and public institutions in the rural Kansas Mennonite community where he lived, taught, farmed, and preached. With a voice of beneficent authority he counseled young missionary candidates where to go to school, advised church members to vote for the Republican party, and told public schoolteachers which dramas would or would not be acceptable for production on the local stage.

Richert endeavored to hold onto the core of Mennonite values in an age of upheaval. At one level, he shared some of the progressive views which were popular at Halstead Seminary and at the Bethel Academy, where he taught from 1898 to 1912. Mennonites, Richert believed, were in advance of the world by virtue of their democratic church organization and their understanding of biblical nonresistance. To one young man who chafed under his authoritarian control, he wrote that Mennonites "have been since the time of the reformation 400 years ahead of the time, and are still ahead of the times in our principles."[8]

At another level, Richert stoutly resisted the contemporary American trends—both American militarism and the popular "new theology"—which he believed threatened the Mennonite way of life and belief. The new theology had various names, most of which carried a pejorative sting—"liberalism," the "social gospel," and above all, "modernism." Mennonites who attended university graduate schools in the first decade of the century and returned to teach at Bethel and Bluffton colleges were said to be infected by the theory of evolution and by the method of biblical "higher criticism" which cast doubts upon the truth of the Bible.[9] For Richert the key issue was the authority of the Bible. In his tenacious endeavor to preserve orthodoxy, he adopted the practice of separating out suspected nonbelievers on the basis of whether they would sign certain doctrinal statements of fundamental belief. In this process Richert and other Mennonites acted out roles in an American Protestant scenario which was a diversion both from the wholeness of early Mennonite mission work and from the Anabaptist understandings of the church.

Mennonites might have been able to resolve satisfactorily the tensions of the liberal-conservative, or modernist-fundamentalist, debates if it had not been for the First World War. That war, for Mennonites as well as for North Americans generally, was a great polarizing event which destroyed the self-confidence of the Progressive Era. The war wrought a peculiar trauma for German-speaking pacifist Mennonites, who came under suspicion of treason in an America mobilized against Prussian militarism. Mennonite draftees were persecuted and court-martialed in military camps for refusal to bear arms, while Mennonites at home were scorned for their German accents and intimidated into purchasing war bonds. The wartime burden of guilt and isolation generated internal conflicts among General Conference Mennonites. One set of issues had to do with the extent to which Mennonites should cooperate or refuse to cooperate with war-making endeavors such as the bond drives. Richert, while counseling drafted young men to be true to the Bible and their nonresistant heritage, did cooperate with the war bond campaigns and personally collected war bond donations in a Bethel College financial drive after the war. Another issue was General Conference membership in the Federal Council of Churches, especially when so many FCC churches became rabidly militaristic in the wartime crusade. The General Conference, already suspicious of Federal Council churches for modernist tendencies, voted to withdraw from the council in 1917.

A third arena for the bitter ventilation of Mennonite wartime malaise was a crisis at Bethel College, where a dispute between two Bible teachers about the date of authorship of the Book of Daniel grew into a major confrontation over the range of modernist-fundamentalist issues. The conservatives, led by P. H. Richert, won the battle and forced the resignation in 1919 of a number of Bethel's most articulate faculty members on grounds of religious unorthodoxy. The board drafted a list of rules and regulations, including a set of twelve fundamental doctrines, which faculty members had to sign as a condition of continued employment.

As secretary of the mission board, Richert introduced a similar procedure to screen out present or future missionaries with liberal or modernist views. All missionaries on the field—including such veterans as P. A. Penner and H. J. Brown—were required to certify with their signature that they were safely orthodox. The key questions were as follows:

> "Do you believe the scriptures of the Old and New Testament to be the inspired word of God, the only infallible rule of faith and practice?
>
> "Do you accept the 'Apostolic Creed' in full?
>
> "Do you believe in the Deity of Christ?
>
> "Do you believe in the scriptural atonement, 'the propiation [sic] through faith in his blood'?
>
> "Have you any opinion at variance with the doctrines of our church as expressed in the Ris confession and in the constitution of the Mennonite General Conference of N.A. (Article 2)?
>
> "Do you believe that personal effort to lead souls to Christ is the paramount duty of every missionary?
>
> "Do you propose to make such effort the chief feature of your missionary career, no matter what other duties may be assigned to you?"[10]

This missionary screening document needs to be seen in the context of disillusionment after World War I. American Protestantism experienced something of a religious recession in the 1920s and 1930s. The optimism of religious progressivism needed to be corrected. For the most part, Mennonites turned to the language of American fundamentalism to express the new mood. It was now the deity of Christ that mattered, rather than Jesus' loving acts in behalf of the sick and the poor. It was now the blood atonement that was important, rather than Jesus' call to discipleship. Missionaries now were to save individual souls rather than build Christian communities. Although P. H. Richert and his generation intended this fundamentalist corrective to be a return to orthodoxy, it was in fact an innovation and a deviation as certainly as was the "new theology" it was meant to correct. Lost in this shuffle was the Anabaptist-Mennonite focus upon the church as a body of believers committed to a life of discipleship. The doctrine of nonresistance was not separately specified on the Mennonite list of fundamentals, even though the church had been so strenuously tested on this doctrine during the war.

The fundamentalist "corrective" in the 1920s and 1930s did not have a great impact upon Mennonite missionary strategy overseas. No new mission fields were opened in these decades to test new ideas. In India, China, and the Congo the prevailing pattern of mission work around developed missions compounds never came under question. No one on the mission board balked at appropriations for hospitals and schools. While the board insisted that the paramount goal was to lead souls to Christ, the majority of missionaries engaged primarily in tasks of Christian nurture, institutional development, and leadership training. The evolution of mission-church relationships on the field tended to shift responsibility for direct evangelism to national church workers and away from the missionaries. It was easier to put the national workers in charge of evangelism than to give them responsibility for running the mission schools and hospitals. Thus a kind of schizophrenia was built into the missionary calling. Missionaries had to promise to give primacy to soul winning "no matter what other duties may be assigned," but the assigned duties in most cases did not have evangelism at the forefront. In general the missionary practice was more wholistic than the missionary theology.

It was P. H. Richert's role to keep lines of communication open between both modernists and fundamentalists around the common cause of missions. Richert did not fit in either camp. Modernism was the more insidious danger, he believed, but the fundamentalists were also untrustworthy, as was obvious in their refusal to accept the truth of biblical nonresistance. Richert's endeavor to hold the middle ground for the General Conference can be illustrated by his relationship to two Mennonite missionaries who became educators and who represented opposing poles in this argument. The two men were C. H. Suckau, missionary to India who became the first president of Grace Bible Institute, and E. G. Kaufman, missionary to China who became president of Bethel College.

2. *C. H. Suckau.* Suckau graduated from the Bethel Academy in 1906

and from the Union Missionary Training Institute in 1909. On the India mission field from 1909 to 1928, he and his wife, Lulu Johnson Suckau, were founders of the Korba station. He was president of the India Workers' Congress for two terms and president of the mission conference from 1923 to 1928. He was known as a strong leader, dynamic preacher, and enthusiastic evangelist. There was a thread of dissonance, however, in Suckau's relationship to the mission board and to his fellow missionaries. A. B. Shelly confided to fellow mission board members in 1907 that he feared Suckau had "more zeal than judgment."[11] Missionaries in India complained that Suckau was very independent minded and resisted mission policies with which he disagreed. Theological differences may have played some role in this disagreement, for Suckau became an ardent premillennialist in India. In 1918, during the crisis of World War I, Suckau asked the mission board for released time to translate into the Hindi language the popular premillennialist book by William E. Blackstone, *Jesus Is Coming*. P. H. Richert, like A. B. Shelly before him, considered it an unfortunate diversion from the central missionary message to focus upon the doctrine of Christ's imminent return to usher in a thousand-year reign. The mission board denied Suckau's request with the explanation that the translation would take too much time and that the Christians in India were not sophisticated enough to compare Blackstone's book with the Bible to see which was true.[12] Suckau later went on to translate the Blackstone book after all, presumably on his own time.

In 1928 when Suckau was on furlough from India and serving as interim pastor of the First Mennonite Church in Berne, Indiana, Richert received a letter signed by all twenty-two missionaries in India (including two members of the Berne congregation, Martha Burkhalter and Loretta Lehman) recommending that Suckau not be allowed to return to the field.[13] The specified charges against Suckau seem trivial in retrospect. They had to do with the disposition of certain properties including a piano, a communion set, and some cattle. Differences over theological questions or missions policy were not mentioned. Richert tried hard to resolve the dispute between Suckau and the India missionaries. When the rift proved to be irreparable, Richert tried to put a good face on matters by asking the India missionaries formally to release Suckau from mission service so he could take up the invitation from the Berne church to continue as their pastor. Suckau asked Richert to conduct his installation service at the Berne church.[14]

It was of utmost importance for Richert to maintain cordial and respectful relations with Suckau, because the large Berne congregation was an important source of missionary candidates and financial giving to missions. Suckau was a highly successful pastor, and he was outspoken in his premillennialist views and his critique of modernist tendencies at Bethel and Bluffton colleges. If his dispute with the missionaries had not been moderated by P. H. Richert, it would have been quite possible for Suckau to lead a fundamentalist schism in the General Conference. As it turned out, the Berne church continued its strong support of the mission board. Suckau left the Berne church in 1943 to be the first president of Grace Bible Institute in Omaha, Nebraska. This new Bible school, which began with the support of six different Mennonite groups, was designed to be an alternative to the established liberal arts colleges. Grace Bible Institute produced many missionaries for work under the General Conference as well as other mission boards from the 1950s onward.

3. *E. G. Kaufman.* Kaufman, like C. H. Suckau, was a missionary who did not return to the mission field because of the opposition of fellow missionaries. From 1917 to 1925 Kaufman worked on the mission field in China, where he chafed under the conservative leadership of the mission founder, H. J. Brown. During his furlough, Kaufman got a B.D. from Garrett Biblical Institute and a Ph.D. from the University of Chicago, in preparation to return to China as a teacher at a Christian university where students from the Mennonite field would study. At the 1929 meeting of the General Conference in Hutchinson, Kansas, H. J. Brown, who had recently returned from China, spoke against the proposal to send Kaufman back to China in this capacity. Kaufman's attendance at the University of Chicago was particularly offensive to Mennonite conservatives, because that school was believed to be a hotbed of modernism. Kaufman came under such suspicion that a special meeting was held after the 1929 meeting to determine whether he should be allowed to itinerate and preach in Mennonite churches, as did most missionaries on furlough.[15]

P. H. Richert, who in 1929 was both secretary of the foreign mission board and president of the Bethel College Board of Directors, was as supportive of Kaufman as he had been of Suckau. Richert had been Kaufman's faculty adviser during student days at Bethel College, and he now played out the role of mentor. He spoke up in defense of Kaufman as a good missionary and an orthodox Christian, and he wrote privately to Kaufman, "I hope you won't disappoint me." Kaufman eventually decided not to return to China. After three years on the Bluffton College faculty, he accepted the call to become president of Bethel College, a position he held from 1932 to 1952. Like the more conservative Suckau at Berne and Grace Bible Institute, Kaufman was deeply committed to the Mennonite missionary enterprise and delighted in teaching and inspiring young people for missions service.

P. H. Richert probably had a hand in the decision of the mission board to subsidize publication of Kaufman's doctoral dissertation, *The Development of the Missionary and Philanthropic Interest Among the Mennonites of North America.*[16] That study chronicled the rise of missions work among all Mennonite groups in the context of "the religious sect cycle." The book was vigorously critiqued in Mennonite periodicals for its liberal bias. [17] Valdo Petter, Mennonite missionary in Montana who had attended Moody Bible Institute, wrote in his copy of the book:

> A Poisonous Volume. Not fit for Christians to read who cannot quickly discern Modernism. . . . The book is a blot on the Mission Board. It is a shame that they ever backed it up! [18]

A Commitment in Common

P. H. Richert and the mission board had to absorb criticism from both the right and left in the stormy decades from the first through the second world wars. But all parties concerned shared a common commitment to overseas missions, and that core of agreement helped keep the General Conference from disintegrating. Although the fundamentalist-modernist polarization had little immediate effect upon overseas missionary strategy, the argument had considerable long-range effect upon the recruitment and education of missionaries.

The General Conference struggled for decades with only limited success to establish a seminary which would gain the confidence of constituent churches for the education of pastors and missionaries. Witmarsum Theological Seminary, established at Bluffton, Ohio, in 1921, originally aimed to become a unifying institution for all Mennonite branches. About twenty future missionaries took some study at Witmarsum during its decade of existence. But Witmarsum became a storm center for antiliberal hostilities, and it folded up in the Great Depression after experiencing low enrollments and a financial crisis in 1931. Not until the mid-1940s did the General Conference again create a seminary, the Mennonite Biblical Seminary in Chicago, associated with Bethany Biblical Seminary of the Church of the Brethren. S. F. Pannabecker, former missionary to China, served as president of Mennonite Biblical Seminary (following Abraham Warkentin in 1947) for a decade until the removal of the school in 1958 to Elkhart, Indiana, in a cooperative venture with the Mennonite Church (MC). Over the years the mission board recruited missionary candidates not only from Mennonite colleges and seminaries, but also from non-Mennonite Bible schools such as Moody Bible Institute in Chicago and the Bible Institute of Los Angeles (BIOLA). At the same time, many Mennonite young people who attended non-Mennonite schools were a rich source of missionaries for non-Mennonite mission boards. A study in 1978 tentatively estimated that General Conference Mennonite churches supplied as many missonaries to nonconference mission programs as they did to mission programs of the General Conference itself. Many of these missionaries working in nonconference programs were graduates of Grace Bible Institute in Omaha, Nebraska. [19]

A Church in Transition: Americanization

1. *Acculturation.* The transformation of the General Conference Mennonite Church in the twentieth century has been dramatic and thoroughgoing. While much sound and fury has been generated over certain theological questions, the more pervasive processes of acculturation proceeded often without notice. Mennonites were an upwardly mobile, German-speaking, religious ethnic group who gradually adopted the cultural ways of Protestant North America. Thus, while Mennonite missionaries were taking the gospel in a particular cultural form to people overseas, the cultural forms they had known at home underwent radical change. Worship patterns were altered in many ways. The common communion cup, symbol of congregational unity, was displaced by separate cups. Foot-washing ceremonies were abandoned. Organs were installed and competed with congregational singing. American flags appeared in sanctuaries. Congregations stopped kneeling for prayer. Revivalist songs with worldly rhythms invaded first the Sunday schools and then the worship services. Separation of men, women, and children broke down as families started sitting together for worship. Professionally educated full-time pastors displaced part-time lay elders. Elaborate new church buildings, often with steeples and stained glass windows, departed from traditions of Mennonite simplicity.

Different congregations made changes at different times depending upon the history and leadership of the group, the recency of arrival from Europe, and the extent of contact with surrounding society. Those of the GC Eastern District were the first to become Americanized, to switch from the German to the English language. Those of the 1870s migration from Russia did not switch from German to English until after the First World War. Those who came in the 1920s and later, mostly to Canada, retained the German language until after the Second World War, and many congregations in Canada continue to use German in the 1970s.

One aspect of Mennonite Americanization has been gradually improved standards of health, education, and material comforts. Missionaries returning home on furlough were often astonished by the rising standard of living among their families and friends. It was painful to see how seldom Mennonites reflected about Christian stewardship in a hungry world as they bought new automobiles, farm equipment, electrical applicances, radios, and television sets. "Everybody has but *one* aim," complained P. A. Penner in 1916, "and that is to make money and get the most out of life. . . . There is a screw loose somewhere when autos can be bought by the hundreds, and the [Mission] Board has a debt of $10,000."[20] Penner's lament has been echoed by dozens of furloughing Mennonite missionaries until the present day.

2. *Secularization.* Another dimension of Mennonite Americanization has been the phenomenon of secularization, or the tendency to take

over not only the cultural forms but also the core values of secular society. Mennonite colleges were typically founded for the primary purposes of training Mennonite teachers, church workers, and missionaries, but the percentage of students preparing for church vocations decreased over the decades. Education for many became a means of escape from the environment of the rural religious-ethnic enclave.

There were also many Mennonites whose economic success in worldly terms tended to pull them away from Christian and Mennonite values. In the rhythm of Mennonite movement from village-to-town-to-city there have taken place many subtle shifts in language and belief which have separated Mennonites from the Bible and the relevance of biblical categories for their lives.[21] North American life was complex, individualistic, competitive, materialistic, and relativistic. The threats to Christian faithfulness were more subtle but just as hazardous in North America as in totalitarian Russia from which many Mennonites fled.

3. *Second-generation missionaries.* The missionary movement was itself one chapter in the history of Mennonite adaptation to the North American environment. The pattern of Mennonite missionary recruitment suggests a broad pattern, although by no means an entirely consistent one, in which the missionary movement has the greatest appeal and vitality in the second generation—the children of the immigrants. Immigrants themselves are preoccupied with the trauma of transition to a new environment and with the difficult tasks of settlement in a strange new world. Children of the immigrants find themselves in the creative tension between their German-speaking, rural religious-ethnic enclave and the beckoning, modern, English-speaking world outside. Becoming a missionary was one meritorious way for the second generation to move out of and beyond the ethnic enclave into the outside world of adventure and opportunity, and to do so on terms esteemed by both the home community and the world. The first overseas missions thrust of the early twentieth century was led by this second generation—persons such as P. A. Penner, H. J. Brown, C. H. Suckau, E. G. Kaufman, and Aganetha Fast, all born of immigrant parents.

Another great missions thrust took place in the General Conference after World War II with the opening of new mission fields in Japan, Taiwan, and Colombia, and expansion of the CIM in Zaire. Prominent in this new thrust were many missionary volunteers from Canada, children of immigrants who had migrated from Russia in the 1920s and 1930s. The first Canadian to serve in General Conference overseas mission was Anne Penner of Rosenfeld, Manitoba, who went to India in 1946. She was followed by dozens of other Canadian Mennonite children of immigrants who expanded horizons for themselves and their home communities through missions work.

Missions provided a window to the world for Mennonites who were undergoing acculturation. Missionaries had a kind of religiously legitimate cosmopolitan allure. They wore the colorful garb of foreign lands when they sat up front in places of honor at Mennonite conferences. They exhibited exotic artifacts, including examples of the "idols" for heathen worship and the cloth that bound children's feet. The only place in Mennonite literature where photographs of bare-breasted women could appear was in illustrations of how unbelievers were clothed before their conversion. Although there may have been some naive and patronizing aspects to missionary portrayals of foreign cultures, particularly in the early years, there was great educational value in the information they shared with their relatively isolated home congregations. The missionaries were on a pedestal. But their position helped put Mennonites at home in touch with worlds beyond the normal limits of community and nation. Eventually the ease and speed of modern transportation made it possible for many Mennonite lay people—beginning with the close relatives of missionaries—to visit "the field" personally. And those at home had opportunities to meet and hear Mennonite national leaders from the overseas churches as they made fraternal visits to North American churches.

In the mid-1970s two Mennonite sociologists made a comprehensive survey of attitudes and behavior of five Mennonite and Brethren in Christ denominations, including the General Conference.[22] The survey provided a sophisticated measurement of Mennonite acculturation, although the statistics did not measure changes over time and did not include those who had left the church in the acculturative process. The data showed Mennonites to be religiously and socially conservative, ranking well above North American Protestants in their doctrinal orthodoxy, Bible knowledge, church participation, and devotionalism. Mennonites were revealed as relatively unaffected by modernism, but deeply influenced by fundamentalism. The study also endeavored to measure Mennonite commitment to Anabaptist principles, and discovered that a substantial majority of contemporary Mennonites do in fact agree to the distinguishing principles of Anabaptism. The meaning of an imputed Anabaptist identity remained clouded, however, because contemporary Mennonites, unlike their left-wing forebears, tended to right-wing political attitudes. Moreover the study revealed that Mennonite groups which have been most successful in evangelistic outreach at home (notably the Evangelical Mennonite Church) are those which have the lowest commitment to Anabaptism. General Conference Mennonites who have sponsored vigorous overseas missions programs have been singularly limited in their efforts to evangelize in North America.

Local Dynamic of Missions

The missionary movement in the General Conference seemed to grow along family lines. Hundreds of young people were inspired to volunteer for missions work by the example of parents, aunts, uncles, or cousins.[23] It was a matter of special pride to have relatives working on the mission field. When Matilda Kliewer Voth went to China, she carried greetings from her brother-in-law, Peter Schmidt, to his "seven cousins in China." As she met these relatives in China, "they figured out how we were related, who we were, and returned the greetings."[24] The return of a relative on furlough became the occasion for large family gatherings which celebrated the witness of a family member who was serving God in a special way.

The family of Frank F. and Anna Wiebe Jantzen, both of whom were born in Russia, set the Mennonite record for production of missionaries. Mr. Jantzen served as unsalaried pastor of the Mennonite congregation at Paso Robles, California (1903-64); he and his wife sent nine of their ten children to the Bible Institute of Los Angeles (BIOLA). Six of them became overseas missionaries (Albert, Aaron, Richard, John, Lubin, and Ruth), serving in China, India, Zaire, Nigeria (with Sudan Interior Mission), and North America.

Women in particular have played key roles in GC missions history as missionaries, as mothers who nurtured and dedicated their children to missionary vocations, as organizers and participants in women's missionary associations, and as writers and publicists of mission work. The first Mennonite missionary sewing societies were organized in Danzig in 1848 and in Holland in 1852. The first women's missionary society in America was organized by Marie Risser in the Salem congregation at Ashland, Ohio, before the conference mission board itself came into being in 1872.[25] The number of women's missionary societies grew from eighteen in 1890 to eighty-seven in 1923. Susannah Hirschler Haury (veteran missionary to Native Americans) became the first president of the Women's Missionary Association when it was formally organized in 1917.

In addition to sewing projects, material aid, and financial help, women produced much of the literature which was used for educational purposes in the congregations and Sunday schools. S. F. Pannabecker, in his history of the General Conference, wrote, "Leaflets, packets, dramatizations, biographies, and maps flowed from their center to local societies along with reading courses and study outlines."[26] The Women's Missionary Association official periodical, at its height a sixteen-page monthly, was ·entitled *Missionary News and Notes* (1926-65), later renamed *Missions Today* (1965-73), and then *Window to Mission* (1974-   ).

Missionary recruitment, support, and celebration were also concerns for the church congregations. A number of congregations became prominent in the General Conference for their extraordinary record in supplying missionaries and in raising funds. In some cases the development of strong missions interest grew out of the work of an outstanding leader, such as S. F. Sprunger in Berne, Indiana. In general, the congregations which gave money most generously were those who had their own members in mission work, or in the words of executive secretary Andrew Shelly, "those who had blood on the field."[27] Congregations with outstanding records of missions support included the First Church of Berne, Indiana; the First Church of Pretty Prairie, Kansas; the Emmaus Church of Whitewater, Kansas; the North Star Church of Drake, Saskatchewan; the First Church of Reedley, California; and the Salem Church near Freeman, South Dakota. Some congregations sent members out under "faith missions" and gave substantial support to missions work outside of General Conference channels. It has been estimated that the amount of GC funds given for missions outside of the conference was equal to the total given for missions through the conference. One study revealed that those congregations which had a record of generous giving outside of the conference in general also gave substantially for missions through conference channels.[28]

Mission Board Modernization

For the seventy-five years that A. B. Shelly and P. H. Richert served as executive secretaries of the foreign mission board, the board operated on an informal and unprofessional basis. The board consisted of farmer-preachers who had no international experience and who did not presume to establish priorities and policies for operations on the field. Their goal was to send missionaries who would proclaim the gospel and do the things that missionaries do. The board endeavored to generate financial support for the missions program, to keep a watch on the budget, and to keep the churches informed and alive to the missions program. Just as the General Conference was organized on the principle of congregational autonomy and lacked bishops or synods to lay down rules, so the mission board allowed maximum autonomy on the mission field. When a letter would arrive from India or China with questions about a particular situation, Richert would circulate the letter to board members, each of whom would pen some comments on the margin or an attached sheet. Then Richert would summarize the board's wisdom and ask missionaries on the field to make decisions in the light of the board's feelings and general guidelines. The mails moved slowly. Months would pass between the posing of a question on the field and the receiving of an answer from the board. With P. A. Penner in India and H. J. Brown in China, the board knew that decision making would be in experienced, responsible hands.

It was a landmark event when J. W. Kliewer, president of the board, became the first board member to travel to the foreign fields in 1920. Kliewer resigned as president of Bethel College to take one year for the world tour and another year to report to churches in North America. He was accompanied overseas by J. P. Habegger of Berne, Indiana, an old friend from the days when Kliewer was pastor in Berne. Kliewer and Habegger were received with triumphant celebrations, with baptism ceremonies, and with festivals on the mission field. At Kai Chow, China, they were greeted by Chinese schoolboys and schoolgirls singing "Onward Christian Soldiers" and "Gott ist die Liebe" under the arch leading to the mission compound. An American flag, a Chinese flag, and a banner with the Christian cross lent color and meaning to the reception.[29]

Kliewer's recorded impressions from his tour were not unlike those of Mennonite missionaries upon their first arrival. The Taj Mahal at Agra (and St. Peter's cathedral in Rome) impressed him not as architectural masterpieces but as colossal memorials built by the rich at the expense of the poor. British imperial rule in India was a force for order and justice, now being discredited "by the seditionist Gandhi."[30] Hinduism in India supported the caste system and veneration of the cow, and needed to be replaced. "Christianity is human," Kliewer wrote. "Hinduism is bovine. New conceptions of God, of man, of sin, of salvation is what India needs."[31] The Kliewer-Habegger visit resulted in no critique of mission strategy or change in mission policy. The purpose of this administrative visit, and of subsequent visits through the 1960s, was basically to establish contact and confidence which would lead to mutual trust between home and field, and to strengthen the support structures for the mission program.

The mission board underwent an organizational transformation in the years after World War II. The change was due in part to growth in size of the mission program, in part to the complexities of mission work in an age of decolonization, and in part to myriad forces in North American life which affected the organizational development of all institutions. The General Conference adopted a new constitution in 1950 and again in 1968. The place of foreign missions in the conference was critical for each reorganization, because missions had a large share of the overall conference budget and because many churches were more eager to give financial support to missions than to other areas such as administration or publications. In 1950 the Board of Missions was divided into a foreign section and a home section, with the latter placed in charge of mission work with Native Americans. In 1968 the Native American work was placed under a new Commission on Home Ministries, while all mission work abroad came under the Commission on Overseas Mission.

The mission board secretaries in the postwar period were Howard Nyce (1948-54), John Thiessen (1954-58), Orlando Waltner (1959-60), Andrew Shelly (1960-71), and Howard Habegger (1971-). Nyce was the pastor of the Pretty Prairie Mennonite Church, one of the strong missions-supporting conference churches. Thiessen, a former missionary from India, was the first secretary who did not operate out of a pastor's office. But the biggest changes in organizational procedure came in the 1960s and 1970s. Andrew Shelly brought to the executive secretary's office a strong commitment to efficient administrative management. While himself a fervently consecrated man, one of Shelly's favorite quotations was, "No amount of consecration can make up for the wastefulness of unplanned work."[32] Shelly not only organized his own activities for maximum productivity (spending, for example, forty nights one year sleeping on the train to save the days for work), but he developed and reorganized procedures for personnel, publicity, office management, budget procedures, itineration among churches, and standardized policies for missionary support. The thrust toward efficient organizational management continued in the 1970s. The mission board offices in 1978 included five full-time executive staff positions (executive secretary, personnel secretary, director of missions services, secretary for Asia, and secretary for Latin America) plus three secretaries.

New missions procedures were needed in the 1970s to take account for the changing roles of executive officers, mission board, missionaries, and national church leaders. Mission board members were increasingly persons of international missions experience who were capable of a more active and well-informed role in establishing policies. National church leaders, formally heading independent churches but in fact dependent upon funds and personnel from North America, demanded a larger voice. Missionaries were caught in a squeeze as they saw their decision-making power flow to more aggressive national churches on the one hand and to a more directive mission board and executive on the other hand. In this context the mission board called an unprecedented conference on "Goals, Priorities, and Strategy" for the spring of 1972, where missionaries, nationals, board members, and executive together considered the challenges of the coming decade. Out of that meeting emerged a set of eight priorities for COM work. These were as follows:

1. Evangelism and Church Planting
2. Leadership Training
3. Transfer to National Leadership
4. Anabaptist Faith and Life
5. Economic Development
6. Urban Witness
7. Missionary Preparation
8. Program Evaluation

It was planned that a follow-up national goals, priorities, and strategy conference be held in each country where COM worked.

In the historical context of Mennonite mission policy evolution, the eight priorities of 1972 denote some significant changes. The top priority of evangelism and church planting was hardly new; the goal of proclaiming the gospel had been at the top of every missions goals statement from the beginning. But absence of concern for health and education from the list of priorities was striking for a mission program whose earlier energies had been so heavily invested in schools, clinics, and hospitals. The interest in an urban witness was a change from earlier years. Another shift was signaled by the high importance (number 4) assigned to emphasis upon "Anabaptist Faith and Life." Mennonite churches at home and abroad were now exhibiting a new interest in the distinctiveness of their particular history and doctrines within the Christian community.

Mennonite Identity

At the far end of the process of acculturation lies the loss of distinctive identity, or, as E. G. Kaufman said in his 1931 history of Mennonite missions, "the complete fusion of the Mennonite sect with the outside community."[33] If the North American melting pot was in fact what it was alleged to be, Mennonites by the last quarter of the twentieth century could be expected to be virtually indistinguishable from mainline American Protestants. But the Mennonites, including the General Conference Mennonites, proved to be stubbornly unmeltable in some key respects. The durability of distinctive Mennonite identity was nowhere more evident than in the changing tides of opinion on the mission board. When Mennonites belatedly joined the Protestant missionary movement in the late nineteenth century, they borrowed their theology and their strategy from the outside. Missionary candidates were examined for Protestant orthodoxy. But by the 1970s the GC mission board was committed to a distinctively Anabaptist-Mennonite witness, and missionary candidates were asked where they stood on issues of discipleship and nonresistance which distinguished them from Protestant missionaries in general.

Why did the Mennonites remain so self-consciously Mennonite? Part of the answer has to do with the Mennonite response to warfare and conscription in the twentieth century. World Wars I and II taught Mennonites that they were significantly different from Western Christendom. Other Christians went to war, but Mennonites refused to fight. To be sure, there was some erosion of the Mennonite doctrine of nonresistance as Mennonites came under pressure to fulfill patriotic military responsibilities. About half of the drafted Mennonites in World War II accepted noncombatant or combatant military service, but the percentage of pacifists in the church went up in the postwar decades, particularly during the Vietnam War. While other Christians faced each other across battle lines, Mennonites took their cues from the Jesus who rejected the sword.

The twentieth-century wars drove Mennonites of various branches into closer cooperation with each other. One product of World War I was the creation of a Mennonite Central Committee (MCC) to coordinate relief efforts for victims of civil war and famine in South Russia. MCC's work in the 1920s and 1930s was directed mainly toward helping Mennonite sufferers and refugees. After World War II MCC became an international agency for development as well as relief. Through work together in MCC peace and service projects, thousands of Mennonites from the different branches of the denomination learned to work with each other and to appreciate their common heritage.

Another dimension of Mennonite identity preservation was an exercise in historical self-discovery which came to be known as the "recovery of the Anabaptist vision." General Conference Mennonites had not lacked an interest in Anabaptist-Mennonite history, as was suggested by the publication of peoplehood histories from the Reformation to the present by C. H. A. van der Smissen in 1895, C. H. Wedel in four volumes from 1900 to 1904, and C. Henry Smith in 1920. For over fifty years Smith's book, *The Mennonites,* was the only one-volume, single-author history of Anabaptism-Mennonitism in print.[34] Mennonite historical consciousness flowered in a new way during and after World War II, galvanized by H. S. Bender's stirring presidential address to the 1943 meeting of the American Society of Church History, entitled "The Anabaptist Vision." As Bender spoke, several thousand young Mennonite men were serving as conscientious objectors to war in Civilian Public Service camps, separated from the rest of Christian America by their religious convictions. This generation responded enthusiastically to Bender's appeal to rescue historical Anabaptism from its detractors and to help establish a new consciousness for Mennonites as a separate people of integrity and relevance. Bender highlighted the Anabaptist teachings of discipleship, the church as a community, and the ethic of love and nonresistance.[35] Mennonites increasingly saw their teachings not only as valid and distinctive, but also as unlikely to be accepted by Christianity in general for the forseeable future. Walter Klaassen struck a responsive chord for Mennonites in the title of his 1973 book, *Anabaptism: Neither Catholic nor Protestant.*[36]

In a more general sense, it can be said that Mennonite identity was shaped by the failure of the progressive Protestant missionary dream. The optimism expressed in J. W. Kliewer's 1901 missionary sermon faded with the passing decades. The world was not won for Christ in a single generation. The twentieth century did not turn out to be the Christian century. A Christendom fractured into warring imperialist powers was a poor model to hold up for non-Christian peoples. One way for Mennonites to deal with the resulting disillusionment was to turn toward fundamentalist premillennialism, and to argue that the contemporary collapse presaged the second coming of Christ. Another option was to remember an Anabaptist-Mennonite experience which had always been pessimistic about the salvation of the world but was optimistic and urgent about the possibility of Christian discipleship for regenerated people within the world. Mennonites became increasingly aware of Anabaptism-Mennonitism as a religious option in its own right. This helped them to resist the postwar polarization of Protestantism into opposing camps of evangelicals (National Association of Evangelicals) and ecumenicals (National Council of Churches and World Council of Churches). Most Mennonites were comfortable in neither camp. Their position was a third way which too long had run the risk of being absorbed and dominated by others.

A desire to emphasize the Anabaptist-Mennonite witness in missions was one reason for the establishment in 1972 of the Overseas Missionary Training Center (OMTC) at the Associated Mennonite Biblical Seminaries, Elkhart, Indiana. The Commission on Overseas Mission encouraged missionary candidates, as well as career missionaries on furlough, to attend the OMTC for courses in missiology, intercultural communication, Bible, theology, etc., in the context of an inter-Mennonite (GC and MC) seminary community. In addition, COM adopted a leadership training program which brought overseas Mennonite church leaders to Elkhart for periods of study which included Anabaptist history and thought. The driving force of this Anabaptist emphasis was not denominational self-preservation nor ethnic survival; rather it was an effort to recover, to preserve, and to reform the Mennonite witness to a biblical faith in Jesus Christ as Lord.

The Kobe Garage Group. Takashi Yamada is second from the left in the front row. In the back row are missionaries Laverne and Paul Boschman, Lois Voran, Bernard Thiessen, and Verney Unruh.

6 Japan

The Kobe Garage Group

The General Conference Mennonite Church in Japan was born in a garage. This first fellowship was not known as a "congregation" but as a "group"—the Kobe Garage Group (KGG). The missionaries did not want to recognize them as an official congregation. The story of the Kobe Garage Group is a delightful monument to missionary inadvertence, as well as a unique tale of how the gospel can take root.

It happened that the first General Conference missionaries studied Japanese in the city of Kobe in a language school sponsored by the Southern Presbyterian Mission Board. Kobe was on the main island of Honshu, rather than the southern island of Kyushu where the future mission work would be. There was an informal comity agreement with the Mennonite Church (MC), whose work was on the northern island of Hokkaido, and the Mennonite Brethren, who were following up Mennonite Central Committee work on the main island of Honshu in Osaka, just a few miles from Kobe. The new group of young missionaries spent two years in language study and lived in the close quarters of a two-story house which had an attached garage.

Even though their future mission work was to be on Kyushu island many miles to the south, and even though they were supposed to spend full time in language study, these enthusiastic young missionaries could not be held back from their calling to evangelize. The result of their teaching and testimony was the emergence of a small group of new Japanese Christian believers, who held their meetings in a garage adjoining the missionary residence. The first baptism in Kobe was in October 1952, about fourteen months after the mission house had been purchased. But into what had the new believers been baptized? There was no organized General Conference Mennonite church in Kobe, nor was one planned. So there was a problem when these believers asked the missionaries that they be organized into a recognized and legitimate congregation.

What should be done with this request? The missionaries were polled and asked to submit written responses. Their answers are in the 1953 folder in the Japan mission files in Miyakonojo, an amazing document in the history of General Conference missions. The missionaries were unanimous in their opinion that these believers should not be organized into a congregation for which the mission would take responsibility! Why not? There were various reasons: Kobe was too far away from Kyushu, where the main work was to be; the mission work should not be divided; Kobe was really in Mennonite Brethren territory; let this group join the Mennonite Brethren or another evangelical group. One missionary expressed his opinion that this group should never have been started in the first place!

In November 1953 this new group of Japanese Christians wrote a letter responding to the decision of the mission, as they said, to "close the Kobe Mennonite Church." They respectfully thanked the missionaries for their zeal, guidance, and kindness. They observed that in early Christian history, as well as in the early Meiji era in Japan, Christians had gathered in humble dwellings and schoolrooms. They said they didn't want to join any other group: "It is our hearty desire to continue Church Services by ourselves and keep our fellowships in faith as we have had, only if it is God's will." So they asked for continued use of the Kobe mission garage to hold meetings on Sunday mornings and evenings, and on weekdays as necessary. They were on their own now. They resolved to continue even if they were not accepted as a General Conference Mennonite congregation. They would be pleased to meet in the mission garage.

Of course, in 1953 no one could know the future significance of this Kobe Garage Group which the Mennonite missionaries were so eager to give away or wish out of existence. Takashi Yamada, Hiroshi Yanada, and Masami Homma of the Kobe Garage Group all became pastors of GC Mennonite churches in Kyushu. Yamada and Yanada served terms as chairpersons of the Kyushu Mennonite Christian Church Conference. Homma later took a position in Tokyo as research secretary for Japanese Bible translation and publication. Another Kobe Garage Group member, Torao Abe, remained in Kobe as a dedicated lay elder who kept the Kobe congregation in existence when the others left for study and work elsewhere.

These men came to the Kobe Garage Group from a variety of backgrounds in postwar Japan which seemed to prepare them to receive the Christian gospel. Yamada, the founding member of the group, was a veteran of the Japanese navy and was employed by a shipping company in Kobe. He met the zealous Mennonite missionary Peter Voran in

General Conference Mennonite Mission Area in Japan

English language classes and decided to become a Christian the first time he heard the gospel in English at Peter and Lois Geiger Voran's home.

Yanada was in his last year in high school when he was baptized. He was working out a relationship with his authoritarian and embittered grandfather, whose fervent Japanese nationalism had been shaken by the defeat of the empire.

Homma had been attracted to the student Communist movement and, although not a Communist party member, had attended a Communist political rally the day before he was baptized.

The Christian fellowship experienced by these men, and by others gathered with them in the Kobe Garage Group, was both intense and joyful. Yamada had some extra income from his shipping company job, which he donated to the fellowship for the creation of a mutual aid fund. Members were able to borrow money from the fund and pay it back with extra donations. This fund was used to help with expenses of those who left Kobe for Christian college or seminary education in Tokyo. The fact that the Kobe Garage Group was thrown back upon its own organizational and intellectual resources was significant for the members' future role as church leaders. They defined their own existence in a special way. Indeed, their very basic decision to remain constituted as a worshiping and learning congregation was made apart from, and in opposition to, the clearly expressed will of the missionaries. It was an exercise in self-reliance.[1]

The excitement of new Christian fellowship and commitment in the Kobe Garage Group remained a fond memory and spiritual resource for many years to come. But the mountaintop days of discovery could not last indefinitely. These men were to become leaders in a new church which would have an arduous struggle for independence and authenticity. Takashi Yamada told of this transition in a striking personal testimony to the First Asia Mennonite Conference meeting in Dhamtari, India, in 1971:

> Fortunately right after I became a Christian I was nurtured and brought up in a small group of young Christians where we had little institutional organization and much genuine, warm Christian fellowship based upon brotherly love and spiritual freedom. Together with other members of this group I really enjoyed and spent the early part of my Christian life here. This continued for some years. Then, later I moved to the area where our missionaries were working, and took up the work of the pastoral ministry in a local church. I lost most of the freedom and the spontaneous, joyful spirit I used to enjoy in the previous group. My long distressing labourings to wrestle with various difficult issues and problems of evangelism and church planting in the mission field began.[2]

The General Conference Mennonite Church in Japan had two beginnings. The first was inadvertent—the Kobe Garage Group. The second was carefully planned—evangelism and church planting on the island of Kyushu.

Missionary Strategy Beyond China

Mennonite mission strategy for Japan was forged out of the wreckage of China. In mainland China the missionaries had established big Western-style mission compounds and institutions which were beyond the capacity of the local Christians to support. This time the missionaries resolved to travel lightly. William C. Voth, experienced China missionary who pioneered the work in Japan, warned at the outset that missionaries might only be allowed a short time in Japan.

Voth made an initial survey in Kyushu island on his way home from China in 1950, and returned for another survey with Verney Unruh in summer 1951. The Voth-Unruh report noted that there were only three or four Christian missionaries in Miyazaki Prefecture in a population of about one million. The Christian groups there, most of which had very small membership despite years of work, welcomed Mennonite involvement enthusiastically. Voth and Unruh recommended that Mennonites begin first in Miyazaki City, then in Miyakonojo, and that top priority be given to the neglected rural areas. Both Voth and Unruh had grown up in "neglected rural areas"—in Oklahoma and Montana, respectively—and the proposing of a rural strategy was for them as natural and as "Mennonite" as eating borscht and zwieback. They were optimistic about prospects for planting churches and expanding quickly. In Unruh's words, "We must not only win believers to Christ but at the same time make plans for their continued growth in Christ. Further, I feel that as soon as a church is firmly established we should move on to new areas. In brief, the indigenous Church is our goal."[3]

Ten General Conference missionaries arrived in Japan in 1951; ten more came in 1953-54. While the younger missionaries who planned for careers in Japan were studying language in Kobe, W. C. and Matilda Kliewer Voth moved to Miyazaki Prefecture (southeast coast of Kyushu), in 1952. Decisions about what kind of buildings to build or buy were not easy ones. Mission board secretary John Thiessen wrote to Voth insisting that all church or institutional buildings "be geared to an indigenous church and property be such as can be owned and controlled by the church."[4] The sprawling bungalows of India and the massive church buildings and schools of China were not to be duplicated in Japan. In fact, the only GC missionary "institution" (in a traditional sense) built in Japan was the Kei Ai [Grace-Love] Kindergarten built next door to the missionary home in Nichinan in 1955. The anti-institutional policy of the mission did not always have unanimous support among the missionaries, but it did make the character of the mission and the church quite different from the Mennonite work in other countries where more energy went into schools and hospitals.

The GC missionaries to Japan were something of a microcosm of the heterogeneous General Conference in their theological points of view. Their ability to work together in a common denominational enterprise without major division or attrition was, in its way, one test of whether the General Conference was a viable entity in the postwar era. Some of the missionaries had attended Grace Bible Institute and were oriented to strict biblical literalism, premillennialism, and the doctrine of eternal security. Others who had attended Bethel or Bluffton colleges were more inclined to amillennialism and a historical-critical view of the Bible. "We were all thrown together in that one house in Kobe for language study," remembered Peter Voran, "and there we knocked off each other's rough edges!"[5] The degree of polarization should not be overemphasized, however. Some missionaries had been helped through the fundamentalist-modernist thicket at Mennonite Biblical Seminary in Chicago. Seldom did missionaries divide on consistent liberal-conservative lines in matters of mission policy. The cement which held these young missionaries together was their fervent common commitment to the Christian evangelical enterprise. "Set your face like a flint" was their mutual admonition as they worked at the daunting task of learning Japanese. At their worship services and business meetings they often sang the hymn "Far and Near the Fields Are Teeming."

The "old China hands," the Voths, at work in Miyazaki, were not planning to be in Japan for the long term, and so did not take the time necessary to learn the language. The pattern of employing local workers (interpreters and teachers, in this case) as had been done in China, became a bone of contention. The new generation of young missionaries were insistent upon avoiding the problems of Western institutionalism. To employ Japanese workers, they believed, would set a pattern of dependence upon North American funds. At a missions business meeting of 14 April 1954, the missionaries agreed "that as a guiding principle for our mission for the next five years we do not hire regular national workers for such work as pastors, evangelists, Bible women, and Bible teachers for a period of more than 6 months."[6]

This decision did not exclude the employment of translators and the use of Japanese evangelistic teams to conduct short-term tent campaigns. But it did set a policy of restriction on the employment of nationals which had to be re-evaluated when Japanese churchmen began to take positions as pastors of the newly emerged churches. Would these pastors receive a salary from the mission on an ongoing basis? And should that salary be sufficient to support a life-style comparable to that of missionaries? Or should Japanese pastors be required to earn their own income through secular employment, and eventually become full-time pastors only after indigenous church growth and church giving provided sufficient support? This difficult and complex problem could not be avoided, for the mission produced more dedicated and well-qualified pastors than the church could support. The question was complicated further by the issue of missionary income and life-style. How great could the disparity between missionaries and Japanese workers be without interfering with basic brotherhood and trust?

There were a number of stages in the evolution of policy for mission employment of Japanese, but the concern to limit the dependence of the local church remained more dominant in the Japan GC Mennonite mission than in other GC mission fields. The mission worked out a sliding scale of graduated reductions in missions subsidies to congregations for pastors' support, not unlike the pattern which had been attempted earlier in China. The Japanese congregations were not always happy with this overall policy. They argued that subsidies be determined on a case-by-case basis to allow flexibility and to avoid the crippling effects of reduced or terminated subsidies for congregations which could not support pastors. The question of financial support for pastors remained problematic even after Japan's remarkable economic recovery in the 1960s and 1970s. Congregations were invariably small, and pastors had to seek alternative means of income.

Births of Congregations

W. C. and Matilda Voth led in founding of the Oyodo Christian Church congregation and moved (as new missionaries finished) down to Miyazaki Prefecture, establishing new mission locations. In the 1950s new work was started in five places, each eventually resulting in the establishment of a church congregation: the Namiki Christian Church at Miyakonojo, the Aburatsu Christian Church at Nichinan, the Kobayashi Mennonite Christian Church, the Hyuga Christian Church at Hyuga, and the Atago Christian Church at Nobeoka. Additional work was started at Takajo, Oita, and Kagoshima in the 1960s, and at Fukuoka in 1977. A second congregation in Miyazaki grew out of student work there in the 1960s. The Kagoshima effort was an experiment in cooperative mission-church evangelism. The Kobayashi church sent Mr. and Mrs. Tsutomu Okutsu to Kagoshima as lay evangelists. They worked for a short time in a team with North American missionaries, but no ongoing congregation emerged from this effort.

Early evangelistic work began with children's classes, Bible studies, and preaching services. Japanese postwar fascination with Americans helped stimulate attendance at street meetings and English classes. The most highly visible evangelistic technique of the early years was the tent campaign, which usually lasted about ten days in a single location. The tent campaigns were led by a Japanese evangelist and a team of Japanese Christian workers, sometimes including Mennonite students on vacation from school. The campaigns included afternoon children's meetings, nightly evangelistic services, house-to-house visitation, and tract distribution. The evangelistic message was the gospel theme of human sinfulness and God's offer of salvation through Christ. With postwar economic recovery, and particularly the general availability of television, attendance at the tent campaigns dwindled, and the mission turned to other methods.

The rapid establishment of Christian fellowships in Japan was a marked contrast to India, where P. A. Penner worked twelve years before even rudimentary church congregations could be organized. The first baptism in Miyazaki was in July 1952, half a year after the Voths settled there. High points for mission celebrations included baptismal ceremonies, Bible camps with guest speakers, the arrival of the first Mennonite Japanese pastor in Kyushu (Yamada to Nichinan in 1956), and the sending of six young men from the churches to Tokyo to prepare for Christian service (1955). The new churches met for two-day spiritual life conferences at New Year's time. These meetings became the embryo of the Japanese church conference.

Confronting the Culture

In Japan, as in other countries where Mennonite missionaries have worked, the presentation of the gospel message involved a confrontation with traditional religious belief and custom. The manner of the confrontation varied according to different circumstances. One dramatic moment occurred in Nichinan in 1955 at about the time of the first baptisms there. The new Christian converts decided to testify to their break with the past by having a public bonfire to burn some books and other objects which symbolized their old religion. One elderly widow, in defiance of her neighbor's warnings of dire consequences, brought for the burning her family god-shelf where the spirit of her husband and those of the ancestors were said to be enshrined. But the burning brought an unexpected crisis. According to missionary Peter Voran, "Within the next week after this woman burned the god-shelf, she had a stroke. A blood vessel burst in her head. One half of her face turned purple and she was paralyzed. The neighbors all said, 'See, we told you!' "[7]

The new young Christians refused to accept this setback for their new faith. They had read in the New Testament letter of James (5:13-16) that a sick person in the congregation could be raised up through prayer and anointing with oil. Voran, who had never before participated in a spiritual healing service, accompanied them "in fear and trembling" to the woman's bedside, where they had a prayer meeting, anointed the woman with oil, and claimed the victory for the Lord. "I sure didn't let those believers know how I felt on this inside," said Voran. But within the next few days the woman was fully healed from her stroke and paralysis, and attended church on Sunday morning. In Voran's words,

"It had to be an answer to the faith of those early Christians who just would read the Word and believed it without any prejudice or doubt in their minds. . . . They taught me something."

The bonfire ceremony at Nichinan was an exception rather than the rule, but there was never a doubt in the Japan churches that to become a Christian involved a decisive break with old ways. The church did not make hard and fast rules forbidding attendance at traditional religious and national festivals of Buddhism and Shintoism. Syncretism appeared to be no temptation. Takeomi Takarabe, who turned down a good position in a Japanese bank to attend Japan Christian College and become a Mennonite pastor, reports how he worked at maintaining relationships with his non-Christian mother and brothers. At one point he decided that in behalf of family relationships, he would pay formal respects at the traditional family altar, while personally withholding himself and denying the religious significance of his act. But when he came to the place for the ritual, he was unable to go through with it. He could not reconcile prayers to the ancestors with his faith in Christ.

The appropriate cultural form for Christian worship and church organization was a question which demanded increasing attention, particularly as the Japanese church became independent in the 1960s. Mennonites adopted patterns from missions which had arrived earlier. The missionaries had introduced a Western worship pattern in which people sat behind each other in straight rows facing a preacher who stood behind a pulpit. Would it be more authentically Japanese for the worshipers to sit on the floor on woven rice-straw mats? The churches occasionally experimented with different forms, but the issues were never clear-cut or obvious, especially in a Japanese culture which was itself being rapidly westernized. Pastor Hiroshi Yanada has said that it is the responsibility of the Japanese to take off imposed Western trappings from the Christian gospel, but that stereotyped pictures of cultural authenticity must be avoided in an age of cultural diffusion. Activities at some sectarian Shinto shrines in Japan today include preaching to persons sitting in rows of benches. "Western" music is so common today in Japan that it no longer sounds Western. In Miyazaki City, 96 percent of the homes have television sets. In this context is is best to admit diversity, to refrain from judging something to be inauthentic, and to concentrate upon the effect of the gospel in the life of the believer.[8]

Missions as Teaching

The character of Mennonite mission work in Japan was different from the work in other countries in one decisive respect. In Japan the missionaries took on a role as teachers; the Japanese seekers and converts became learners; the gospel message itself was something that was studied and learned. The predominance of the teacher-learner model for mission was not something the missionaries planned. Indeed, they specifically avoided the establishment of mission schools. This outcome was rather due to the special character of Japanese society.

"By nature the Japanese people like to be taught," says Pastor Hiroshi Isobe of the Namiki Church in Miyakonojo.[9] Teachers receive special honor and status, as well as special responsibility, in Japanese society. Teachers in primary and secondary schools are held responsible for the behavior of their students in nonschool hours, as well as during the school day. For parent-teacher conferences, the teachers come to visit in the homes of the parents. The high value attached to education and the limitations on university enrollments lead to intense competition among students and diligent study both in and out of school.

The Japanese were particularly fascinated with American culture and language in the immediate postwar years. The old empire had been destroyed and discredited. Japanese survivors eagerly looked for new alternatives. Mennonite missionaries discovered that one of the best methods for establishing personal contacts was through the teaching of English classes. Such teaching did not require full command of the Japanese language, and it allowed for additional contacts through Bible study or worship. The English-teaching method of evangelism proved to be more long-lasting than some other methods. Radio evangelism was discontinued in 1966; tent campaigns seemed to lose their appeal with the coming of television. But the English classes remained popular. In the 1960s a number of short-term mission workers were recruited for the mission, in some cases fulfilling American Selective Service obligations, and these workers usually engaged in English teaching.

A number of consequences seemed to flow from the teacher-learner context of mission work. People were won to the church not in groups but as individuals who had done some wrestling with Christian theology. The Christian faith among Japanese Mennonites probably had more intellectual content and appreciation than in other Mennonite mission fields. The size of Mennonite congregations remained small. Whether led by missionaries, or later by Japanese pastors, the congregations did not grow above classroom size. Every change of leadership for a congregation seemed to create a crisis. The problem was not primarily the lack of good leaders to replace the missionaries, but the strength of the attachment to a particular teacher. "The Japanese are loyal to leaders," said Masami Homma, "so they became loyal to missionaries rather than to Christ and the church."[10]

The distinctive teacher-learner character of the Mennonite church in Japan has been the source of significant strength for the mission and church. Although the church has remained small, Japanese Mennonite pastors and church leaders have demonstrated a theological understanding and maturity which stands out above any other church resulting from General Conference mission work. The quality of preaching in Japanese Mennonite churches is high. Mennonite pastors are theologically well informed. Takashi Yamada, pastor of Kirishima Brotherhood since 1959, has served as mentor to other Japanese Mennonite pastors and as a pioneer thinker and strategist for church development in Kyushu. Yamada has been a leader in the wider Mennonite scene with work for the Japan Mennonite Fellowship, the Asia Mennonite Conference, and the Mennonite World Conference. The close working relationship between missionary Paul Boschman and Pastor Yamada has been cited as a rare case—perhaps the only one in Mennonite missions history—where the national member in such a partnership is the more aggressive and dominant member of a harmonious and productive team.

Professor Gan Sakakibara of Tokyo is another person who symbolizes the intellectual strength of Japanese Mennonites. Sakakibara was an active Presbyterian layman who earned a distinguished reputation as a scholar of the history of economic thought. Through his contacts with Paul Peachey, Mennonite Central Committee peace worker in Japan, Sakakibara became interested in the tradition and contemporary expression of Anabaptist communitarian groups. In the Hutterite colony of South Dakota, the Reba Place Fellowship in Chicago, and other communal groups, Sakakibara made the discovery of Anabaptism which inspired him to bring, as he said, "my past academic work to a providential finish."[11] In the 1960s and 1970s he wrote, translated, and published nine books in a Japanese "Anabaptist Series." The series included the history of the Hutterites, a survey of contemporary communitarian groups, a study of the Classical Age of *Radicalism,* an *Anabaptist Genealogy of Conscientious Objectors,* and others. Sakakibara's interest was not just academic. He became a Mennonite himself and actively led in the establishment of an Anabaptist center in Tokyo.

Church Growth and Social Structure

A major disappointment for the mission and church in Japan was the unexpectedly slow growth of the church. Early hopes had been high. General Douglas MacArthur, whose stirring call for a thousand missionaries had been a stimulus to Mennonite entry, had said that there was a spiritual vacuum in Japan. The successes of Mennonite evangelism in Kobe and in southern Kyushu in the early 1950s seemed to confirm the belief that the Japanese were ripe for the Christian gospel. But by the 1960s the first hopes had to be revised. Church growth was slow and difficult. By 1964 there were seven churches, five pastors, and a total membership of 321. But the attrition rate had been high—over 50 percent. The church had to struggle just to replace members who were leaving the community or dropping out.

In the mid-1960s the mission and church became increasingly aware of ways in which Japanese social structure affected the life and growth of the church. A series of missionary and church pastor seminars were held to examine the issues and evaluate alternative strategies. Missionary Paul Boschman and Pastor Takashi Yamada published a book in 1968, *Experiments in Church Growth: Japan,* which outlined the results of their research and thinking.[12] (Boschman studied under missiologist Donald A. McGavran at the Institute of Church Growth in Eugene, Oregon, in 1964.)

Boschman observed in the book that although Mennonites originally intended a rural strategy, only nine farmers in twelve years had joined the church. Most of the church members were from "transient segments of Japanese society," salaried persons (29 percent), housewives (19 percent), and students (12 percent). Salaried persons and students were very mobile; housewives in non-Christian homes were handicapped in expressing their faith. The result was a highly unstable church membership. The critical group to win in order to achieve stability and growth, according to Boschman, was the Japanese grouping of households called *buraku.* The proper mission strategy was not to call individuals out of their social context where they must bear the burdens of ostracism, but rather to win people as part of their natural group.

Pastor Yamada carefully and minutely analyzed the patterns of conversion from his experiences with evangelism in Kobayashi City and Nishimorokata County. He observed from work with students that they tended to come to the Christian faith in small groups of friends, rather than as isolated individuals. Although Dr. McGavran wrote a glowing foreword to *Experiments in Church Growth: Japan,* there were fundamental differences between the Mennonites and the church growth school with which McGavran was identified. Yamada had little interest or intention in starting a large-scale people's movement, and he discussed his differences at length with McGavran when the latter visited in Japan. In his vision of the church and of Christian discipleship, Yamada has emphasized "an intense attitude of confrontation" with secular political powers—a theme which has not been prominent in the school of church growth missiology.[13] The dialogue in church and mission about church growth and social structure in the 1960s, however, served an important function in helping Mennonites to critique their own work.[14]

Anabaptism and the Peace Witness

Hiroshi Hidaka, youthful Japanese interpreter for William C. Voth, remembers the old missionary as a "born storyteller." Included in the Voth repertoire were stories of the American Mennonite experience in World War I, which Hidaka remembered in vivid detail a quarter-century later.[15] As they drove along the Miyazaki Prefecture countryside, Voth told how the German-speaking Mennonite young men were drafted into American army camps in 1918 and were persecuted for their refusal to take up weapons in the war against Germany. The military officers forced these religious pacifists to go on long hot marches with heavy gear, threatened to run over one of them with a truck if he wouldn't put on a uniform, and held them to scorn and ridicule from their peers. But Hidaka does not remember that Voth made Mennonite nonresistance a part of his evangelical message, or that he ever expounded upon the relevance of the Anabaptist-Mennonite experience and tradition to a war-disillusioned Japan which was eager for a pacifist message.

"If the Mennonites had clearly articulated their peace position," says Gan Sakakibara, "they could have won the Japanese people to their way."[16] As it was, the Mennonites allowed the moment of greatest receptivity to pass without clearly formulating and projecting the evangelical Mennonite peace witness in a way that would link up with Japanese postwar needs and aspirations. Hiroshi Yanada, member of the Kobe Garage Group, put it this way: "Practically everything I know about Anabaptism I learned not from the missionaries but from Japanese study. If the missionaries know a good thing, they should not hide it."[17]

Why did the GC missionaries not emphasize their Anabaptist heritage and the doctrine of nonresistance? In this regard the missionaries to Japan were not different from GC missionaries to other countries. Mennonites in general learned their missionary strategy and message from prevailing Protestant models and not from their Anabaptist heritage. Moreover, GC Mennonites in North America had fallen victim to theological fragmentation on typically Protestant liberal-conservative lines. Mennonite leaders of liberal inclinations were in danger of emphasizing the "peace witness" as separate from the evangelical thrust of the gospel. Missionaries in Japan reacted against this manifestation of an incomplete gospel. Meanwhile, North American Mennonite leaders of conservative inclinations—often connected with the Bible Institute movement—were in danger of emphasizing the doctrines of sin and salvation to the virtual exclusion of nonresistance and the peace witness.

Peter Voran, a graduate of Grace Bible Institute and of Bethel College, outlined a conservative position in a 1959 paper entitled "A Missionary Looks at the Peace Witness." Missionaries should "start with the gospel of saving grace," said Voran. Not only did peace activism have the danger of "unholy alliances" with the non-Christian peace movement, but it was a diversion from the primary missionary calling. "I am afraid that if we get sidetracked into one particular teaching and try to build upon it or even try to lead to Christ through it we will find ourselves 'Busy and occupied' but not getting the job done."[18]

Voran's assumption that Mennonites were evangelical Christians who had a secondary peace witness was typical for Mennonites ever since S. S. Haury went to Indian Territory in 1880. But this assumption began to undergo some revision in the 1960s and 1970s, and missionaries began to shift emphasis. Robert Ramseyer, another Mennonite missionary to Japan who became director of the Overseas Mission Training Center in Elkhart, outlined an alternative position in a 1976 paper, "The Christian Peace Witness and Our Missionary Task: Are Mennonites Evangelical Protestants with a Peace Witness?"[19] Ramseyer argued that the way of peace was an integral part of the gospel of salvation, rather than derivative from it. "Living as a disciple of Jesus Christ is living in this world in the way in which we were created to live," said Ramseyer. "Being a disciple of Jesus Christ means living in the peace of God."[20] For missions this means testifying to the ultimate claims of Christ over against the claims of the nation, even though this position may make the church unpopular in ecumenical circles and suspect in the eyes of governments.

The Mennonite peace witness in Japan evolved as something separate from mission board programs. In 1955 the Mennonite Central Committee sent a representative from its Peace Section to work as a Mennonite peace ambassador with headquarters in Tokyo. The work of this office, which was first held by Melvin Gingerich (1955-57) and Paul Peachey (1958-60), included the holding of peace seminars and arranging for the publication in Japanese of Mennonite peace literature. It was in this work that Peachey first made contact with Sakakibara. One drawback of MCC sponsorship of the Japan peace witness, however, was that it represented an institutional separation of missions and peace, added to the theological separation which was common among missionaries. The peace witness was something which Mennonites through MCC "added onto" the missions program started some years earlier. By its institutional identification, and by its location in Tokyo, this peace witness was somewhat removed from missions activity proper, even after missionary Ferd Ediger took the position of peace representative in 1960. In 1976 the GC Commission on Overseas Mission placed a worker with the World Friendship Center in Hiroshima, but again the relationship between that assignment and the life of the Japanese Mennonite Church was somewhat ambiguous and needed to be developed.

The peace witness of the Kyushu Mennonite Christian Church Conference has been primarily directed against current manifestations of the revival of Shintoism as a Japanese state religion. The conference passed an official resolution against government legislation to nationalize the Yasukuni shrine, a Shinto shrine which before World War II had been a focus of Japanese religious nationalism and militarism. Copies of the resolution were sent to every member in the Japanese parliament. In another case, some Mennonites have contributed to a fund for the legal case of a Christian woman whose deceased husband was enshrined, against the woman's will, as a "national guardian" in a local Shinto shrine. And in a third instance, Mennonites in Miyazaki assisted in a successful protest against mandatory civil-religious rituals in the local police force. The local police chief had been requiring all policemen to pray or pay respects to an amulet from a Shinto shrine so that they might be successful in capturing a certain thief. These confrontations have elicited opposition. Pastor Yanada tells of having received telephone calls accusing him of being a foreigner and inviting him to leave the country.[21] Mennonites have been cooperating with other Christians in these confrontations.

Another kind of Japanese Mennonite peace witness has been organized in Tokyo by Michio Ohno, a former Congregationalist who was attracted to the Mennonites by the peace emphasis. Ohno studied at the Associated Mennonite Biblical Seminaries in 1964-66. In 1974 he initiated a movement of conscientious objection to military taxation, and began to refuse payment of a percentage of his tax equivalent to the military portion of the budget. For fiscal 1977 this was 5.9 percent. Compared to the expenditures of the world's industrial military powers this is a small amount, but tax refusal in Japan has the additional argument that militarization of Japan is a violation of the postwar peace constitution. Because the Japanese government does not want a major confrontation or legal battle on the issue, tax resisters usually have not been pressured or punished by the government. In 1978 Pastor Ohno presented his understanding of the Christian basis for resistance to militarism in a seminar at Bethel College and at the Tenth Mennonite World Conference.

Church Independence

Pastor Takashi Yamada in 1970 outlined six stages of developing maturity in the relationship of older churches in North America and younger churches in Asia. These stages were as follows:

1. (Babyhood) - Period of *unconscious overall dependence* upon the older churches in North America.
2. (Childhood) - Period of *conscious overall dependence.*
3. (Preadolescence) - Period of *resisting against,* and yet *depending on,* the paternalistic approach of the mission and the older churches.
4. (Adolescence) - Period of *spiritual independence.*
5. (Adulthood) - Period of *cooperation and interdependence* with the older churches.
6. (Matured Adulthood) - Period of *significant contribution and service* of younger churches to the older churches.[22]

Yamada did not identify the moment, or the year, in which the Kyushu Mennonites achieved "adulthood." It can be said, however, that the maturation process in Japan proceeded more rapidly than it ever had before on General Conference mission fields. One reason for this was the leadership abilities of members of the Kobe Garage Group who accepted challenges of pastorates or other work related to the new churches in Kyushu. Yamada became pastor of the church at Nichinan in 1956; Yanada came to Miyazaki, and then to Miyakonojo, in 1959 and 1960, after studying at Japan Christian College; Homma became pastor at Miyazaki in 1958. The mission's record in educating pastors from the Kyushu churches was not as good, however. Four of the first five students sent out for theological education failed to return to positions of church leadership.[23]

The question of church-mission relationships was in the fore in the 1960s. The Kyushu Mennonite Christian Conference emerged gradually out of a pattern of policy-making meetings in the early 1960s, and was officially born with six member churches in 1965. But the official status of the mission remained unclarified. The Japanese leaders were wary of mission paternalism; the missionaries feared that dissolution of the mission might cause problems for budgeting, expansion, and other decision making. The Japanese revised the top-heavy organizational structure inherited from the missionaries. They questioned mission strategy and made a number of changes, such as the dropping of radio work in 1966. A Bible school which was planned to begin in 1963 never materialized, in part because of the preoccupation with problems of mission-church relationships.[24] In the late 1960s, some missionaries were so discouraged by what they considered unfair criticism from the Japanese Christians that they considered resigning. The "adolescent stage" was not easy.

One indication of Japanese church independence was their questioning of the assumptions behind the 1972 COM Goals, Priorities, and Strategy (GPS) meeting. COM had adopted a set of seven priorities for mission work and asked that the national churches hold parallel meetings in their own countries. The Kyushu Conference leaders were less than enthusiastic about holding a similar meeting. Didn't the very pattern of North American GPS initiatives and expected Asian responses, they wondered, contradict the ideals of equality and independence? Could not the Kyushu Conference set goals for itself at a time and with an agenda of its own choosing, rather than dealing with a particular set of priorities written in North America? Such questions were in themselves a test of how seriously the COM took its own stated priority number 3, "Transfer administrative authority, responsibility, and accountability to national leadership. . . ." If such a transfer had in fact actually taken place in Japan, the North American mission board could not expect unquestioning response from Japan to North American initiatives and requests, whether it was for a given priorities evaluation or for more articles about Japanese Mennonite church life to publish in North American Mennonite church papers.

Tokyo Inter-Mennonite Conference

Mennonites avoided the city of Tokyo in the first round of mission church planting around 1950, but the flow of Japanese Mennonite church members to the capital city eventually led to the establishment of Mennonite churches and an inter-Mennonite church conference. Cooperative inter-Mennonite planning for work in the Tokyo area began in the early 1960s. In 1974 the General Conference Mennonites, Mennonite Church (MC), and Brethren in Christ formed an official Tokyo Area Mennonite Evangelism Cooperative Conference (Keihin Dendo Kyoryokukai), which consists of eight small churches, two of which have property and buildings. KDK cooperative activities include an annual two-day Christian Life Retreat, leadership training programs, and fellowship meetings.[25] The General Conference missionaries active in the Tokyo conference have been Ferd and Viola Duerksen Ediger. The Edigers, who had worked with the GC mission in Japan since 1953, initiated an alternative form of missionary financing when they became self-supporting in 1965. At first they kept their own income, but then an arrangement was made that their salary (Ferd Ediger is a tenured professor at Rikkyo University in Tokyo) be forwarded to the mission treasurer and they receive compensation on the same scale as other missionaries.

Conclusion

In 1961 S. F. Pannabecker surveyed and predicted Japanese General Conference mission-church development as a three-stage process, with the first stages taking one decade each: 1951-61, the decade of missionary predominance; 1961-71, the decade of joint participation; 1971- , the era of Japanese predominance. But events moved faster than Pannabecker and the missionaries expected. The Kyushu church conference was formed already in 1965. Despite the difficulties of moving quickly from missionary domination to missionary servant-hood, there was strong continuity in missionary leadership and personnel from 1951 through the 1970s.

The witness of Japanese Mennonites, however, was inhibited by the small size and limited growth of the churches. In this regard the Mennonites were similar to Protestant churches in Japan generally. The Kyushu Mennonite Church Conference in 1978 claimed 588 members, but many of these were nonresident or inactive.[26] It was, for the most part, a middle-class church whose members were growing in economic prosperity. But the church's resources for program development were restricted by limited numbers. This meant continued dependence upon the North American mission board in a number of respects, although there was no doubt that the church would survive even if all North American missionaries would have to leave and all foreign subsidies would be cut off.

In no country other than Japan did there emerge so quickly a group of spiritually dedicated and theologically articulate Mennonite leaders who could communicate the gospel with freshness and persuasiveness. In the space of a few short decades, North American Mennonites found themselves sitting at the feet of Japanese teachers to learn the meaning of biblical Christianity in the Anabaptist tradition! This is not to say that the Japanese Mennonites solved their problems of leadership recruitment and development. The absence of a Japanese Mennonite seminary or training school and difficulties in finding good church leaders remained a problem area for the church.[27]

The Kyushu Mennonite churches quickly developed an interest in overseas mission outreach. Teruko Yano, of the Hyuga church, served two terms with the Mennonite Central Committee in Vietnam. The churches helped support an MC missionary family, the Kanekos, in Quito, Ecuador. The Mennonite congregation at Oita provided regular monthly support for Richard and Marilyn Carter Derksen, missionaries in Banga, Zaire, under the Africa Inter-Mennonite Mission. The Oita church members knew Richard personally as the son of Japan missionaries, Peter and Mary Klaassen Derksen, and they considered him to be one of their missionaries. Japan Mennonites have also been liberal supporters of the inter-Mennonite endeavors of Asia Mennonite Services. There has been much discovery and growth since those early days in the Kobe Garage Group.

Behind a Buddhist temple in Taipei, Taiwan, Paul Lin (in 1960) tells the story of the lost sheep.

Photo by Lola Friesen

7 Taiwan

The Beginnings

"Of all the fifty or more denominations who began mission work in Taiwan after the war," said Lillian Dickson, "only the Mennonites were invited."[1] Lillian and James Dickson had been missionaries in Taiwan with the Canadian Presbyterian mission since 1927. In 1948, three years after Taiwan had been liberated from Japanese rule, James Dickson went to Shanghai to try to persuade the Mennonite Central Committee to begin medical work with mobile clinics among the aboriginal mountain tribes in Taiwan. Dickson's invitation was accepted. MCC was being excluded from China along with all other Christian missions and relief organizations, and was ready to grasp a new opportunity for service to the needy in the name of Christ.

After several years of pioneering medical and social service, MCC handed over its work in Taiwan to the General Conference Mennonite mission board in the early 1950s. The mission began to establish a Mennonite church in Taiwan, a church which by 1978 had nearly a thousand members in sixteen congregations.

The People

Those living on the island of Taiwan—or Formosa as it was named by Portuguese navigators in the sixteenth century—could be divided into three major groups. The differences between these groups and their troubled relationships with each other were important for the founding and the development of the Taiwanese Mennonite church.

1. *The mountain people.* A number of aboriginal tribes, probably of Malay origin, were the people who had been on the island the longest. They maintained their distinct languages and culture but were the least developed and most impoverished of the island peoples. Taken together,

these tribes were less than 2 percent of the population. The Japanese, who ruled Taiwan from 1895 to 1945, had forbidden Christian missionary contact with the mountain people, but during and after World War II a rapid movement toward Christianity took place in a number of these tribes. The Dicksons worked among these people and became aware of their great needs for literacy, health care, and economic development. Mennonite Central Committee mobile clinic work among the mountain people was combined with a spiritual ministry which helped set the stage for the rapid planting and growth of Christian churches.

2. *The Taiwanese.* Over 80 percent of the population on the island— some ten million people—could be designated as Taiwanese, or Minnan Chinese. The Taiwanese were descendants of early immigrants from the Chinese mainland provinces of Fukien and Kwantung. The national Taiwanese patriot-hero is one Koxinga (Cheng Ch'eng-kung), who overthrew Dutch rule of Taiwan in 1662 and attempted to use the island as a base to oppose the new Manchu Dynasty on the mainland. The Taiwanese spoke a Chinese dialect much like that spoken in the Amoy region of Fukien province, and distinct from the Mandarin and Cantonese Chinese languages.[2]

3. *The mainland Chinese.* When the Communists defeated the Nationalists on the Chinese mainland in 1949, General Chiang Kai-shek brought military personnel and government civil servants, along with a flood of escaping war refugees, to the island of Taiwan. This most recent wave of Chinese immigration—some two to three million people—was made up of people who did not consider Taiwan their home and who looked forward to their day of return to the mainland. The Nationalists claimed to be the rightful rulers of all of China. Their claim was supported with economic and military aid from the United States and the anti-Communist West. Taiwan was alleged to be a bastion of freedom, a staging ground for the eventual overthrow and defeat of Communism on the Chinese mainland.

For the Taiwanese people, however, the rule of these immigrant mainland Nationalists did not represent freedom or self-government. Their former Japanese rulers had been replaced by Chinese mainlanders who treated the Taiwanese majority like captured enemies. In the spring of 1947 the Taiwanese revolted against Chinese rule, but they were defeated in brutal reprisals that took over ten thousand Taiwanese lives. Potential Taiwanese leadership was further suppressed in a "land reform" program which broke the power of the rural Taiwanese gentry.[3] In subsequent decades the Chinese Nationalists succeeded in establishing political control and stability—albeit under continuing emergency and "wartime" conditions—and in fostering the conditions for great economic growth and social progress to the island. The Taiwanese lacked political self-rule but gained material prosperity.

The Choices

In this context of political hostility, it was a critical matter for Mennonite missionaries in the early 1950s to decide with which group they would begin the work of evangelism and church planting.[4] The possibility of working with the immigrant Mandarin-speaking Chinese was attractive as a link of continuity with the Mennonite mission work in Hopei province on the China mainland. Several former China missionaries who had command of the Mandarin language were available and could begin work with the people immediately. Moreover, if Chiang Kai-shek's dream of Communist collapse and Nationalist takeover of the mainland came to fruition, the Mennonites would be in position to return to their former field. Three former China missionaries worked in the mission in Taiwan in the 1950s—William C. and Matilda Voth, and Marie J. Regier. They did find it possible to contact a few people from the mission area in Hopei province. Matilda Voth, for example, wrote of meeting Liu Hsiu-chung, who as a child had attended a Mennonite school taught by W. C. Voth. He now had served as a doctor for eight years in the China Air Force medical corps, and was approached to work at the Mennonite hospital at Hwalien.[5]

The former China missionaries tended to have a positive view of Chiang Kai-shek and the Nationalist government. In the text for a proposed mission film on Taiwan, the missionaries not only neglected to mention Chinese Nationalist brutality in taking control of Taiwan, but acclaimed the Nationalist government as "a model of democracy" whose political stability was "a boon and blessing to the Christian church and to Christian missions carrying out 'the Great Commission.' "[6] A number of considerations, however, led the GC mission to decide against the Mandarin-speaking immigrants as the primary mission field. There was, in fact, a surplus of Christian missionaries for this group, because many other missionaries who had been excluded from China had come to Taiwan. Moreover, the number of contacts with Chinese from the former Mennonite mission field in Hopei were very few and provided no real base for church development. With each passing month and year, the prospects for return to the Chinese mainland diminished.

Another option was to follow up Mennonite Central Committee mobile clinic work among the tribal peoples with a program for church planting in the mountain villages. Glen Graber, who had been working with MCC on the China mainland prior to 1949, developed and coordinated the mobile team, which went out to mountain villages for up to two weeks at a time, often treating several thousand patients on a trip. By 1953 there were two mobile clinics in operation—on both the east and the west sides of the island—and the goal was to reach every aboriginal village in Taiwan once per year.

The mobile clinic work combined evangelism and medical services. The team would begin in each village with a preaching service, followed by medical care for people with a great variety of ailments, and concluding with a slide show in the evening. Lu Chhun-Tiong, a Taiwanese Presbyterian pastor and evangelist, was in charge of evangelism for the mobile clinic teams. He often spoke to the tribal people in Japanese, a language required in schools during the long Japanese occupation. The people, Lu reported, were remarkably responsive. The team would teach the people a simple gospel chorus on one visit, and return a year later to discover the people doing indigenous dancing and drumming to that same melody![7]

The MCC mobile clinic work was an important part in a strong people's movement toward Christianity among the mountain tribes in the early 1950s. The mobile clinic has been credited with setting the stage for the establishment of more than four hundred mountain churches by other denominations.[8] None of these were Mennonite churches, although one of them has a marker identifying Glen Graber as the founder. The Mennonites were not greatly concerned that other denominations were reaping this harvest. Executive secretary Andrew Shelly wrote of the medical mountain work after one trip to Taiwan, "While in a sense we 'lose ourselves,' the cause of Christ gains."[9]

Although the early mission board planning had foreseen the possibility of work among the Hakka people or the Amis tribes, by the time the Mennonites were ready for church planting work in 1955 it was clear that the more open and challenging field was among the Taiwanese people who formed the large majority on the island. There were more Taiwanese villages without Christian churches than there were unchurched tribal villages.[10] And so it happened that Taiwan became a Mennonite mission field in its own right, rather than a temporary stepping-stone for return to China. A suggestion of continuity with China was preserved, however, in the name chosen for the missionary newsletter published for North American supporting churches. The defunct *China-Home Bond* was followed in July 1956 with volume 1, number 1, of *Taiwan-Home Bond*.

Mennonite Presbyterians or Presbyterian Mennonites

The character of the Mennonite church which emerged from mission work among the Taiwanese people was profoundly shaped by the Mennonite relationship to the Taiwanese Presbyterian Church. English Presbyterians were the first Protestants to take up mission work in Taiwan in the nineteenth century, when work in China was extended to the island in 1865. Canadian Presbyterians subsequently undertook mission work in the northern part of the island. By 1940 there were nearly twenty thousand Presbyterian communicants in Taiwan, and the church was sufficiently rooted to survive and grow during World War II when the Japanese expelled the missionaries, closed the seminaries, and took over the church schools.[11]

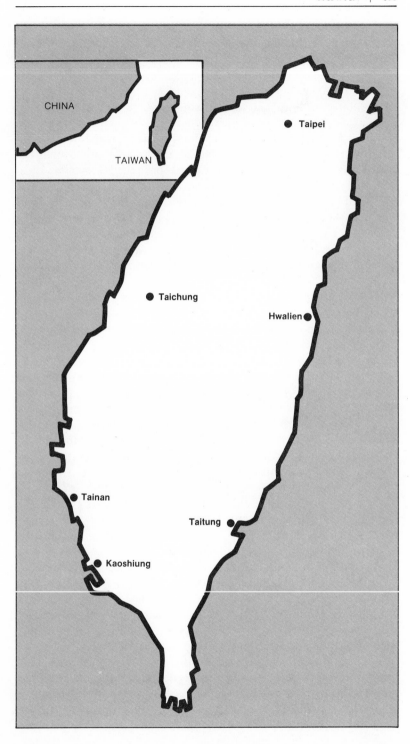

In 1954, at the time that Mennonites were preparing to begin church planting work in Taiwan, the Presbyterians inaugurated a Double-the-Church Movement with the goal of doubling the number of churches and also of church members in ten years. The movement was a great success. Both goals were achieved, and by 1965 the Presbyterian membership was more than sixty-five thousand. It was in the context of this successful expansion—which included growth among the Taiwanese and the mountain tribes—that Presbyterians helped Mennonites get their evangelism and church planting efforts under way. Not all the Presbyterian church leaders were eager to have the Mennonites begin church-planting work in 1954. It had been their understanding that MCC had promised in 1948 not to establish churches. Yet the fact that the Presbyterians experienced rapid growth in these years, as well as the open and cooperative attitude of Mennonite missionaries, helped smooth the way for the Mennonite mission work. Thus Taiwanese Mennonitism emerged as one chapter in a history of Presbyterian expansion.

The "founding father" of Mennonite churches in Taiwan was a man who did not become a Mennonite himself—the same Presbyterian evangelist Lu who had worked with Glen Graber and the MCC mobile clinic team. Pastor Lu was a deeply devout Christian and a dynamic public speaker. It was said that he could hold an audience spellbound for 2½ hours. Pastor Lu was greatly impressed that Mennonites had unselfishly developed the mountain medical work which led to the growth of Presbyterian churches. He noted that Mennonites even turned down a request from one tribal Presbyterian congregation which was disaffected with the presbytery and asked to join the Mennonites. Other mission groups who moved into the same field were more inclined to denominational competition for converts and churches. Pastor Lu now took a leading role in evangelism for Mennonite congregations, in recruiting Presbyterian pastors for Mennonite churches, and in assisting Mennonite missionaries to identify new areas for church planting.

The founding of the first Mennonite congregation in Taiwan—the Lin-Shen Road Mennonite Church in Taichung—was a prime example of Mennonite-Presbyterian cooperation. That congregation grew out of a children's Sunday school and youth English Bible classes organized by Glen and June Straite Graber in the yard of the Christian Children's Fund Babies' Home in 1954.[12] When attendance grew and the weather turned too cold for outdoor meetings, the Grabers built a simple bamboo chapel in their own backyard. Evangelist Lu came for a series of evangelistic meetings in November 1954, and the response to his vigorous messages was so great that regular congregational meetings were instituted and a larger meeting place sought. It happened that the Presbyterian church had purchased a Japanese house nearby with the intention of starting a new congregation. At Graber's request, the

Presbyterians sold the house to the Mennonites and wished them well in establishing the church. A Presbyterian evangelist, Sia Eng-Lam (Samuel Hsieh), who graduated from Taiwan Theological College in 1955, became the first pastor of the new congregation in July of that year. The Lin-Shen Road Mennonite Church grew rapidly to about sixty members by 1958 and fairly steadily to over one hundred members in 1964.

The mission established five additional churches in Taiwan in 1957 and 1958. Two of these, the Hsi-Tun and the Ta-Ya churches, grew up in market towns in the Taichung area at the initiative of Glen Graber and his Taiwanese helpers. Two more were started on the other side of the island at Hwalien. The Meilun church was located in a northern suburb of Hwalien near the small Mennonite Christian Hospital which had opened in 1950. This church grew out of the evangelistic work of W. C. and Matilda Voth in 1957. It was the only Mennonite church in Taiwan with significant Mandarin-speaking Chinese participation, a fact due both to the Voths' interests and to the involvements of Chinese hospital personnel in this congregation. The worship services have been dual language—Taiwanese and Mandarin—throughout the history of this congregation. The Meilun congregation grew slowly over the first ten years to about fifty members. The Po-Ai congregation in downtown Hwalien was begun by missionary J. N. (Han) Vandenberg, a Dutch Mennonite working with the GC mission. The first Mennonite church in the capital city of Taipei grew from the work of missionaries Hugh and Janet Frost Sprunger, together with seminary student Lin Ching-Ho (Paul Lin) and Ruth Chen, director of a home for blind children. Here, as in other places where the Mennonites planted churches, the evangelistic work of Lu Chhun-Tiong was essential in attracting seekers and winning converts.

It has been a concern of the Mennonite churches in Taiwan that many converts enter the church as isolated individuals rather than as families who could lend stability and continuity to the ongoing fellowship. There was one family, however, which provided exceptional leadership and talent for the church—the family of Wung Tien-Min. [13] Mr. Wung was from a typical rural Taiwanese family. He was converted to Christianity at age twenty-four under the influence of the famous Chinese evangelist, John Sung, and was later called to preach. Wung's mother, fearing that she would have no son to mourn at her funeral, opposed his interest in Christianity and hid his Bible and hymnbook. Eventually, however, both Wung's mother and his wife, Chuang Chang, became Christians and joined him as members in the Presbyterian church. "Becoming a Christian," said Wung, "causes a revolution in the family—like the revolution of Sun Yat-sen." [14] In 1957 Wung accepted a call from the Taichung Mennonite Church to take charge of the outstation chapel in the Hsi-Tun suburb; under his leadership the fellowship increased to forty members. He later served as pastor of two other Mennonite churches, as chairman of the evangelism committee of the church conference, and in other offices. Three of Pastor and Mrs. Wung's sons became pastors—two in Mennonite churches and one in the Presbyterian church. (He was moderator of the Presbyterian church in Taiwan in 1978.) Another son in 1978 was in his last year of residency as a surgeon at Mennonite Christian Hospital in Hwalien.

A Place to Meet and Worship

One characteristic of Mennonite church planting in Taiwan was the special significance of gathering or worship *places*. The typical strategy for founding new congregations was not to begin with a group of local believers, but rather to begin by renting a building in an unchurched area and then buy or build a church later. The church structures were usually quite modest in size—certainly never as large and imposing as the church buildings in Kai Chow and Taming Fu in the China mainland interior had been. But it seemed important in Taiwan that Christians have a place to meet and to worship which would be more respectable and more clearly set off than the living room of a missionary home or than a bamboo shack in Glen Graber's backyard. The early leaders Pastor Lu and Samuel Hsieh emphasized the importance of proper worship places in Taiwanese society where people were used to going to temples or shrines for religious services.

The orientation of mission and church toward buildings has been criticized both by missionaries and by Taiwanese nationals. Simon H. H. Wung, a Taiwanese Mennonite pastor, noted that not only is church life "centered around the church building and the activities that take place there," but that there is an overemphasis upon the role of the pastor. The church, wrote Wung, "makes the layman a hearer of the gospel and the bystander to the Church's ministry."[15] The same critique, of course, could be made of Mennonite churches in North America. The Taiwanese Mennonite church did in fact experience a rate of growth greater than that of the sending churches in North America. Taiwanese Mennonites founded, on the average, one new congregation every two years. By 1978 there were seven congregations in the Taichung area, six congregations in Taipei, and three congregations in Hwalien.

Church-Mission Relations

Relationships between missionaries and Taiwanese have been notably cooperative and cordial, especially compared with the troubled decades in China. The church conference, the Fellowship of Mennonite Churches in Taiwan (FOMCIT), was organized with seven church congregations in 1964. A Taiwanese pastor served as chairperson of the FOMCIT executive committee, and a missionary served as vice-chairperson. The two major FOMCIT committees were in charge of education and evangelism, with a literature committee added later. As the Taiwanese church grew in numbers and in maturity, it took increasing initiative, including responsibility for the calling and assignment of new missionaries. The church took control of the mission legal body (juridical person) in 1975.

In quest of appropriate policies for the transfer of mission-owned properties to the churches, the missionaries in Taiwan sought information in 1966 from Mennonite missionaries in Japan, India, and Zaire. Responses from Vernon Sprunger in Zaire, George Janzen in Japan, and Edward Burkhalter in India suggested that there were major difficulties on all mission fields. In Taiwan the churches and parsonages were legally owned by the church conference. In some cases initial costs were partially covered by grants from North America. It was typical, however, for the local congregation to be responsible for the gradual repayment of loans from the Church Extension Service, a North American agency which financed church and parsonage buildings at home and abroad. By 1977, only four of the sixteen FOMCIT churches were financially independent for current expenses and clear of loan repayments for property purchases, but the capacity of the Taiwanese to work toward self-support was aided by rapid economic growth in Taiwan in the 1960s and 1970s.

Goals, Priorities, and Strategy in the 1970s

Taiwan Mennonite church leaders and missionaries responded enthusiastically to COM's 1972 call for a review of church-mission goals, priorities, and strategy (GPS). In November 1972, twenty-five Taiwanese pastors, elders, and deacons met for a conference with the missionaries and COM representatives. This meeting agreed on a list of ten goals for the following ten years. The top three goals were (1) increase (double) church membership to fifteen hundred, (2) increase offerings, (3) establish five new churches. Other goals included encouragement for whole families to become Christians, strengthened training for laypersons, recruitment and training for five new pastors.

The Taiwan church had been at something of a growth plateau. There had been only one congregation founded between 1968 and the 1972 conference. The 1972 "Goals, Priorities, Strategies" meeting was a Spirit-filled occasion, and proved to be the launching pad for aggressive church planting. The church conference held a second GPS meeting in September 1976 to assess progress and make revisions in goals. The goal of five new congregations had already been achieved in the first four years of the projected ten-year period, so the goal was adjusted upward to plan for two more new congregations. Significant progress was reported in the achievement of the other goals as well, although the recruitment of students for seminary training and pastoral work seemed to be a problem.

The 1976 Taiwan GPS meeting added two new goals to the list of priorities, both of which suggested lines of future development. One goal was to "select and send suitable persons to be trained as Mennonite-Anabaptist theologians." Another was to "send out one missionary overseas." The training in Mennonite-Anabaptist theology was to be for Taiwanese Mennonite scholars who would study at Mennonite Biblical Seminary in Elkhart, Indiana, and return to teaching positions in Taiwanese institutions—presumably at Presbyterian seminaries in Taipei or Tainan. In 1977 Timothy Liau became the first person to enroll in this program. Plans for a Taiwanese Mennonite overseas missionary remained to be developed. In April 1977 Simon Wung and Hugh Sprunger made a trip to the Philippines to investigate possibilities there, but a lack of suitable persons to send as missionaries delayed the opening of this work. [16]

Medical and Social Services

The GC Mennonite mission programs in Japan and Taiwan were both initiated in the post-Second World War period, and were both under the same mission board. But mission strategies varied widely between the countries. The Japan missionaries, reacting to the collapse of the China missions programs, endeavored to keep mission work in Japan as noninstitutional and as indigenous as possible. The Taiwan program, meanwhile, inherited from Mennonite Central Committee a strong medical and social service program. The Mennonite missionaries in Taiwan not only continued the MCC programs, but expanded the medical work in important ways and sought other avenues to stimulate the consciousness of social responsibility in the new Taiwanese Mennonite churches. One consequence has been that the number of missionaries assigned to evangelism in Taiwan has always been fewer than the number assigned to medical or other kinds of work. In most years there were no more than six missionaries engaged primarily in evangelism. Yet in the early 1970s, Taiwan was the second largest of all GC mission fields, in budget as well as in personnel.

The founder and director of Mennonite Christian Hospital in Hwalien was Roland Brown, son of H. J. and Maria Brown who founded the GC mission in China. Under Dr. Brown's leadership a thirty-six-bed hospital was officially opened on 3 January 1955. The hospital continued as the center for mobile clinic work in the mountains. In 1962 the mobile clinic inaugurated a new system of regular visits to strategically located villages nearer the hospital, rather than attempting to reach every village throughout the island once a year. The hospital itself has carried on a vigorous spiritual ministry both to the staff, about one-half of whom are Christians, and among the patients. Since 1964 the hospital chaplain has been Paul Lin, who worked with MCC in 1949 and later became the first ordained pastor of the Mennonite church in

Taiwan. At the end of 1977, Lin reported that seventy-five patients who had been introduced to Christianity through the hospital in the previous year had made decisions to attend Christian churches.[17]

The Mennonite Christian Hospital's broader concern for public health and community development was expressed in a special project in the two mountain villages of Shwei Yuan and Da Shan from 1971 to 1973. This project was called the Taroko Community Development Program and was directed by William Siemens. The project employed a Taiwanese agriculturist, a public health nurse, and other workers to mobilize community improvement for crops, livestock, cottage industries, education, savings and loans, health and nutrition. Funding for the program came primarily from a special Poverty Fund established by the General Conference in North America. In the view of one evaluator, the Taroko Community Development Program successfully integrated religious, economic, and social dimensions of development and was "the most thoroughly planned and best administered program I have yet seen."[18] The hospital was the base for sponsorship of additional Poverty Fund projects in the Hwalien area.

Mennonite Christian Hospital continued to expand in the 1970s, even though the Commission on Overseas Mission had not included hospitals or medical work on its list of priorities in the 1972 Chicago GPS meeting. M. J. Kao became the hospital administrator in 1975, but the hospital was unsuccessful in recruiting Taiwanese or Chinese medical doctors for long terms. In the 1976 annual report, Mr. Kao said, "It has been over twenty years since the hospital was established, but we still have not been able to secure one single national Christian doctor who shows willingness, or has the vision, to serve his own people at MCH with the same Christian love as that of the missionary doctors."[19] By 1978 the process was under way to take the hospital away from mission control and put it under a church-related, but not directly church-controlled, association in which the power to elect board members was based upon financial contributions from individuals or churches. The Taiwan church conference in 1977 decided to inaugurate a financial drive for NT $1,000,000 (US $26,300) toward hospital development.

Five of the Taiwan Mennonite church congregations have used their church facilities for kindergartens or day-care centers. The Hsi-Tun church in Taichung has had a special ministry to college students, has operated a credit union for church members, and has administered a Bible study correspondence course for 762 enrollees from 1975 through 1977. A new institution on a different frontier came into existence in 1977 with the founding of a school for retarded children, the New Dawn Developmental Center. The school, planned for sixteen children and two full-time teachers, was held in the former kindergarten facilities of the Meilun Mennonite Church.[20]

Nonresistance and Military Dictatorship

The issues raised by Mennonite teachings on peace and nonresistance had a particular urgency and relevance for the Mennonite mission and church in Taiwan. Taiwan was a highly militarized society—officially at war with the People's Republic of China. Taiwan represented the first case in GC Mennonite overseas missions history where church members faced compulsory universal military training, and where church educational institutions were required to include military training in the curriculum. The potential for conflict with the prevailing political order was great, especially since Mennonite missionaries were working primarily with people who were not ethnically identified with the ruling Chinese Nationalist minority.

The first major test on the issue of nonresistance arose in 1955 and 1956 out of the mission's plans to establish a registered nursing school.[21] A thirty-bed hospital had been opened in Hwalien in 1954 to meet hospitalization needs of mountain people as well as of others. Funds for the hospital, as well as for the proposed nursing school, were available from the Joint Commission for Rural Reconstruction. It was learned, however, that registered nursing schools were required to include in their curriculum military combat training taught by a faculty member from the Chinese military. Roland Brown, the director of Mennonite Christian Hospital, proposed to the Nationalist party officials and to the government Department of Education that the nurses in the Mennonite school be allowed to substitute alternative training not involving military weapons, but including such things as stretcher drill and field sanitation.[22] When the government rejected the alternative proposal, the Mennonites refused to establish a registered nursing school, even though it meant turning down available funds. Not all the Mennonites agreed with this refusal to compromise. Bessie Plant, an MCC nursing educator, thought the mission was "straining at a gnat." Why should the Mennonites attempt to be the consciences of nonpacifist girls who want an education? Wouldn't the Mennonite hospital have to depend in any case upon registered nurses who had had military training in other schools?[23]

Instead of a registered nursing school, the mission began a practical nurse training program and, later, a nonregistered nursing school at the vocational level. In 1971 the government issued new regulations which required the upgrading and registration of private nursing schools. The new regulations required military training for all nursing students, as well as expensive improvements in facilities. Rather than offer military training at a Mennonite school, the mission decided to close its nonregistered, vocational-level nursing school. In the place of a Mennonite school, the mission worked out a relationship with a Presbyterian school, the Mackay Memorial Hospital School of Nursing in Taipei. The Mackay school accepted for entrance examination students chosen by Mennonite Christian Hospital. Graduates were to receive diplomas from Mackay. Military training would be included in their curriculum.

The decision to close the school was made by the mission and not by the Taiwanese church, because the hospital and school were not under church conference control. Roland Brown, however, did discuss the matter with Pastor Paul Lin, who was chairman of the church conference as well as hospital chaplain. Brown reported Lin's judgment that "under the circumstances most of our national church members pastors or leaders would not be in a position to make any comments one way or the other, and many of them really would not understand the problem, basically."[24] It cannot be known for certain what the Taiwanese Mennonite church would have decided if the nursing school issue had been in their hands, but it is likely that they would have opted to keep the nursing school open and to comply with government regulations regarding military training.

The issue of compulsory military service for young men was a life-and-death matter in Taiwan. People who refused military service in Taiwan were given long prison sentences and were drafted once again after being released. Mennonite missionaries were themselves conscientious objectors to military service, although over one-half of drafted General Conference Mennonite young men in the United States accepted military service in World War II—despite the availability of legal civilian service alternatives. Given this context, it is not surprising that refusal of military service was not made a precondition of Mennonite church membership in Taiwan. But neither was the peace teaching ignored. There were special meetings for peace-teaching emphasis, highlighted in 1957 and 1963 by visiting Mennonite speakers from Japan, Melvin Gingerich and Ferd Ediger. Ediger conducted a three-day peace seminar for thirty-five church workers and students, including testimony from four missions Pax workers who were fulfilling their American Selective Service obligations with alternative work in Taiwan. Ediger's message was reported in *Taiwan-Home Bond:* "Immense problems confront peace-loving Christians in Taiwan because the country is in a state of war. Is it expedient, practical, advisable, or even possible, to follow positive, non-resistant teachings of love in action? . . . But the message from God is unchanged." Ediger was aware of the sensitivities of calling the Taiwanese Mennonites to costly discipleship and to possible martyrdom. "A prophet must rise and speak in the name of the Lord from experience within the situation," Ediger said.[25] One Taiwanese Mennonite pastor later wrote on peace and nonresistance for his seminary graduate thesis. Another college student translated into Taiwanese a 1955 booklet by Harley J. Stucky, *The Doctrine of Love and Nonresistance.*[26]

The mission evangelistic committee made an effort to provide literature about Anabaptist-Mennonite history and doctrine for the Mennonite church and others in Taiwan. Harold Bender's landmark essay, *The Anabaptist Vision*, was translated and published in 1960. Subscriptions to North American Mennonite church periodicals *The Mennonite, Mennonite Life, Mennonite Quarterly Review,* and *Christian Living* were provided, along with basic books on Mennonite history and doctrine, for seminaries in Taipei and Tainan.[27] In the 1970s the peace emphasis was continued in a number of ways including visiting lecturers, the attendance of Taiwanese pastors at Elkhart in the Overseas Missionary Training Center, and plans for a Mennonite teacher in a Taiwanese seminary where Mennonite pastors were trained.

The dilemma of a Taiwanese Mennonite youth facing the draft was poignantly portrayed in one man's testimony:

> After graduation from the university, I was recruited to serve in the Chinese Marine Corps as a lieutenant. It was a painful struggle in my heart as a Mennonite young person to be engaged in the career of killing. I prayed to my God and I talked over the problem with my pastor.
> Finally we got a conclusion that if I refused to be enlisted, I would immediately be put in prison without even a trial. I would stay there at least ten years or vanish like vapor without a sound. Nobody in the world would remember me anymore. No newspaper would be permitted to expose the problem to any people. I believe that was not the sacrifice God wanted. Therefore, I accepted the challenge. During last year I did not kill any man. I did not even hate any man. I was enduring the most difficult time in my life.[28]

The political climate in Taiwan reached a new level of volatility as American foreign policy moved toward recognition of the People's Republic of China, and thereby denial of the Chinese Nationalist claim to the mainland. The Taiwanese Mennonites favored changes in government toward democracy and majority rule on the island, but no Mennonite leader could openly criticize the government without placing himself in danger of harassment or imprisonment. Mennonites knew that there were potential informers in every congregation and that the government could use the continuing emergency conditions or martial law to put dissenters out of the way without benefit of charges or trial. When the Presbyterians in 1976 issued a forthright "Declaration on Human Rights" (which was immediately suppressed by the government), some Taiwanese Mennonites were able to express private support of the Presbyterian declaration. But they knew that a similar statement by Mennonites would elicit similar government action. The Taiwanese people had difficulty making known their case for freedom to a world which was used to seeing the Taiwan problem solely in terms of the conflict between Communist China and Nationalist China.

Conclusion

The Mennonite mission in Taiwan published a special calendar for the year of 1960, marking twenty-two days for celebration of historic occasions of significance for the identity of Mennonites in Taiwan. The calendar was a revealing blend of political and religious high points, as well as a linking of Anabaptist-Mennonite history with Mennonite church growth in Taiwan. Three of the selected dates marked Taiwanese political celebrations: Sun Yat-sen's birthday, the anniversary of the Republic of China, and the coming of freedom for Taiwan in 1945. Six of the dates were religious holidays such as Christmas, Thanksgiving, Bible Day, and Pentecost. The notable dates for Mennonite history included the dates of the founding of Mennonite churches and institutions in Taiwan in the 1950s, alongside events associated with Anabaptist founding fathers 400 years earlier (Menno Simons, Georg Blaurock, Felix Manz). This 1960 calendar seemed to express the hope for a new synthesis in Taiwan—for a church which would be both truly indigenous and truly conscious of standing in the historical Christian-Mennonite tradition.

Mission and church development in Taiwan held numerous surprises for the Mennonites. It was a surprise that church planting took place among the Taiwanese people, rather than among the mountain tribes or the mainland Chinese immigrants. It was another surprise that the work in Taiwan proceeded under conditions of political stability—a stability of long-term crisis but nevertheless allowing a longer uninterrupted period of mission work than had ever been possible for Mennonites on mainland China. And there was the surprise of rapid Taiwanese economic development that set an urban-industrial context for Mennonite missions, which was radically different from pre-World War II mission work in rural India, Africa, and China.

In some ways Taiwan was a unique mission field for the GC Mennonites. Taiwan was the only overseas country where GC Mennonites carried on mission work without the presence of other Mennonite branches in the same country. In Taiwan the mission work was uniquely determined and shaped by preceding Mennonite Central Committee work. Only in Taiwan were Mennonite fortunes so closely bound up with another Protestant denomination—the Presbyterians. Finally, the Taiwan mission was singular among GC Mennonite missions for the cordiality of relationships between missionaries and nationals—a fact which surely owes much to the sensitive leadership of the four Mennonite missionary couples of longest tenure on the island: Roland and Sophie Schmidt Brown, Hugh and Janet Frost Sprunger, J. N. and Martha Boschman Vandenberg, and Peter and Lydia Pankratz Kehler.

There were, of course, many unresolved questions and challenges for the Taiwanese Mennonite church as it faced the waning decades of the twentieth century. Did the Mennonite mission burden the church with so great a weight of institutional responsibility—hospital, church conference apparatus, inter-Mennonite Asian and worldwide programs—that the church would be perpetually dependent upon the wealthier North American churches? Would Anabaptist-Mennonite teachings of church, discipleship, and nonresistance come to have concrete application in the volatile and dangerous Taiwanese church-state situation? What would it mean to be a faithful Christian and a Mennonite in Taiwan in the 1980s and beyond?

In 1978 a twenty-voice Mennonite women's choir from Taiwan toured North American churches and sang at the Tenth Mennonite World Conference in Wichita, Kansas. The director of the choir was Ruth Chen Lin, a graduate of Bluffton College who had recently been named one of the ten outstanding women in Taiwan. The choir's ability to finance its own international travel, as well as its distinguished promotion of Christian fellowship across boundaries, was one more indication of a new day in mission-church relationships.

Mission buildings near Cachipay, Colombia.

146

8 Colombia

The Wedge Project

W. C. Voth caught typhus in Bogotá, and that made all the difference for General Conference missions in Latin America. Voth was the pioneer of GC Mennonite missions in the post-China period. In Colombia, Japan, and Taiwan he broke new ground with missionaries of a younger generation at his side. Traveling with Voth in 1943 on a Latin American tour in quest of a new mission field was Gerald Stucky of Berne, Indiana, a recent graduate of Bethel College and New York Biblical Seminary. Because of Voth's typhus, the investigating team stayed three weeks instead of three days in Colombia. In this interval, Stucky made the contacts which led to the choice of Colombia as the country for the first GC Mennonite mission effort in Latin America.

Stucky visited the Colombian colony for people with Hansen's disease called Agua de Dios (Water of God), which had a population of some seven thousand people of which less than half had the disease. At the colony was a small Presbyterian church where the people expressed their need for an evangelical primary school for their healthy children. Protestants were discriminated against in the Catholic schools. The American Leprosy Mission, based in the United States, was ready to supply funds for school building and operations. A boarding school for the children of Protestant parents suffering from Hansen's disease would be the "wedge project" by which Mennonites would gain entrance into Colombia. The school would provide a great service to needy people and an opportunity to evangelize both among students and in the surrounding community.

The first four missionaries arrived in Colombia in the fall of 1945— Gerald and Mary Hope Wood Stucky, Janet Soldner, and Mary Becker. Soldner was a nurse, also from Berne. Becker was from the First

147

Mennonite Church in Newton, Kansas, and had turned toward Colombia after waiting long for a visa to India. They acquired a site and began school in 1947.

Mission strategy in Colombia in the early years was dictated by practical possibilities and limitations, rather than by a prescribed missions philosophy or mission board direction. The result was the creation of a kind of Mennonite mission "compound"—although it was quite different from Mennonite mission compounds in India, China, and Africa. The site chosen for the school was a fifteen-acre (six-hectare) farm nestled in the Andes Mountains about fifty miles (eighty kilometers) west of Bogota. It was an idyllic isolated environment—lush with orange and banana trees and bordered by a rushing mountain stream. About one mile (1.6 kilometers) distant by burro path was the village of Cachipay (Cah-chee-pie); its five hundred inhabitants came to the market twice a week in the village square which sloped down from the imposing Catholic church. The local economy was geared to coffee production. An enterprising German had built a two-story hotel-house on the farm in about 1939, having brought all the building material up the path by beast of burden. The hotel-house and farm were planned to be a retreat and cultural center for Germans in Colombia. Like many German dreams, this plan had to be abandoned with German defeat in World War II. The Mennonites first rented and then bought the property and turned it into the physical and spiritual center for mission work in Colombia.

There was room in the hotel-house for twenty-eight children and the missionary staff of four, if everyone was willing to squeeze into small quarters. A spirit of family togetherness permeated the community from the beginning. In addition to schoolwork assignments, everyone had assigned duties for school and farm operations. Discipline was strict, as it had been in the Stucky, Soldner, and Becker homes in Indiana and Kansas. Everyone had to attend devotions every morning and evening, Bible study Wednesday evening, and worship services Sunday mornings and evenings. There were times for play and celebration as well, often with a distinctively North American flavor. At Easter time they painted and hunted Easter eggs. On October 31 they had "a Hallowe'en Party with masks and everything that goes with it." On November 27 they dismissed school to observe the United States Thanksgiving Day. At Christmastime the children received gifts both in stockings and under the Christmas tree—mostly practical things, but also a little perfume for the girls and dark glasses for the boys.[1]

Gradually the school at the Cachipay farm expanded in response to the needs of the many applicants. With financial aid from the American Leprosy Mission, additional buildings were constructed—three student dormitories with quarters for missionary residence, a classroom building, dining hall, laundry, shop, and clinic. The school was designed

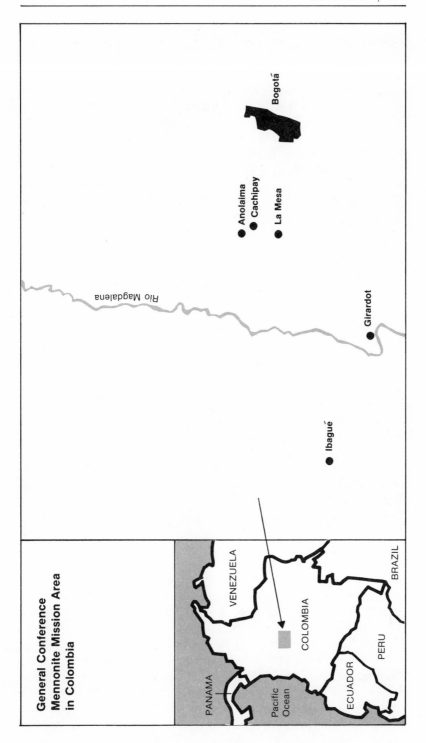

General Conference
Mennonite Mission Area
in Colombia

to teach the elementary grades, with children ages six to fourteen. For graduates unable to get a place in a secondary school, a limited program of vocational training was organized. The school grew to about one hundred students, with the percentage from the leprosy-patient colony dropping from 80 percent to about 50 percent. The North American mission staff remained fairly small for the first ten years, usually consisting of two or three missionary couples and two or three single women. Evangelistic forays—"gospel invasions" the missionaries called them—were made into Cachipay and other surrounding villages. But the mission school-farm, a half-hour's walk from Cachipay, remained the center and the sanctuary of the work. When executive secretary Andrew Shelly made his first visit to Colombia in 1960, he was surprised how concentrated the Mennonite work was at this one location. Only two missionaries were living away from the "compound."[2]

Mission Work During "The Violence"

The Mennonites were in genuine need of a protective sanctuary in the first decade of their work in Colombia. It happened that this decade coincided with a period of destructive civil strife known in Colombia as La Violencia—"The Violence." From 1948 to 1958 the competition between Colombia's two traditional leading political parties—the Liberals and the Conservatives—broke out into prolonged bloody terrorism and civil warfare which resulted in the death of some 200,000 people.[3] The roots of the violence were fundamentally political—a struggle of parties contending for power—rather than ideological or religious. But there was nevertheless an anti-Protestant, antievangelical dimension to the upheaval. According to one account, 126 Colombian Protestants were "killed because of their religion."[4] Protestant worship services were disrupted, schools closed, and church buildings destroyed.

The Catholic church had exercised an exceptionally powerful influence in Colombian life from the time of the Spanish conquistadores. The alliance between church and state, somewhat weakened by the liberalism of the movement for independence in the early nineteenth century, was consolidated under Conservative rule between 1886 and 1930. The Catholic claim to jurisdiction over education, baptism, marriage, and burial—as well as to exclusive control over two-thirds of the country's territory—was formalized in a Concordat with the Vatican in 1887 and a Treaty on Missions of 1953. As a result, the Catholic church had more influence upon national and civil life in Colombia than in other Latin American countries.

Protestants in Colombia were too few to exercise political influence. The Presbyterian Church of America began mission work in Colombia in 1856, but a religious census in 1937 showed a Protestant (or Evangelical—the terms are interchangeable in Colombia) membership of 1,196 in a total population of nearly 9 million.[5] By 1948 Protestants in

Colombia still numbered less than 1/10 of 1 percent of the population (7,908). But the number of Protestant missionaries was increasing. The Mennonites were only a tiny fraction of the large North American mission force which had been shut out of China and now looked for new openings in Latin America. Although Catholic dismay at Protestant advances may have had some part in the expressions of The Violence, it was because Conservatives saw Protestants as allies of the anticlerical Liberals that Protestants were often victimized.

Gerald Stucky was on his way from Cachipay to Bogotá to buy some furniture for the mission on 9 April 1948 when the popular left-wing Liberal Jorge Eliécer Gaitán was assassinated and Bogotá exploded with killings and burnings that initiated the violent decade. Stucky succeeded in making his purchases, which fortunately were not in the city center, and in being passed through roadblocks on the way home. He later heard on the radio that some two thousand people had been killed in Bogotá and that the violence was spreading through the countryside. The new missionaries knew that Colombia in its history had already suffered through ten national civil wars, and they assumed that the situation was one which simply had to be accepted as normal for the country.[6]

The area of GC Mennonite mission work in fact experienced relative calm during the violent decade. No GC missionaries were imprisoned or killed. No Mennonite churches were burned. But the atmosphere of political and religious tension created problems for both the educational and evangelical work of the mission. The most dangerous event of overt violence against Mennonites took place in December 1950 at the village of Anolaima, several miles north of Cachipay. At the mass celebrating the Immaculate Conception of Mary, the local priest announced that he would lead a procession against the Protestants after the second mass. The crowd, which included the local mayor and chief of police, came to the home where missionaries Arthur and Helen Morrow Keiser had lived the last two months. The priest raised up a statue of Mary before the house, pronounced his condemnation upon all who would enter there, and led the crowd in the repeated cry, "Satan's house, Satan's house. . . ." Windows on two sides of the house were broken by flying rocks. Several days later missionaries Gerald Stucky and LaVerne Rutschman came with the mission truck at 4:00 A.M. to evacuate the Keiser household back to Cachipay under cover of darkness.[7]

Catholic harassment of Mennonite educational and evangelistic work took a variety of forms. Missionary Alice Bachert of Kitchener, Ontario, reported how insults were shouted at her on the street. Mary Hope Stucky handed out gospel portions in Cachipay one day, and later saw them being burned in the public square. A health inspector came to the Mennonite school and demanded that a newly dug cesspool be moved one yard (about one meter) from where it was. The mother of a girl student who had been disciplined brought suit against school director Gerald Stucky with trumped-up charges that Stucky had made improper advances to her daughter. (She later withdrew the charges.) Persons renting meeting places to Mennonites were pressured to terminate the rental agreements. A new school at La Mesa had to be closed three times because of opposition. Occasionally there were cases of economic reprisal, such as the boycott against Tulio Pedraza, a blind coffin maker of Anolaima who became a Mennonite. He lost his business when a competitor convinced the local priest the Protestant coffins should not be used in Roman Catholic burials.[8]

Opposition to the Mennonite school near Cachipay peaked in 1955 after the government passed a law to require all private schools to get a license, and then made the standards so high and the procedures so complex that the Protestant schools could not comply with the regulation. On 3 July 1955, the mayor of Anolaima came with a policeman and the secretary to the inspector of police to the Mennonite school near Cachipay and announced that he was going to close the school because they had not received a license. Missionaries Keiser and Rutschman asked to see the written government order—which the mayor could not produce—and said they would keep the school open even if the mayor would throw them in jail. Armando Hernández, a Cachipay tailor who had become a Mennonite, joined the argument and complained about the lack of liberty in the country. The mayor asked if Hernández was a Colombian and invited him to leave the country if he didn't like it there.[9] The mayor departed, and the school stayed open. In 1956 the Colombian Ministry of Education granted a license to the school—the first such license granted to a Protestant school in the country during the Violence period.

The missionaries in Colombia did not always agree with the mission executive in North America how much publicity should be given to the stories of Catholic opposition. In 1952 general secretary John Thiessen vetoed the publication of an incident involving a drunk policeman who called a worshiper out of a Mennonite service, beat him with his fist and rifle, and took him to jail. Thiessen feared that newspaper publicity about this incident might lead to additional trouble and possible closed doors in Colombia. The missionaries believed that international publicity would rather bring pressure to bear upon the Colombian authorities to adopt more enlightened policies.[10] The Mennonite missionaries cooperated with the Evangelical Confederation of Colombia (CEDEC), whose information secretary, Presbyterian minister James E. Goff, diligently researched and publicized incidents of violence against Protestants in Colombia.

In the 1960s relationships between Catholics and Protestants in Colombia underwent great improvement. Political peace was finally established in 1958 when the Conservative and Liberal parties joined in a National Front coalition in which the presidency alternated between the parties. The reforms of the Vatican II Council brought a gradual opening and increasing tolerance on the part of the Catholics in Colombia. A moment of healing in relationships took place in Cachipay on the day after the assassination of John F. Kennedy, Catholic president of the United States. The priest in Cachipay, who had long been hostile to the Mennonites, walked down the path to the mission school and farm to express condolences to the missionaries who had lost their national leader. The missionaries reciprocated with a return visit to the priest's home after the death of Pope John XXIII.

Most GC Mennonite missionaries welcomed the Catholic rapprochement. Strong anti-Catholic sentiments had been expressed among some of the Mennonite missionaries—fearing Catholic domination in America as well as in Colombia and seeing in Catholic power a sign of the Antichrist and second coming of Christ.[11] But on the whole, the Mennonite mission was more open to dialogue and cooperation with Catholics than were most other groups.

Despite the persecution, Protestant churches in Colombia experienced significant growth. In the five years from 1948 to 1953, a period in which forty-two church buildings were destroyed and 110 Protestant primary schools closed, the membership of Protestant churches increased from 7,908 to 11,951.[12] The Mennonite church-planting efforts were in their earliest stages in these years, with the first formal organization of the Mennonite Church of Colombia taking place on 1 January 1952. Members of the new organization included baptized believers from the villages of Cachipay, Anolaima, and La Esperanza. The first Mennonite missionary to work exclusively with evangelism—and the only missionary in the first decade without direct involvement in the Mennonite farm and school near Cachipay—was Alice Bachert of the Stirling Avenue Mennonite Church of Kitchener, Ontario. Bachert had worked with the Latin America Mission in Costa Rica and in Colombia before joining the Mennonite mission in 1948. In that same year LaVerne and Harriet Fischbach Rutschman arrived. They were from the Swiss Mennonite Church at Whitewater, Kansas. Rutschman took charge of the evangelistic and literacy work of the mission and gave special attention to the village of Cachipay. He also started the work in Anolaima and La Esperanza.

As with mission work elsewhere, it was not always easy to evaluate the sincerity and conviction of professed believers. One elderly woman in Cachipay came to Rutschman with the request, "Sir, . . . I would like to accept your religion, but I want you to help me rent a room."[13] One young man apparently sought baptism as one step in an unsuccessful attempt to develop a romantic attachment with one of the single missionary women. But there were others who were baptized in the face of community opposition and who suffered socially and economically for their decision to join the church. The Mennonites called upon the services of Latin American evangelists to conduct campaigns in the villages. In 1954 the twenty-four-year-old evangelist Francisco Liévano spent ten days at Anolaima, La Mesa, and Cachipay. Seventy-six conversions in response to Liévano's preaching were recorded.[14]

The mission aimed for an independent national church from the time the first congregations were organized. "The Mission Board has urged us," said a 1953 article in the *Colombian News,* "to take immediate steps of self-government, self-support, and self-propagation in the groups now functioning in Colombia under our oversight."[15] The first four copastors of the Cachipay congregation, elected at the end of 1953, took correspondence courses in Bible study and instruction in practice preaching to develop leadership potential. The occupations of these men—tailor, barber, carpenter, and baker—suggested that the first core of the Cachipay congregation was made up of village artisans. The tailor was Armando Hernández, a gifted person who became the outstanding Colombian leader of the church for the next twenty years. Hernández attended the Latin American Biblical Seminary in San José, Costa Rica, and was ordained at his home church in Cachipay in 1965. He was the founder and pastor of the Mennonite church at Ibagué, and served as Mennonite representative and officer for various ecumenical inter-Protestant and inter-Mennonite meetings and associations. Hernández developed a special interest in religious radio broadcasting. He initiated a half-hour weekly broadcast in Ibagué which involved counseling with people who responded to the program. After three years in Ibagué, the broadcast was moved to the capital city of Bogotá. Hernández left Colombia for Puerto Rico in 1973 to become the executive director of the Latin American Executive Board of Mennonite Broadcasts.

By 1959 there were 112 members in the GC Mennonite churches in Colombia: 50 in Cachipay, 22 in Anolaima, and 40 in La Mesa. Nearly twenty years later (1977) the number of active members in these same three village congregations was just about the same. The Mennonite village churches failed to grow. A key explanation for this lack of growth was the high mobility of church members. Educated people—and Protestant membership tended to be identified with education and upward mobility—tended to move out of the village to seek jobs in the cities, especially in nearby Bogotá. The most qualified national pastors and church leaders sought more stimulating and challenging locations for work.

Gerald and Mary Hope Stucky in 1961 began regular monthly meetings in Bogotá to follow up former students so they would not be lost to the church. These students formed the core of a new Mennonite congregation in Bogotá, organized by new missionaries Howard and Marlene Short Habegger in 1964. By 1967 the congregation dedicated a modern new church building in the Berna district of Bogotá. The Berna congregation quickly became the premier Mennonite church in Colombia in terms of vitality and leadership.

At the annual church assembly of 1968 the General Conference mission and the Colombian Mennonite church were officially integrated into one governing body. Authority to make decisions was placed in a central church council, the Mesa Directiva, which included representatives from each of the organized churches. All mission properties were signed over to the new conference, which was called the Evangelical Mennonite Church of Colombia. Armando Hernández played a major role in pushing for this new structure, which ensured that Colombian nationals would have a voice in all decision making.

Antonio Arévalo, a charismatic pastor of Pentecostal background, became pastor of the Berna congregation in 1972. Under his leadership the congregation grew to 260 active members by 1977, more than twice the membership of all eight other Mennonite GC congregations in Colombia combined. Arévalo provided significant leadership in the Colombia Mennonite church conference, as well as in Colombian ecumenical Protestant associations. The Berna congregation opened a day-care center in church facilities for fifty children in April 1977.

A second Mennonite congregation in Bogotá grew out of the ministry of Gerald and Mary Hope Stucky, who returned to Colombia in 1973 after spending a number of years in the United States. The core of the new group was again formed of ex-students from Cachipay, including some who had helped begin the Berna church. In 1978 this new group, which met in the Stuckys' apartment in the Chapinero section of Bogotá, numbered forty-four members and faced decisions regarding church building and leadership for the future. It seemed clear that the growing edge of the church was in Bogotá and that new Mennonite groups might emerge in the city in coming years.

Mission, Church, and Economic-Social Development

For two decades the GC mission and churches in Colombia concentrated their efforts upon education and evangelism. In the mid-1960s the mission initiated programs of a new type, called "community development." There were two phases in this work. The first projects were carried on by young short-term missionaries in and around the Cachipay area. The second phase involved inter-Mennonite cooperation under Colombian leadership with projects in widely separated parts of the country. The concept of *community development* had an innovative, up-to-date, and somewhat theologically questionable ring in the 1960s. Community development was in fact a new statement of an old theme in Mennonite missions. In the decades before World War I Mennonite missionaries had assumed that gospel proclamation entailed manifold community changes.

1. *Community development.* Peter and Claire Landis Harder of

Lansdale, Pennsylvania, were assigned to Cachipay in 1966 with the simple job description, "the maintenance of mission property and community development."[16] Harder came with the assumption that economic development would mean introduction of new seeds and fertilizer, but he soon learned that the expressed need of the small farmers in the Cachipay area was for improved roads and for better prices for goods which could be produced in abundance. Harder organized a marketing cooperative which enabled farmers to sell directly to big supermarkets in Bogotá and bypass the traditional local market. Prices to the farmers were tripled as a result. Membership in the co-op was not dependent upon or related to association with the Mennonite church. The co-op grew to include sixty farmers and the shipment of a thousand boxes of oranges per week to Bogotá. This project, in its days of greatest success, was acclaimed not only for its benefits to members but also for its potential as a model for other groups.[17]

Another great need was not only to get goods from Cachipay to Bogotá at fair prices, but also to build roads so goods could be transported from the farms to Cachipay. Harder mobilized fourteen community action groups in the Cachipay area to combine into a single agency which applied for and received the loan of two bulldozers from the American Agency for International Development (AID) to enable the building of roads. The work of the bulldozers, ceremoniously christened El Comunero ("the commoner") and La Amistad ("friendship"), enabled farmers in an 80-square-mile (208-square-kilometer) area around Cachipay to get to market by motor vehicle on passable roads rather than by mule on rugged mountain paths. Some three thousand families were said to benefit from the 100 miles (160 kilometers) of new roads built.

There were other projects tried as well. A "candy factory" was built on the site of the Mennonite school, to enable the processing of perishable raw fruit into a nonperishable marketable product. There was also a feed mill operation in addition to rabbit, duck, and fish projects to provide protein supplement to the local diet. In the long run, however, nearly all of these development projects, with the exception of the roads, ended unhappily. The marketing cooperative failed not long after Harder's departure from Cachipay in 1969. The candy factory likewise failed, and the building put up for that purpose was torn down. The projects apparently were too dependent upon the boundless energy, organizational ability, and mechanical genius of one volunteer missionary. The projects were never closely integrated with the Cachipay Mennonite congregation or the broader life of the Colombian Mennonite church. The relationship of community development to the Mennonite mission and churches remained clouded.

2. *Mencoldes.* A second effort at Mennonite community develop-

ment work in Colombia came almost a decade later in 1975 with the formation of the Mennonite Colombian Foundation for Development (Mencoldes). Mencoldes was an inter-Mennonite foundation which brought together four groups: The General Conference Mennonite Church of Colombia, the Mennonite Brethren Church of Colombia, the Mennonite Central Committee (MCC) of North America, and the Mennonite Economic Development Associates (MEDA) of North America. Mencoldes operated under a six-member board, five of whom were Mennonite citizens of Colombia and one of whom was a missionary. The Mencoldes director was Luis Correa, who had been in the first year (1947) of classes at the Cachipay school and was among the first students baptized there. Correa had studied at the Mennonite seminary at Montevideo, Uruguay, and was a founding member of both the Berna and the Chapinero Mennonite congregations in Bogotá.

Mencoldes' first center of community development work was related to the Mennonite Brethren congregation at the town of Bebedó on the San Juan River in the Chocó district west of the Andes Mountains. An existing credit cooperative of church members provided a base of operations. The development projects included a rice mill for selecting, drying, and threshing the grain; a sugar mill; a boat for river transportation; medical supplies; and a rat eradication project. Mark Claassen of Beatrice, Nebraska, Mennonite mission agronomist, worked with the project at the outset. A Colombian agronomist engineer, José María Ríos, was employed to continue the work. Young volunteers from the Colombian Mennonite churches were recruited for short-term assignments on the project in an additional effort to develop a closer relationship between Mencoldes and the churches.

Mencoldes also began work on the eastern slope of the Andes Mountains at the village of Uribe in Meta district. Uribe had about six hundred inhabitants, many of whom were evangelicals, but it did not have a Mennonite congregation. The first projects at Uribe were the building of three suspension bridges for improved local transportation and the improvement of several public school facilities. Through the Mennonite Economic Development Association, Mencoldes also received funds for small business loans which were granted mostly to Mennonite church members in Bogotá and in La Mesa.

It was too early in 1978 to evaluate the success of Mencoldes as a church development organization. The efforts both in Bebedó and Uribe suffered when key local organizers in each place died in drowning and airplane accidents in 1977. But the Colombian national leadership base remained strong, and represented a contrast to Mennonite Central Committee administration in such countries as India and Zaire, where MCC offices were headed by North American Mennonite directors. Mencoldes was integrated with the Mennonite churches in Colombia. Its success would depend upon developing this strong local base, as well as upon continuing financial support from North American Mennonite agencies and from possible alternative private and government development support agencies. The final evaluation would also depend upon whether Mencoldes projects would in fact assist needy people in cooperative work to improve their living conditions.

Changing Relationship with Catholics

The Catholic International Eucharistic Congress was held in Bogotá in 1968, and was attended by Pope Paul VI—the first official visit by any pope to the Americas. In connection with the Congress, the pontiff invited leaders of all churches in Colombia to an interfaith meeting at the Vatican embassy in Bogotá. Most evangelical groups refused the invitation, but Glendon Klaassen and Luis Correa represented the Colombian Mennonites at the meeting and were granted a few minutes of conversation with Pope Paul. The meeting symbolized a new era in relationships between Mennonites and Catholics in the country. In a country which was so overwhelmingly Catholic, virtually any church activity outside the walls of the church or beyond the Mennonite schools at Cachipay and La Mesa involved relationships with Catholics.

In 1968 John and Elma Giesbrecht Wiebe of Carrot River, Saskatchewan, took the pastorate of the La Mesa church and began a small bookstore operation there. This bookstore began to thrive through sales of religious as well as secular materials to a Catholic market. In 1972 the Wiebes established another bookstore in Bogotá, which in time became the best Protestant bookstore in the city and which also enjoyed brisk sales of Bibles and religious materials to Catholic buyers. The bookstore ministry included a mobile van—which circulated to outlying areas—and a service for showing religious films in churches. The films were requested mainly by Protestant groups.

A new experiment of Mennonite mission among Catholics began in 1974 when Glendon and Reitha Kaufman Klaassen moved to a middle-class area of Bogotá to begin evangelistic work directed more toward Catholic renewal than toward the establishment of a Mennonite church. The Klaassens developed a ministry through natural neighborhood contacts. They were greatly encouraged by Catholic interest in spiritual renewal through Bible studies, prayer groups, and youth work, but it was clear that one precondition of the hearty reception of their ministry was their explicit disavowal of intentions to plant a church, to convert Catholics to Protestantism, or to relate the work directly to the Mennonite church of Colombia. The experiment ended when Klaassens returned to North America in 1977. While the Mennonite church and mission recognized the experiment as a fruitful ministry and an illustration of great improvement in Catholic-Protestant relationships since the 1960s, this type of missions work seemed too lacking in ongoing results to be duplicated elsewhere.

Cachipay and Beyond

The story of the GC Mennonite mission and church in Colombia begins with the development of a strong rural base centered at the farm and school near Cachipay, and unfolds with an extension outward through ministries of evangelism, church planting, economic development, and follow-up work with graduates of the Mennonite boarding school. Somehow the Mennonite reference point for Colombia always remained at Cachipay. This pattern of outward movement from a rural home base paralleled the experience of Mennonites in North America during the twentieth century. Mennonite roots were in the country—in Mountain Lake, in Steinbach, in Goessel—and the challenge of the church was to make the transition to an urbanized, modern world outside.

In 1967 the school near Cachipay became a day school only, after twenty years as a boarding school. Graduates of the boarding school, all of whom came from a poor background and many of whom were children of parents with Hansen's disease, established a remarkable record of educational achievement and professional accomplishment in subsequent years. Among their number were teachers, nurses, pastors, lawyers, administrators, and workers in a variety of technical and professional fields. Thirteen of the Cachipay students eventually became permanent residents of the United States, and others had opportunities for travel and other experiences in North America. Former students who had significant positions of responsibility in Colombian Mennonite institutions included Otilia Lugo, principal of the Cachipay school; Elisa Prieto, principal of the Mennonite school at La Mesa; Luis Lugo, administrator of the church retreat grounds at Cachipay; Luis Correa, director of Mencoldes; and José Naranjo, pastor and church planter.

Despite this outpouring of talent from the Cachipay school, the recruitment of leaders for the Colombia Mennonite church remained a continuing problem. Candidates for the ministry received their seminary training at a number of Bible institutes and seminaries. Jaime Caro, who came from La Mesa, studied at the Bible Institute in Armenia, the United Biblical Seminary of Medellín, and the Latin American Seminary in San José, Costa Rica. For a number of years beginning in 1969 with the initiative of missionaries George and Margaret Voght Ediger, the Mennonites organized their own decentralized Bible Institute which loosely associated with the seminary at Medellín. In 1978 there were five Mennonites in church leadership preparation, four at a Baptist seminary in Cali and one at a Christian Missionary Alliance Bible Institute in Armenia.

Coming Together

The movement outward from Cachipay over the years involved a gradual cultural accommodation or "Latin Americanization" of the Mennonite churches. The culture gap between North America and Colombia was not as great as experienced by missionaries to Africa and Asia. One indication of this cultural bridge was the fact that three women working with the Mennonite mission married Colombian men. Mary Becker, who was in the first mission group, married Hector Valencia in 1950. Dr. Valencia was for many years prominent in the Presbyterian educational program in Colombia. In 1975 he joined the North American staff of the GC Commission on Overseas Mission as secretary for Latin America, a staff appointment which suggested increasing internationalization of the Mennonite missions movement.

Mennonites in Colombia have been influenced by the Pentecostal movement which has been in the forefront of rapid Protestant growth in the 1960s and 1970s. Antonio Arévalo, pastor of the large Berna church in Bogotá, has shown in his ministry how emphasis upon the Holy Spirit could be combined with concern for human social and economic welfare. The worship services at the Berna church were characterized by more freedom of religious expression than had been the case in churches pastored by missionaries. (It is interesting that this development took place in Colombia at the same time that a charismatic movement took hold in some Mennonite circles in North America.)

Colombia was geographically and culturally closer to North America than were Mennonite mission fields in Africa and Asia. Indeed, Colombia was more accessible in an age of airline transportation than had been the Cheyenne and Arapaho tribes in Indian Territory 200 miles (320 kilometers) away from Halstead, Kansas, in 1880. Mennonites of North America took advantage of Colombia's nearness in a variety of ways. Executive Andrew Shelly made six official visits to Colombia from 1960 to 1971. The number of short-term mission workers increased in the 1960s. Mennonite lay people on vacation tours put the Colombia mission on their itinerary, especially in 1972 en route to the Mennonite World Conference in Curitiba, Brazil. In 1974 the MENNO (Mennonites Encountering New Neighbors Overseas) program was initiated to enable church families from North America to have a work camp experience of several weeks in Colombia. The MENNO volunteers usually did maintenance and building work on the farm and school near Cachipay.

Mennonite students in North America became acquainted with Colombia through programs sponsored by the Council of Mennonite Colleges. Héctor G. Valencia, who taught at Bluffton College in 1964-65, administered a number of these programs beginning in 1967. Included were a summer seminar in connection with a bicultural center in Bogotá, a year abroad program at the University of the Andes, and a practice teaching program in English at the Colegio "Nueva Granada" in Bogotá.

Conclusion

The "theology of liberation" which received so much attention among Latin American and North American church leaders in the 1970s held little attraction for Colombian Mennonite leaders. Colombian Mennonites had personally experienced liberation through evangelism and education; they were more oriented to models of development than of revolution. The political situation in Colombia in the 1970s was beset with corruption and inequality. Luis Correa wrote in 1977 of the country being dominated by a series of "mafias," including the military, emerald, coffee, and cocaine businesses.[18] But the political situation was much more stable and favorable than in the years of violence.

The Evangelical Mennonite Church of Colombia was a small group in 1978—about five hundred in eight congregations in a country of twenty-five million people, some 2 percent of whom were Protestants. It was sure that the future of this small fellowship would be shaped both by its particular history of Mennonite mission origins and by its response to a rapidly changing Latin American environment.

Kakese Gasala, Ngongo Ngolo, Reuben Short, and Milo Nussbaum signing documents which "fused" the mission and the church in Zaire (14 January 1971, Djoko Punda).

Africa Inter-Mennonite Mission

9 Post-Independence India and Zaire

"It seems as though the Africa missionaries are still deeply under the delusion that the African Christian cannot be responsible. . . . We humans want to domineer where we possibly can. Missionaries are no exception to this. They need our intercession in these matters too." John Thiessen, 1956

Missions on the Defensive

A kind of domino theory played about in the minds of Mennonite mission leaders in the years after World War II. The General Conference Board of Missions had three major dominoes—three historic overseas mission fields. China had been the first to fall. When would the missionaries have to leave India and Zaire? And would the church in these countries survive the collapse? The winds of nationalism and of anti-imperialism were blowing through Africa and Asia. It was not an easy time to be a missionary or a missions executive, especially in countries where both church and mission were rebounding from half a century of the mind-set of colonial domination.

John Thiessen, career missionary in India who had become executive secretary of the GC Board of Missions in 1954, traveled to the mission fields in Zaire and India in 1956. This was his first visit to Zaire, where the mission work was separately administered by the Congo Inland Mission. He noted some key contrasts between the two fields. "In Congo Africa," he wrote, "it is considered an honor to be a Christian. In India if a person turns to Christ he is so often despised and persecuted."[1] People were flocking to Christianity in Zaire. "The doors of entrance into the Christian Church are literally bombarded. People must be kept back from being baptized." The Mennonite church had grown to some twenty thousand baptized members, but a leading Zairian pastor, Kazadi Lukuna Muadianvita, told Thiessen that not more than 25 percent of those baptized were "really Christian." Despite the presence of many who were Christians in name only, the Christian faith and values were sufficiently pervasive to "make an impression on society as a whole." African Mennonite church leaders had influence not only in the church; they were often accepted as "trusted elders in the village" by non-Christians as well.

In India, by way of contrast, Christians in 1956 were victims of ostracism and persecution. Mennonite pastors had no influence in the civic community outside the church. The rising tide of nationalism was putting pressure upon foreign missionaries as well as Indian church members. Church leaders were scorned rather than honored in their own society. The church was not growing. Thiessen reported that due to anti-Christian pressures, "several hundred of our Christians accepted 'shudie,' that is, being cleansed from Christianity and become Hindus again."

Despite their many fundamental differences, Zaire and India had two conditions in common as mission fields. On one hand, both countries had great needs for educational and social development, which mission resources could help to meet. There was opportunity for significant missionary expansion. On the other hand, Mennonite churches in both countries needed to develop patterns of self-reliance and self-support. These two conditions presented the GC mission board with an agonizing dilemma. Was it possible to have *both* missions expansion *and* national church self-reliance? How could the national churches in Zaire and India have growing missions programs, bigger missions budgets, and additional missionary personnel, and at the same time have church members and leaders who could overcome the psychology and reality of dependence upon their wealthy North American benefactors? Missions strategy in the post-independence period was caught on the horns of this unavoidable and complex dilemma. Not long before returning from India, John Thiessen wrote from Champa, "Our mission condition and church condition in India is so puzzling that my head whirls. I do hope that I will have a clearer vision when I get farther away again."

India: 1947 to Present

Locked away in the safe on each GC Mennonite mission compound in India during World War II were contingency plans in case of missionary evacuation. Who among the Indian Christians would be given responsibility for mission schools, churches, and hospitals? To whom would be given the keys to the missionary bungalows and supply rooms? Who would be given authority to draw funds from the missionary account? Answers to these questions were not made public, because the evacuation never took place.

The great war ended in 1945; India became independent in 1947; and Hindus and Muslims fought each other and divided into the separate states of Pakistan and India. Through all these political and social upheavals, the civil order in that part of Madhya Pradesh (Central Provinces) where GC missionaries worked remained so stable and peaceful that the missionaries never had to hand over the keys and the property to the nationals. In Zaire some missionaries who underwent the agony of evacuation in 1960 and 1964 later came to see the upheavals as a blessing in disguise for the achievement of independence of the Zairian church. Could it be that the nonevacuation in India was a misfortune disguised as a blessing?

There were three stages of development in church-mission relationships in the postwar period, which can be roughly divided according to the decades. The 1950s saw great ferment, anti-Christian agitation, and exploration of new alternatives. The 1960s were more quiet. Church and mission worked together in a structure which came to be known as "partnership." In the 1970s there were troubled relationships between church, mission, and mission board, which eventually led to the dismantling of the mission organization. By 1978 only a few missionaries remained. The future was in the hands of the self-directing church.

Political Independence and Pressures

The Indian independence movement led by the Congress party, the party of Mohandas K. Gandhi and Jawaharlal Nehru, had the favor of Indian Mennonites as well as the missionaries. The GC Mennonites were in a relatively isolated and rural area, however; few church members were politically active. The Congress party was attractive to Christians because it promised a *secular state*. If this promise were kept, it would mean freedom of religion for India, rather than the establishment of Hinduism as a state religion.

One dimension of this new freedom was the opening to Christian evangelization of certain districts where the British had excluded missionaries by agreement with the local rajahs. In the Surguja district, for example, about 75 miles (120 kilometers) north of Korba, the departure of the British—with resulting home rule—meant that Christians could evangelize among non-Hindu tribal peoples for the first time. There followed a rapid people's movement to Christianity in the tribal areas. More than four thousand members of the Uraon tribe in the Surguja district converted to Christianity in 1952, with the Lutheran church particularly active in this field. Missionaries Paul A. Wenger and Edward H. Burkhalter initiated Mennonite evangelistic work in Surguja district, and in 1953 the first baptism into the Mennonite church took place there. Pastor Puran A. Banwar and his wife, Lily, became the first resident GC Mennonite missionaries, and in 1961 the Calvary church,

Surguja, became a member of the church conference. This meant the entry into the Indian Mennonite church of a new group of people—with distinctly different language and culture—in addition to the three groups which had emerged previously (the mission compound churches in the North, the Gara caste church in the South, and the church at the Bethesda Leprosy Hospital).

The state government of Madhya Pradesh was one of the most conservative and anti-Christian states in the new nation of India, and it viewed with alarm the evidences of Christian growth in the tribal areas. High officials in the Madhya Pradesh government charged that the spread of Christianity was due to the alien influence of foreign missionaries and was connected to a political separatist movement and opposition to the Congress party in the native states. The state government then created an investigative commission to gather information about Christian missionary activity throughout the state. This Niyogi Commission, named after its chairman who was a retired chief justice, toured fourteen districts of Madhya Pradesh in 1954, contacted 11,360 people, received 375 written statements, and published its findings in three volumes.[2] The effect of the Niyogi inquiry was, in the view of Bishop Gurbachan Singh who represented the United Church of North India to the commission, the same as happens in all cases where a powerful majority investigates a minority. It created a psychological environment in which the Christian minority was terrorized.[3]

The Niyogi Commission held hearings which elicited anti-Christian charges in the centers where Mennonites worked—Ambikapur, Korba, Champa, Basna, and Jagdeeshpur. In Ambikapur, evangelist Puran Banwar was falsely accused of urinating on a Hindu shrine. In Champa, Mennonite hospital officials were charged with discriminating in favor of Christian patients. Many of the accusations attempted to prove that missionaries had used illicit inducements and pressures to seduce unwitting people into conversion. The published conclusions of the Niyogi Commission paid token tribute to missionary contributions in the fields of education, medical relief, and social reform, but expressed more basic alarm that Christianity was an alien and subversive influence in India. For example:

> Evangelization in India appears to be a part of the uniform world policy to revive Christendom for re-establishing Western supremacy and is not prompted by spritual motives.[4]

Short-term effects of the encounter with the Niyogi Commission were purifying for the Mennonites in India. Church members rallied around their leaders who courageously testified to the authenticity of their Christian faith. The incidents of public violence in these years were not exceptionally severe—several beatings in the Surguja district and the destruction of one church in Phuljar by a gang of ruffians. But in its long-term effects, the state government's hostility to Christianity had a demoralizing and corrosive influence upon the church and the mission. Anticonversion legislation made evangelism increasingly difficult. Government denial of missionary visas and residence permits frustrated missions programming. There seemed to be an implicit invitation for disgruntled or excommunicated church members to approach government officials in secret to agitate for the expulsion of missionaries from the country.

Lessons from Dhamtari

The central organizational issue before the church and mission in the early 1950s was the question of "amalgamation." From the beginning of the century there had been a commitment to work toward a self-governing, self-supporting, and self-propagating church in India. Ever since the church conference was created in 1922, there had been a dual organizational structure with the Indian church on one side and the North American mission on the other. Had the time come to dissolve this structure, to assign all mission properties to the church, and to put missionary personnel and institutions under the Indian church? A missions indigenization committee struggled with this "amalgamation" issue in the early 1950s, impelled by anti-Christian pressures in Madhya Pradesh and by a desire to move as quickly as possible to a mature and independent church in India. By 1957, however, the decision had been made not to amalgamate church and mission but to continue the dual structure inherited from the past, with some modifications.

One key influence against amalgamation (or "integration," as it was called in Zaire) was a negative response to the experience of the sister Mennonite mission and church in Dhamtari. Vocal Indian leaders arose earlier in Dhamtari to challenge the traditional mission-centered system. From 1945 to 1949 the mission and church there experimented with a constitution which amalgamated Indian Christians into the mission structure. In 1952 a new constitution, imposed upon reluctant missionaries by board secretary J. D. Graber, ended the existence of the American Mennonite Mission (MC) in India and placed mission institutions under the church conference.[5] This decision involved so much ill will and organizational disruption that the GC missionaries were convinced that the amalgamation option had been discredited. Through the 1960s GC mission policy in India was designed to avoid the presumed mistakes of Dhamtari, and the idea of partnership within a dual structure was the chosen method to do so. With virtual autonomy to make decisions on the field, the GC missionaries could chart their own course.

The Achievements of Partnership: 1950 - 1970

The GC mission and church continued the work of education, health care, evangelism, and literature in the 1950s and 1960s, with significant advances in a number of areas.[6] Missionaries and nationals cooperated on committees to produce and distribute Christian literature. In 1955 a Joint Literature Committee was created together with the Mennonite Church in India (MC). This committee adapted, translated, and published materials in the Hindi language for daily vacation Bible schools over a six-year period. Missionary Helen Kornelsen gave leadership for the production of the series, which was used widely in non-Mennonite circles as well. The mission established public libraries or "reading rooms" in Basna (1953), Saraipali (1956), and Korba (1958), and occasionally staffed them with seminary graduates who could use these positions as stepping-stones to pastorates. The Joint Literature Committee published its first peace literature, a collection of peace stories, in 1965. In 1967 it began publishing a quarterly magazine, *Shanti Sandesh.*

A new Inter-Mennonite communications endeavor, the Mennonite Literature and Radio Council (MELARC), began in 1970 and sponsored the training of Indians for radio and literature work. C.S.R. Gier, Udit Sona, Kesho Rao, all of Jagdeeshpur, contributed in writing and broadcasting projects. Theodore Roberts of Korba, son of the first Indian pastor of the Korba Mennonite Church, privately wrote ten full-length Christian social dramas for production in the local church and community. A new generation was emerging which could translate the gospel into authentic Indian idiom and rhythm with new songs, dramas, and other writings

An Economic Life and Relief Council (TELARC) was born in 1968 at the initiative of missionaries Jake Giesbrecht and John Pauls. There had been some famine relief programs in the mid-1960s, and Mennonite Central Committee assisted with funding for long-range community development programs. A major dam-building community project led by Pauls ended prematurely when his residence permit was not renewed in 1976. Development programs in the South continued under the umbrella of a Rural Economic Development and Community Health Association (REACH), with representatives from the hospital, school, and churches in the Jagdeeshpur area. In 1977, MCC entered into a five-year agreement with REACH to fund acceptable projects in the areas of community health, agriculture, and handicrafts.

The hospitals at Champa and Jagdeeshpur expanded their facilities and services during the "partnership" decades. The mission board supplied grants for renovations and new buildings, while the hospitals became self-supporting as far as salaries of national workers and hospital medicines and supplies were concerned. Electricity came to the Champa hosptial in 1958 and to the Jagdeeshpur hospital in 1967. The medical work came under a Mission Conference Hospital Board in 1957, with provision for Indian participation on the board. Mr. Amritus

Sonwani became the first Indian nursing superintendent in the mission hospitals in 1969. The first Indian medical superintendents were Dr. E. S. K. Arthur in Jagdeeshpur (1973) and Dr. T. Mathai in Champa (1974).

The educational work of the mission and church also expanded, despite the closing of the two Janjgir schools—Funk Memorial School for girls and the Union Bible School—in 1959 and 1960. Janzen Memorial School in Jagdeeshpur became a higher secondary school in 1958. Primary schools and middle schools were upgraded in Korba, Champa, and Sirco (near Jagdeeshpur). A new English-medium school was opened in Korba in 1966. In 1970 a total of 2,233 children, 1,126 of whom were of Christian families, attended Mennonite schools. The mission education subsidy from North America was $35,000. Parents bore an increasing share of the cost through student fees. Government grants covered about 50 percent of the expenses.

The village of Korba had long been considered the poorest area of Mennonite mission work in contrast to Champa and Janjgir with their institutional activities. In the 1950s and 1960s the Indian government developed Korba into a great industrial center. The Mennonites struggled with the question of how to relate to Christians from a dozen or more different denominations who were moving in to find jobs in the Korba area. The Christians of different denominational backgrounds were not necessarily eager to come under the Mennonite umbrella, nor was the Mennonite church conference vigorous in its efforts to embrace the possibility. Eventually there came to be at least four groups, in addition to the Korba Mennonite Church, which held services with Mennonite leadership on Sundays. Not all of these groups affiliated with the Mennonite church conference, however. Congregations also were established in the villages near Korba.

Leadership training remained a major concern of the church and mission in the "partnership" decades. The mission had put its emphasis upon educating evangelists and pastors since the founding of the Bible school in Janjgir by W. F. Unruh in 1930. But the need for administrators and leaders with higher education went largely unfilled. Joseph Asna, son of the first Indian evangelist, says that the mission missed an opportunity in the late 1920s by failing to provide higher education for a number of young men and women who were ready at that time. Asna applied to study in North America in 1927, but the application was turned down despite some missionary support for the proposal.[7] The first Indian Mennonite church leaders to study in North America were Puran A. Banwar in the late 1940s and Samuel and Helen Lal Stephen in the mid-1950s. Both Banwar and Stephen filled leadership roles in the church conference and mission work with great distinction. Banwar directed the mission work in Surguja from 1955 until his death in 1971. Stephen became principal of Janzen Memorial

High School in Jagdeeshpur and served for many years as chairman of the church conference.

The need for higher church leadership training was met in the early 1950s when the Mennonites affiliated with the interdenominational Union Biblical Seminary (UBS) at Yavatmal. Martha Burkhalter of the Mennonite mission joined the teaching staff in 1951, and Kenneth G. Bauman served as principal from 1967 to 1972. Shadrak B. Kumar in 1956 graduated from UBS, the first GC Mennonite with the Graduate in Theology degree from that school. Numerous Mennonite students received their education and preparation for church work at UBS in the 1960s and 1970s.

Flaws in Partnership

Despite the achievements of the "partnership" decades until the 1970s, there was a fundamental flaw in the "partnership" structure. The church and the mission were vastly unequal as partners. The church conference was poor, both in finances and status. In charge of pastors, evangelists, church properties, and—for a short period—of primary schools, the church conference struggled each year to meet its budget. By 1951 all eleven pastors were ordained nationals supported from church conference funds. Mission subsidies for evangelism ended in 1959. A sustained effort was under way to make the church self-reliant and self-supporting, but the long history of dependency upon missions largesse made progress very difficult. While it was possible to speak of a self-supporting church in these decades, the hidden fact was that the greatest share of church monies came from the private tithes of missionaries and from nationals employed at mission schools and hospitals where their contribution was regularly deducted from their monthly salaries.

The mission conference, by contrast, was powerful and relatively well funded. There was more status and income associated with jobs at mission schools and hospitals than with employment as pastors and evangelists under the church conference. Missionaries controlled the pipeline of funds from North America and the processes by which nationals could be promoted to positions of greater authority in the institutions and in the mission conference structure. Ideally, the long-range plan was for the mission conference to be taken over by Indian nationals and to lose its character as an overseas-directed "mission." In the 1970s a series of events converged to dissolve the structure of "partnership" and dismantle the mission conference. It was a time of troubles for both the mission and the church.

The Valley of the Shadow

The foreign mission board, or Commission on Overseas Mission (COM) as it became known after the General Conference constitutional change in 1968, began to take a more aggressive role in establishing missions policies in the early 1970s. The historic pattern had been for missions policies to be set basically on the field. The board members, most of whom did not have overseas experience, were responsible for watching budgets and keeping up relationships with constituent churches. After the 1968 constitutional revision, decision-making power began to shift from missionaries on the field to the mission board and the mission executive in North America. Verney Unruh, staff secretary for Asia, noted the changed mood and procedure of the board after an executive committee meeting in 1971. The staff was used to bringing recommendations to the board and having them accepted more or less without question, but now the board was making changes in nearly all recommendations and rejecting some entirely. All the members of this COM executive (Elmer Neufeld, Vern Preheim, Gerald Stucky, and Peter Fast) had overseas experience, reported Unruh, "and we found that this brings in a whole new dimension in the discussion."[8] A new executive secretary took over in 1971, Howard Habegger, who had been on furlough after two terms in Colombia.

Unruh visited India in 1971 and became convinced that progress in transferring positions and authority to nationals was too slow. He noted, for example, that only two Indians served on the twelve-member medical board of the mission conference. On his way Unruh wrote a letter from Bombay calling the missionaries to "take necessary steps to have at least *equal* representation of missionaries and nationals on all boards and in mission conference within *two to three years.*"[9] There were many reasons why missionaries considered this an unwise and virtually impossible demand. There had been cases in which Indians had been promoted to jobs for which they were not competent or which they abused by embezzling funds. It was extremely difficult for missionaries to take orders from nationals who were less qualified. After all, many missionaries had training in technical skills, and it was not easy to lower standards. There was some fear that relinquishing key positions of responsibility would make it more difficult to renew residence permits and get visa extensions. And, of course, there was the unmeasurable and indefinable human reluctance to give up power and authority. But times had changed. There was no alternative to handing over the institutions to Indian nationals and to helping them grow in maturity and responsibility—just as North American Mennonite institutions had grown by trial and error in their own time.

The crisis point for the India mission came in 1973, when a delegation of four men from North America (Howard Habegger, Elmer Neufeld, Robert Ramseyer, and Verney Unruh) came to India for a goals, priorities, and strategy meeting with the missionaries and the national church leaders.[10] It happened that this delegation arrived at a time of considerable tension in church conference relationships between the northern churches and the southern churches. The South had surpassed the North in vitality and influence—a shift symbolized by the closing of the girls school and Bible school in Janjgir (north) and the growth of Janzen Memorial High School in Jagdeeshpur (south). Relationships also became strained in 1972 when all the executive officers elected in the church conference were men working in the North, which resulted in a regional imbalance. Meanwhile there was some misunderstanding between the church conference and the mission conference over the mission's program to transfer mission properties—mission compounds, reading rooms, and various plots of land—to the Evangelical Trust Association of North India. The documents for this transfer were signed in March 1973, but some church conference leaders were unhappy that the property had not been given directly to the church conference.

Before the COM delegation arrived in India, the Indians had somehow gotten the idea that a major rift had taken place between COM and the missionaries, and that the delegation was coming to India to gather evidence against the missionaries and get rid of them. All the dissident and frustrated forces mobilized to deluge the delegation with accusations against the missionaries. Much of the protest came from people who had been bypassed in competition for mission-allocated jobs and scholarships. The delegation's hearings, like the Niyogi Commission of 1954, generated great hostility. It was the first time in GC missions history that the missionaries and the mission board (now COM) had not presented a united front in working with the nationals.

The COM delegation, missionaries, and national leaders had an emotion-charged meeting in Raipur in September to set forth policies for the future. The effect of the Raipur decisions was to reduce the power of the missions conference and to accelerate the timetable for transfer of authority to the church conference. The work of the mission conference Christian Nurture Board and Literature Board was to be transferred to church conference. The hospitals were not to be placed under the church conference, however, but under the independent Emmanuel Hospital Association. In line with the Chicago 1972 GPS priority on evangelism, COM promised funds to the church conference for evangelistic work. This reversed the 1959 decision to end mission-paid evangelism. It would be many years until the decisions of 1973 could be fully appreciated and evaluated. There were some who felt the mission's refusal to adopt the amalgamation option two decades earlier had made an eventual crisis of this kind inevitable. There were others, especially some missionaries, who believed that COM had unwisely and prematurely in the 1970s imposed a settlement that would cause the church to regress in the steps it had already taken toward indigenous methods of evangelization.

A Canceled Celebration

There was to be a seventy-fifth anniversary celebration in 1975 of the founding of the General Conference mission in India by the P. A. Penners and the J. F. Kroekers in 1900. That celebration was not held, however, because of a crisis in the Champa church and hospital. A young Mennonite medical doctor at Champa hospital was dismissed for allegedly performing an illegal abortion on his sister-in-law. He retaliated against the hospital staff and missionaries with the sensational and spurious charge that nursing superintendent Irene Funk, who had died of acute leukemia in March 1975, had in fact been poisoned by persons with her before she died. Funk's body was exhumed for chemical analysis by government officials. The official analysis— reported orally in May 1976—showed the charges of poisoning to have been false. By that time, however, the bitter controversy had nearly split the Champa church and had spread ill will throughout the church and mission. It would take years for the Champa church and hospital to recover from this incident.[11]

India Is Different

The troubles of the GC Mennonite mission and church in India in the 1970s need to be seen both in historical context and in comparison with the situations on other fields. The relationship between Mennonite missionaries and nationals in India was fundamentally different from parallel relationships in other countries. In India the Mennonite converts were generally rural low-caste people who came out of a long tradition of oppression within their own society. The Christian gospel carried for these people a great liberation from their degraded position. Over the years in the twentieth century, the India Mennonites raised themselves in status and position, often with the help of mission education and employment. But they remained a minority in their society, surrounded by people of higher caste and of Hindu religion who resented the fact and condition of their liberation.

The conflicts between missionaries and nationals which seemed to peak in the 1950s and 1970s in India were not due primarily to Indian resentment over the relatively affluent missionary life-style or to alleged colonialist attitudes of missionaries. Missionary paternalism did exist to some degree, but it had different meaning in India where centuries of the caste system had entrenched habits of social deference. In India the nationals were more inclined to defer to the superior status and authority of missionaries. Conflicts between missionaries and nationals in India emerged primarily because of the missionary control over limited resources in the Christian community—jobs, promotion, money, and access to North American authorities. The missionaries were effectively attacked, and sometimes successfully evicted, by nationals who failed to get jobs they wanted, who lost positions because of church discipline, or who were angered when missionaries took sides in local disputes. Missionaries were more vulnerable to attack than were national church leaders, who usually had a hand in the difficult decisions.

Aggrieved nationals had one source of power at their disposal—appeal to their own Indian government for action against missionaries. The state government in Madhya Pradesh was more anti-Christian than in some other Indian states, and was quite willing to hear charges and take action against missionaries. The government could deny visas or residence permits without explanation, so missionaries had no way to answer those who complained against them, or even know for sure who the complainants were. Thus a letter or petition against a missionary, perhaps bolstered with a bribe, could get effective action to exclude missionaries. The fundamental problem was structural rather than personal. As long as missionaries made decisions regarding the allocation of scarce resources, and as long as aggrieved nationals could complain anonymously and effectively to an anti-Christian and antimissionary government, the possible exclusion of missionaries remained to threaten the future of the mission.

The number of GC missionaries on the field in Madhya Pradesh dropped from thirty in 1950 to ten in 1976. Government refusal of visas and of residence permits accounted for only part of this attrition. Missionaries who retired because of age, family reasons, or "troubled relationships" were replaced in their positions by Indians rather than by a new generation of young missionaries. By 1978 there remained only one couple and one single (Edward and Ramoth Lowe Burkhalter and Anne Penner) on the field.[12] Empty mission bungalows in Champa, Janjgir, and Saraipali—ill-suited to the life-style and tastes of Indian nationals—testified to an earlier era of missionary initiative and affluence.

The GC church in India faced a number of significant challenges as it endeavored to move beyond the crisis of the 1970s. Relationships between the North and the South remained problematic, and separation into two district conferences seemed a real possibility. The church faced a continuing struggle for financial self-sufficiency as the link between the church and the missions institutions was weakened. The church could no longer expect the automatic tithes of school and hospital employees. Evangelism remained a concern, for the church had grown only slightly in three decades.

But the church also had significant strengths. There was a core of talented and committed young pastors. The village churches in the South continued with great stability and vitality. Janzen Memorial High School promised to be a continuing resource for church leadership in the future, both in its student body and in its faculty. There were eighteen young people attending seminary in training for church work in

1978. These young people would write new chapters in the history of the GC church in India as the church moved beyond "partnership" to more complete autonomy and initiative.

Zaire, 1960-1978: Integration-Disintegration

The decade of the 1960s began for Congo Inland Mission with a plan and a prayer for "integration." The mission and the church were to be integrated into one legal entity, outlined in the agreement of February 1960, with missionaries and nationals sharing equal representation on committees. The next five years, however, turned into a time of agonizing "disintegration" as things fell apart. The Belgians left their colony precipitously, having failed to prepare the people with the leadership and the institutions appropriate to political independence. The new country exploded with intertribal violence and with conflicts among regional contenders for national leadership. The Mennonite church, caught in the cross fires of rebellion and tribal warfare, suffered through a series of calamities—a church schism along tribal lines, a loss of church leadership, and often-hostile relationships between missionaries and national church leaders.

Compared to India, where the democratic-oriented Congress party established order and stability after the postindependence war and partition between Muslim Pakistan and Hindu India, national unity in Zaire remained indefinitely precarious. There was relief from anarchy when the head of the Zairian army, Mobutu Sese Seko, established control of the country through a military dictatorship in 1965. In the subsequent years Mobutu struggled erratically to find economic and social policies which would enable his country to survive the threats of tribalism, inflation, foreign domination, and secessionism in the copper-rich Shaba province.

Two events highlighted the independence upheavals for Mennonites in Zaire. From North America, the most shocking event appeared to be the evacuation of Mennonite missionaries in July 1960, in the two weeks after independence. In Zairian eyes, however, the more tragic event was fighting between the Lulua and Baluba tribes which resulted in widespread killing, a massive migration, and a formal split in the Mennonite church.

The Lulua were the earlier and the more numerous inhabitants in the western Kasai, where the Mennonite work was located. The Baluba had come from the eastern Kasai and had taken advantage of educational and economic opportunities to rise to leadership positions in the colonial system. The Lulua feared that the departure of the Belgians would mean that political and economic leadership in their areas would fall to the Baluba. Fighting broke out between the tribes already in 1959 before independence, and spread in January 1960 to the Mennonite centers of Mutena, Tshikapa, and Djoko Punda. The Baluba were able to defend themselves for a time in areas where they were more entrenched, but eventually the Lulua triumphed, and the Baluba fled in a chaotic mass exodus to the eastern Kasai. The story of Baluba suffering, and of the relief work of missionary Archie Graber with the Congo Protestant Relief Agency, is told in Levi Keidel's book, *War to Be One*. [13]

Pastor Kazadi Muadianvita, the most capable and authoritative figure in the Zaire Mennonite Church at the time of independence, belonged to the Baluba tribe. Kazadi had been raised in a Catholic family, and was converted as a young person under the leadership of L. B. Haigh, the first missionary to go to the Zaire under Congo Inland Mission. Kazadi served for nineteen years as an evangelist in the village of Basongo, and was ordained to the ministry in 1941. At the time of the revolution he was in the Djoko Punda area, where he had developed some successful coffee and corn plantations together with his sons and sons-in-law.

Kazadi's leadership was desperately needed in the Mennonite church in the revolutionary 1960s, but events forced him out. In the face of mounting anti-Baluba agitation, Kazadi left his home, church, and properties at Djoko Punda and fled to Mbujimayi in the eastern Kasai, some 200 miles (320 kilometers) to the east. Here he founded a new and independent church among his refugee tribespeople. The political prominence of his son-in-law, Munkamba, among the Baluba helped Kazadi's group to gain status and recognition. The new church, known as the Evangelical Mennonite Community of South Kasai, grew to include twenty parishes, sixteen ordained pastors, and a small Bible institute, even though it received no support or missionaries from the Africa Inter-Mennonite Mission. The matter of reconciliation between Kazadi's group and the older church was high on the agenda of mission and church in the 1960s and 1970s, and some significant steps in cooperation were achieved.

Added to the divisive Lulua-Baluba intertribal strife was a Kwilu rebellion which disrupted life in the Mukedi-Kandala area in 1964-65. [14] Behind this rebellion lay broad popular disillusionment that political independence had failed to bring its promised peace and prosperity. The economic situation deteriorated. The new government proved to be often inept and corrupt. Tribal leaders were often resentful and hostile toward new national leaders of different tribal origin. In the Kwilu the forces of frustration rallied around the charismatic leadership of the leftist rebel, Mulele Pierre. Many Protestant and Catholic church members supported the movement in its early stages, but disillusionment set in as the movement failed in its military and political objectives, and as undisciplined rebel partisans terrorized villagers. The Mennonite mission stations at Kandala and Mukedi were burned and ravaged by the rebel youth gangs and had to be evacuated. Unlike the wholesale

1960 evacuation, however, it was possible in 1964 to transfer most of the missionary families to other stations in the country.

Another center of rebel activity in 1964 was at Kisangani (Stanley-ville) in eastern Zaire, where rebels led by Christophe Gbenye declared a Congo People's Republic. Melvin and Elfrieda Loewen had gone to Kisangani to help organize a new Protestant university and were caught in the rebel occupation from August until November, when they were rescued (along with Paxmen Eugene Bergman and Jon Snyder) by Belgian paratroopers.[15]

Zaire's experiment in democracy ended in 1965 when Joseph Mobutu (Mobutu Sese Seko) took over the government and established order through the army and the political party which he controlled. The coming of stability was welcomed with great relief by a country which had suffered now not only from the oppression of colonialism but also from the chaos of independence. In behalf of national identity, Mobutu in 1971 launched a drive for "authenticity" to rid the country of imposed colonialist consciousness. By presidential order, traditional African names replaced European names for cities, provinces, and people. This meant that Western and biblical names, which had often been taken at baptism, had to be abandoned. December 25 was declared to be a normal working day rather than an official holiday. Religious radio broadcasting and literature production were banned for a time.

Mennonite schools were affected by Mobutu's drive for authenticity and national consolidation. Youth cells of Mobutu's political party were supposed to be organized in every school, while political chants and rituals became an obligatory part of school routine. Unlike the Catholics, whose protesting archbishop of Kinshasa, Cardinal Malula, was disciplined and deported for resisting Mobutu's politicizing of religious schools, the Mennonites had no open and direct confrontation with the government. There were moments of tension, however, such as one case in 1974 when a Mennonite Zairian student in the evangelical seminary in Kinshasa accused a Mennonite missionary teacher of opposing involvement in the student political party there. At another politically tense time, Mennonite church officials temporarily stopped distribution of a pamphlet on Mennonite history and doctrine because the pamphlet had so clearly stated the priority of the claims of God over the claims of man.

The Zaire Mennonite church in the 1970s had to respond to government policies which shifted in unpredictable and contradictory fashion. The government nationalized the schools, but then requested the churches once again to take over school administration after two years when the school situation had badly deteriorated. The government attempted to centralize and unify religious organizations. For Protestants this meant that all churches had to affiliate with the one central Church of Christ of Zaire, which had grown up out of the former

Congo Protestant Council and which was now identified with Mobutu's party and political ideology. By 1978 the main problem for the Mennonite church, however, was not the threat of political control but rather the rampant inflation and economic deterioration identified with Mobutu's personal rule.

From CIM to AIMM

The Congo Inland Mission board structure was an inter-Mennonite anomaly in a time when different Mennonite groups in North America were embarrassingly unable to cooperate with each other in missionary enterprise. Separated Mennonites generally could work together in Mennonite Central Committee (MCC) projects of relief and service, but they went their own ways on the theologically sensitive matters of evangelism and church-planting. But CIM was inter-Mennonite from the beginning, and it became more so in the 1960s and 1970s. The founding groups—Evangelical Mennonite Church and Central Conference—had been joined by two board members from the Evangelical Mennonite Brethren in 1938. After World War II the Evangelical Mennonite Conference of Canada (Kleine Gemeinde) associated with Congo Inland Mission. In the 1970s the Mennonite Brethren, who had long had their own mission and church in Zaire, joined with Congo Inland Mission (now AIMM) for its new work with independent churches in southern Africa.

While the inter-Mennonite base of CIM was gradually broadened, there was a trend toward an increasingly predominant role of the General Conference in the organization. The Central Conference affiliated with the General Conference in 1946, and the number of General Conference missionaries from outside the Central Conference increased dramatically from two in 1945 to forty-four in 1960. From 1970 to 1975 the numbers of missionaries from the EMB and EMC groups dropped from twenty to eight, and the General Conference accounted for nearly 80 percent of the AIMM missionary force. James Bertsche, who became AIMM executive secretary in 1974, was committed to increasing recruitment of missionaries from the non-GC groups in order to avoid GC domination of the mission.

The Congo Inland Mission adopted a new name—Africa Inter-Mennonite Mission—in 1972. It was necessary to remove the name Congo from the mission board designation, since Congo had officially become Zaire in October 1971. At the same 1972 mission board meeting the decision was made to send a missionary couple to Lesotho in southern Africa. For the first time AIMM became active in a country outside of Zaire: Missionaries were also sent to Botswana and Upper Volta in the 1970s.[16]

Toward Fusion and Autonomy

When the missionaries returned to Zaire after the revolution, they moved to reestablish the dual mission-church structure rather than to implement the "integration" agreement of 1960. By 1962 a Field Executive Committee without African representatives was making basic policy decisions. The missionaries saw the situation as transitional, but African church leaders often suspected that missionaries were making excuses in order to perpetuate their control. The church situation became particularly volatile in 1970. The annual church conference that year was marked by tribal dissension, and two groups held separate "rump sessions" in Nyanga and Luluabourg after the regular conference ended inconclusively. One separatist group contacted government officials to inquire about possibilities of starting a new church, but they were rebuffed. Government policy was overwhelmingly in favor of religious unity and consolidation rather than separatism and sectarianism.[17] The dissident African church leaders accused missionaries of manipulating intertribal hostilities in order to delay or prevent church-mission fusion.

A new era of stability and cooperation began with the official signing of a fusion agreement at Djoko Punda on 14 January 1971. The mission as such went out of existence. All mission properties were transferred to the African church. All missionaries would be called by the Zaire Mennonite Church and would be responsible to Zairian superiors. Funds from North America, both for missionary support and for church expenses, would flow through the Zairian church treasury.

The Zairian church remained dependent upon North American personnel and funds in the 1970s. There were sixty-five missionaries on the field in 1971; the CIM budget for the Zaire Mennonite Church (apart from missionary support) was $60,000 for that year. Missionaries assisted Zairian church leaders at nearly all tasks of administration. Not until 1977 was the annual church budget prepared without missionary assistance. But there were signs that the church was becoming increasingly self-directing, and this was nowhere more evident than in several cases in which the church leaders made decisions which were unpopular with the missionaries and board. The church unilaterally decided to join the World Council of Churches, despite missionary and board opposition. The church asked that certain missionaries not be returned to Zaire after furlough, and the board accepted the decision. The church decided—against missionary advice—to launch a sawmill project to raise funds for current church expenses. Even though the mission board strongly believed the church should be funded through the stewardship of members rather than through special projects, the mission in North America facilitated the sawmill project by referring the church to MEDA (Mennonite Economic Development Associates) for aid. The Zaire Mennonite Church in the 1970s groped toward increasing maturity and independence. Notable progress was made both in the occasional areas of church-mission disagreement, as well as in the myriad continuing experiments in missionary-church cooperation in the work of evangelism, education, medicine, and economic development.

Leadership Training

The Congo Inland Mission for years had endeavored to provide leadership training which would be able to meet the needs of local rural churches. There did emerge a strong core of evangelists and church workers, but there was also a distinct lack of advanced training for persons at the higher pastoral and administrative level who might replace missionaries in the transition of authority from mission to church. In the early 1960s the Congo Inland Mission began a joint five-year theology program at Kajiji in cooperation with the Mennonite Brethren mission. Kabangy Shapasa, who replaced Ngongo David as president of the church conference after fusion in 1971, was a graduate of the Kajiji program. In 1970 the Mennonites joined other Protestants in a new evangelical theological school with a campus in the capital city of Kinshasa. Mennonite teachers at the school included Peter Buller, Peter Falk, and Richard Steiner. The Mennonite Brethren mission also supplied teachers. By the late 1970s this Kinshasa school was in difficulty because of rampant inflation and high costs in the city and because church leaders felt students educated in Kinshasa were being "spoiled" for the more difficult work in the villages.

As important as it seemed to have well-trained persons for top administrative positions and upper level teaching, the greatest need was for leadership in the local villages. In 1977 there were sixty-eight ordained pastors who served some 140 church centers in the Zaire Mennonite Church. There were 850 villages for which the church would have wanted to supply at least some trained lay leadership. A program of lay theological training by extension was started to try to meet this need. A three-year Bible Institute program operated at Kalonda for students who had completed the tenth grade. It seemed clear that most future leaders would come from the Bible Institute and from the new program for theological education by extension.

MCC and SEDA

The Mennonite Central Committee played a significant role in Zaire in the 1960s and 1970s, often in cooperative programs with the Zaire Mennonite Church. Orie Miller, who was in positions of executive responsibility with MCC from 1921 to 1963, had been a counselor to Harvey Driver in the 1950s, giving particular encouragement to inter-Mennonite contacts on the African continent. In the wake of the independence upheavals in 1960, Miller became a founder of the Congo Protestant Relief Agency which operated as an arm of the Congo

Protestant Council and through which Mennonites and others channeled food, clothing, and medical supplies to victims of war and rebellion.

The MCC program broadened to include agricultural development and church assistance as well as refugee work and material aid. Dozens of North American Mennonite young people served two-year teaching terms in Zairian schools (after a year of French language study in Brussels) in the Teachers Abroad Program (TAP). In 1972 MCC had seventy persons working in Zaire, thirty-four of whom were TAP teachers assigned to church schools. [18]

MCC and the Zaire Mennonite Church cooperated in an agricultural development program, based at Nyanga, which came to be known as the Service for Development of Agriculture (SEDA). SEDA was designed as a grass roots village program for development of improved crops, animal husbandry, nutrition, and Christian stewardship. Fremont Regier became director of the program in 1965, and in 1976 transferred directorship to a Zairian, Ngulubi Mazemba. The work in early years focused upon a farm center at Nyanga and the village extension work of two-person teams, consisting of a young short-term Mennonite agriculturist and a Zairian counterpart. In the early 1970s an extensive program of New Life for All weekend seminars was developed. In Mazemba's words, these seminars were "an effort to put together all the resources at the church's disposal in a team effort to bring new life to rural families." [19] The local village churches were the base for the seminars. The staff included an agriculturist, evangelist, public health nurse, bookseller, woman's worker, and a youth folk-singing group. Worship and evangelism were brought together with practical instruction for community improvement.

The SEDA program received widespread attention both inside and outside Zaire as a model experiment in development, but it had to deal with many problems which threatened its purpose and existence. SEDA became a department of the Zaire Mennonite Church and it confronted issues of tribal jealousies. Was it fair for the Pende tribe of the Nyanga area to receive the greatest benefit for the program? Another great problem was to foster in the Zairians a sense of ownership and responsibility for the program. SEDA was initiated by missionaries and funded by outside agencies. How could Africans, who for so long had been conditioned to dependence upon outsiders, learn the attitudes and habits of self-help and initiative? A particular crisis emerged in late 1973 when the Zairian government threatened to take over SEDA as part of its program to nationalize all foreign-owned enterprises in the country. Government officials at first refused to accept that SEDA belonged to the Zairian Mennonite Church. The testimony of Kabangy Shapasa, general secretary of the church, at government offices in Tshikapa was essential in saving SEDA as an arm of the church. Despite SEDA's many problems, however, it remained one of the best examples of integrated evangelical and economic developments in GC missions history. In the words of director Ngulubi Mazemba, "New life in Christ means a whole new way of looking at everything."[20]

Dependency, Financial Support, and Self-Direction

The Congo Inland Mission, like Mennonite missions in other countries, set itself early toward the goal of a self-directing, self-propagating, and self-supporting church. Self-propagation and rapid church growth through the work of African evangelists were achieved in Zaire earlier and with greater success than in other countries. Great strides toward self-direction came with the "integration" agreement in 1960 and its fulfillment in the "fusion" settlement of 1971. But self-support remained a distant dream in the late 1970s. Church life at the village level was supported locally. District level work, including many village activities, was also supported almost 100 percent locally. But the vital needs of education, health, agricultural development, and central church administration were met by substantial infusions of foreign funds. Reuben Short wrote toward the end of his term as AIMM executive secretary, "Unfortunately, the Zaire church is still economically dependent on subsidy from outside sources. . . . These sources demand some kind of dependency structure before providing the desired help. . . . The dependency problem limits independence and can tend to humiliate depending on attitude."[21]

The decade of the 1970s was less stormy and disruptive for GC Mennonites in Zaire than for those in India. Despite the unpredictability of the Mobutu regime, the Zaire church was able to grow in maturity and cooperate productively with its mission agency in North America. There was no exodus of missionaries from Zaire in the 1970s as took place in India. General Secretary Kabangy wrote in 1975 that he disagreed with the call for a moratorium on missionaries which was currently popular in missions dialogue. Kabangy preferred the term "autonomy of the church" to the concept of moratorium. Missionaries were still needed to work together with, but under the authority of, the Zaire Mennonite Church. Mutual decision making was not always easy, but the missionaries had learned the right spirit. "Among the missionaries placed at the dispositon of the CMZA (Zaire Mennonite Church) by the AIMM," wrote Kabangy, "I've never found anyone who aspired to become a 'chief' within the church; this is a sincere truth." It would take uncommon gifts of love and respect in mutual relationships for Africans and missionaries to continue working in a situation where the goal of church autonomy was contradicted by the dependency structures which seemed an inevitable corollary of North American funding and personnel.

Andrew R. Shelly (in hat at left) talks with Indian Christians after a morning service in Paraguay, 1961.

10 Latin America

Paraguay: The Great Exception

Throughout most of its century-long history, the expectations and the accomplishments of General Conference Mennonite mission work have been similar to those of neighboring Protestant missionaries and mission stations. In lower Latin America, however, there emerged a Great Exception. In the "green hell" of the Paraguayan Chaco there grew up a missionary effort to native Indian tribes which was radically unlike anything Mennonites, or the Protestant missionary movement generally, had ever done before.

Mennonite mission work in Paraguay was not initiated by North American Mennonite mission boards, but by Mennonite settler communities. These communities were nourished by ties of kinship and religious fellowship with North American Mennonites, and they were divided into various groupings which had formal, as well as informal, affiliations with North American counterpart groups. The GC Mennonite churches in Paraguay, Uruguay, and Brazil in fact came to form one conference—the South American Conference—in the Mennonite church. Mennonite settlers in Latin America began mission work not long after their arrival, and they eventually invited North Americans to cooperate in that work.

There were three main waves of Mennonite migration and settlement in lower Latin America, as well as some smaller movement of groups and individuals.[1] The first wave consisted of conservative Mennonites from Canada who fled when Canada's anti-ethnic nationalization policy of World War I and the 1920s began to threaten their control of the schools and their use of the German language. After great hardship, including a devastating typhoid epidemic, this group founded the Menno Colony in the Paraguayan Chaco in 1928 with about seventeen hundred persons in twelve original villages. A second wave was made up of Mennonites fleeing from Stalin's Russia in the early 1930s. About six thousand Mennonites came to Paraguay in 1930-32 and founded the Fernheim Colony. In 1937 about a third of this group left the Chaco and settled in East Paraguay. Some twelve hundred Mennonite refugees from Russia in 1930 settled in Brazil at Witmarsum and Auhagen. Many of these eventually moved to the outskirts of the city of Curitiba. Finally, a third wave of immigration resulted from Mennonite dislocations of World War II. Some seven thousand Mennonites settled in Paraguay after the war, founding the Neuland and Volendam colonies. Mennonites of Prussian origin came to Uruguay in 1948 and 1951, settling at El Ombú, Gardental, Delta, and Montevideo.

Several kinds of peoples in lower Latin America have been the targets of Mennonite mission work: non-Mennonite, German-speaking immigrants; national peoples speaking Spanish or Portuguese; and the unassimilated aboriginal Indian tribes. In the earlier years the Mennonite settlers themselves were often in great need of various kinds of spiritual and material assistance. Some groups had lost their pastors and leaders in the European persecutions and warfare which preceded their migration. North American Mennonites, through a variety of agencies which included Mennonite Central Committee and various mission boards, helped provide mutual aid to their fellow believers. Already before their new settlements were established and secure, however, the immigrant Mennonites laid plans for mission work of their own. The stories of all of the differing GC Mennonite mission efforts in Paraguay, Uruguay, and Brazil deserve to be told in a more comprehensive history, but in this account we will focus upon the encounter of the Mennonites with the Indians in the Paraguayan Chaco.

Transforming Land and Culture

The Paraguayan Chaco is an isolated and forbidding plain of dense bush, intermittent grasslands, and hot winds, which had long defied any dreams of settled, agricultural life. When Mennonites first arrived in 1926, they thought the region was entirely uninhabited. There were in fact several nomadic Indian tribes of carefully limited population which were thinly dispersed in the area. It has been estimated that the total Indian population in the area initially settled by Mennonites consisted of two groups of the Lengua tribe, with fifty to a hundred in each group, plus several scattered bands of other Indian tribes beyond the fringes of the newly settled territory.[2] The Lenguas may have been in the process of dying out as a people. Various Indian tribes suffered severely in the Chaco War between Paraguay and Bolivia, 1930-32.

The establishment of successful Mennonite agricultural settlements in the Chaco transformed the social and economic life of the Indian tribes. It changed their interaction with each other, as well as their relationship

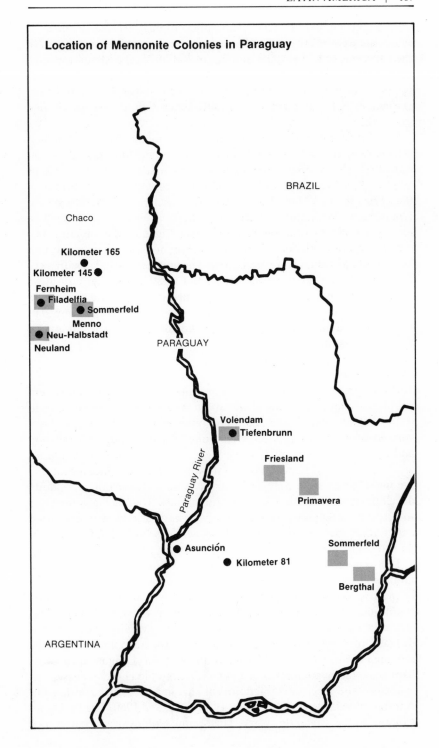

Location of Mennonite Colonies in Paraguay

BRAZIL

Chaco

Kilometer 165

Kilometer 145

Fernheim
Filadelfia
Sommerfeld

Menno
Neu-Halbstadt

Neuland

PARAGUAY

Volendam
Tiefenbrunn

Friesland

Primavera

Paraguay River

Asunción

Kilometer 81

Sommerfeld

Bergthal

ARGENTINA

to the outside world. The Mennonite colonies were a magnet of economic opportunity toward which the various tribes converged. In the half-century to 1975, the number of Indians in the Mennonite area grew from several hundred to over nine thousand. The accompanying processes of modernization may have saved some of these tribes from extinction, but it also entailed virtual obliteration of their traditional way of life.

The Mennonites were clear from the beginning that their mission work among the Indians would involve thorough cultural transformation. Preliminary discussions of plans for mission work were held as early as 1932. In September 1935 members of three Mennonite groups in the Chaco—the Mennonite Brethren, General Conference, and Evangelical Mennonite Brethren (Allianz Gemeinde)—formed a missionary association which they called Light to the Indians. The stated purposes of the association allowed for no separation of body and soul, or of individual and community. The purposes included witness to the living God, teaching of the Bible and Christian doctrine, education for children, teaching for morally pure Christian family life, training in hygiene, and economic and cultural progress. The Mennonites hoped to make the Indians into "true, useful and industrious citizens of the Paraguayan state."[3]

Living with the Sending Church

Unlike previous Mennonite mission work among culturally different peoples, Mennonites in the Chaco did not need to send missionaries to some distant "field." Indians were on Mennonite doorsteps. They worked as hired laborers on Mennonite farms. Through observation and experience they knew that the "sending church" had its scoundrels as well as its saints. The close proximity and interdependence meant that the missionaries were necessarily involved in questions of community development and relationships. A primary task from the beginning was to settle the previously nomadic Indians into orderly, well-organized agricultural communities. The Indians would be given land and taught how to build permanent adobe huts and to cultivate land to earn a living.

The first substantial settlement was started in 1936 with six Lengua families at Yalve Sanga. The missionaries experienced great frustration in the first decade. The Indians would pack up and leave to attend a traditional festival in a distant village, even when their work was critically needed in harvest or planting time. Missionaries found it difficult to teach reading and writing to Indian children. But the settlement survived. In February 1946 seven Lengua men were baptized—the beginnings of a Lengua Mennonite church. These men asked for, and received, larger plots of land in a new village settlement. Additional villages were started in 1958, 1959, and 1960. The Fernheim Colony led the way in this work. The Menno Colony organized its own mission program in 1955. The Mennonite Brethren Church in North America accepted responsibility for outside administration and financing of the mission work, although the association Light to the Indians remained in existence. Members of General Conference and Evangelical Mennonite Brethren churches worked as missionaries under the Mennonite Brethren board.

A Mennonite Martyr

While settlement work proceeded with the peaceful Lengua and Chulupi tribes, Mennonite missionaries also made contact with the more hostile Moro tribe to the north. It was on an exploratory visit among the Moros in 1958 that Kornelius Isaac, a thirty-year-old missionary stationed among the Chulupi Indians in Neuland Colony, became the first General Conference missionary to die a violent death at the hands of native peoples. The incident took place near a drilling camp of the Pure Oil Company, some 175 miles (280 kilometers) north of Filadelfia. Isaac and his associates were in the process of distributing gifts of clothing to the Moros when he was, without warning, stabbed in his side by a spear. At Isaac's funeral in Filadelfia the speakers appealed for missionary replacements for the young martyr, and it was announced that three young men had volunteered to carry on the work among the Moros.[4] Mennonite contacts with the Moros in subsequent years were sporadic, however, and this work was carried on by the New Tribes Mission. Moro isolation and hostility eventually broke down, and members of the Moro tribe were among Indians petitioning for the privilege of joining one of the Mennonite-initiated settlements.

Economic and Cultural Complexity

By 1961 the pressures of the settlement program, with Indians moving in from all directions to request land and settlement aid, had become so intense and complex that the Paraguayan Mennonites appealed to North America for help. The Mennonite Central Committee and several mission boards joined with Paraguayan Mennonite groups to form a new Indian Settlement Board to make policies and to oversee program development. A major settlement program grew up in the 1960s and 1970s, with the help of substantial infusions of funds from Mennonite Central Committee and other agencies in North America and Europe. By the mid-1970s there were five major Indian agricultural settlements, with a total of forty villages and an average of twenty families per village. As more Indians came in to demand land and implements for settlement, additional plans for expansion were made. Future growth and development were not hindered by shortage of land (although the harsh Chaco climate remained far less than ideal for reliable agricultural production), but rather by the myriad problems of administration and management.

In each of the five Indian settlements there was established a mission center from which missionaries carried on church work and evangelism. As the nonreligious dimensions of the settlement program expanded rapidly, the proportion of personnel and funds available for mission work as such was diminished in relation to the project as a whole. Indians were not required to become Christians in order to qualify for settlement. In 1978 some 3,000 Indians out of a total of about eleven thousand had been baptized as Christians.

The Mennonite Central Committee and the Indian Settlement Board in Paraguay called upon research and advice from North American experts for economic policy as well as issues of cultural change. Mennonite anthropologists Jacob Loewen and Calvin Redekop made studies in 1962 and 1972, respectively.[5] The issues of cultural change were fascinating and complex. One set of problems related to mechanisms for population control. Two traditional practices helped Lengua society hold down population numbers so that the tribe would not starve in their situation of severely limited food supply—the mothers killed their unwanted babies, and the parents abstained from sexual intercourse during an extended period of up to five years after the birth of a child. Mennonites were shocked by infanticide because it contradicted the Christian value of all human life, and they were opposed to the long prohibition on marital sexual relations because it led to extramarital relations.

When Lenguas became Christians, they were obliged to adopt Mennonite ways. The result was an immediate population explosion. Suddenly there were new pressures for resources to feed and clothe larger families. In addition, relationships and roles within the Lengua families were forced into agonizing reorientation by the presence of children who joined the family in such unprecedented rapid succession. It was the Indian women who suffered the greatest loss of status and power in these changes. Mennonites found it difficult to understand the workings of Indian conscience. Indian Christian couples who had had no objection to infanticide (the Lenguas did not consider babies to be persons) would feel deeply guilty for having sexual relations in the years after childbirth and would insist upon confessing this sin before taking part in Christian communion.[6]

By the 1960s the dominant factor of Indian demand for land and for the instruments of settlement overshadowed considerations of the rightness or wrongness of certain cultural changes. Successful economic settlements required fundamental changes in the nature of Indian communities. The Indians had to learn new patterns of saving and investment which worked against traditional patterns of communal sharing. A successful farmer could not allow his relatives and friends to come in and consume his entire crop of sweet potatoes a few days after the harvest, no matter how much traditional Indian communal values called for free sharing. Changes in such matters were not unilaterally imposed upon unwilling Indians by authoritarian Mennonites. Changes were rather inevitably required by the new life of agricultural settlement which had become the Indians' number one priority.

Questions and Criticism

The Chaco experiment raised many questions for the Mennonite understanding of the relationship of church and community, or of church and state. The Mennonite Chaco settlements themselves had sufficient autonomy that they could be fairly described as one form of state church, or of *corpus Christianum.* Mennonites in the Chaco were a ruling majority, not a persecuted minority. The Paraguayan government, in an action of 26 July 1921, had granted Mennonites special privileged status which exempted them from normal civic requirements. They controlled their own local political system, their own economic enterprise, and their own educational system. They could import foreign goods without import charges. They were exempted from military service. The Mennonites did have to pay land and income taxes and to allow national health and police officials access into the colonies to carry out national requirements; but they had remarkable freedom and autonomy, in a country formally ruled by a military dictatorship, to organize their common life, as well as the Indian settlement program, in their own way.

The Mennonite mission-settlement program has had its critics both inside and outside the Mennonite communities. The most influential critic has been a Paraguayan anthropologist, Miguel Chase Sardi. At a 1971 symposium on interethnic conflict in South America, sponsored by the World Council of Churches Programme to Combat Racism, Sardi accused the Mennonites of violating Indian culture and of economic exploitation.[7] Mennonite doctors, Sardi wrote, have so mismanaged birth control devices that "cases of death by hemorrhage are frequent." Sardi said that Mennonite farmers become wealthy by employing Indian laborers at substandard wages, and manage the marketing of Indian products in a way which keeps the Indians in debt. Sardi's charges were made in a context of a general indictment of all settler and mission contacts with Indian peoples in Paraguay. The World Council of Churches symposium where it was presented drafted a statement which recommended the withdrawal of all missionaries from contacts with the Indians.[8]

The Mennonites have said that some of Sardi's accusations are fabrications, while others are biased formulations of situations which have been acknowledged and are being dealt with in the settlement program. Calvin Redekop responded to Sardi with an article in the July 1973 *International Review of Mission.* It was Redekop's judgment that the Mennonites, despite failures and exceptions, "have not exploited the

Indians but instead have established schools, hospitals, churches, cooperatives, farms and industries to help the indigenous peoples survive extinction and take their place in the modern world."9

Some Comparisons

The Mennonite missions experience in the Chaco is still in its developing stages in the late 1970s, and a final judgment on the encounter is premature. But this unique program invites comparison at a number of levels with other Mennonite historical experiences in missions endeavor.

The Chaco mission-settlement program has apparently resulted in a more complete obliteration of traditional native culture than is true for any other Mennonite mission program. The Chaco Indian tribes were hunters and herders, unlike the agricultural peoples Mennonites encountered in India, China, and Africa. A more comparable situation would be the Mennonite mission to the Cheyenne and Arapaho Indians, where colonization efforts proved unsuccessful and where Indians held onto more elements of their traditional culture and identity.

The settlement program in the Chaco has been remarkably successful, and may in fact be virtually without historical precedent as a model by which one modernized community aided hunting and herding peoples to make the transition to agricultural life. Compared to the failures of the United States government policy to turn Native Americans into agriculturists on reservations in the nineteenth century, the Mennonite Chaco program is most impressive. Mennonite ideology—particularly the doctrines of nonresistance and missions—had much to do with the evolution of the settlement program. If the Mennonites had not been pacifists, if they had been prepared to destroy the Indians with military weapons as happened on other frontiers, an Indian settlement program may have been neither necessary nor possible.

The issues of economic justice and social separation remained as major ongoing problems, however. Mennonites benefited from cheap Indian labor. The Mennonites were relatively wealthy and the Indians were relatively poor, and this disparity was a source of potential conflict. In their other mission programs, wealthy North American Mennonites had been separated from their economically poor mission churches as in, for example, India and Zaire. But in Paraguay the Mennonites were cast into a situation where they competed for limited economic resources with the Indians who had been converted by their mission efforts. Many of these Paraguayan Mennonites could recall their recent history in Russia where the relatively wealthy Mennonite German-speaking colonists were driven out after the Russian revolution by Russians who resented Mennonite wealth and cultural separateness. The missions-settlement program must be successful to keep the

Mennonites from once again reaping the whirlwind.

The Mennonite communities in the Chaco face continuing social changes of their own in coming decades. Their isolation from Paraguayan society and economy has been gradually breaking down, especially since the completion of the trans-Chaco road in 1961. A slow transition from the German to the Spanish language is taking place. Meanwhile Mennonites are slowly losing mastery and control over relationships with the Indians as Indians are becoming more self-conscious and more articulate in making their demands and in establishing direct contacts with the Paraguayan government. There remain many fascinating chapters to be written in this story of one of the last geographical frontiers on the earth.

Uruguay and Brazil

General Conference Mennonite mission work in Latin America has been marked by increasing degrees of inter-Mennonite cooperation. The Paraguay Chaco work has had an inter-Mennonite base since the founding of Light to the Indians in 1932. A new Mennonite Missions Committee for Paraguay (MMKFP) was organized in 1963 with membership from Mennonite groups in Paraguay and the GC and MC Mennonite mission boards in North America. MMKFP mission projects included radio evangelism and a Christian bookstore at Asunción.

Another inter-Mennonite project was the founding of the Mennonite Biblical Seminary in Montevideo, Uruguay, in 1956 to meet the need for trained church leaders and missionaries in the Mennonite colonies and growing national churches. The GC and MC (Elkhart) mission boards took primary responsibility for providing financial support and teaching faculty for the seminary. Nelson Litwiller, career MC missionary in Argentina, was the first president. Ernst Harder, whose pilgrimage had led from Russia to Germany, Paraguay, and the United States, became president in 1966. Students from the Montevideo seminary, a few of whom came from Colombia and Mexico to join the majority from lower Latin America, took positions of leadership in the churches. Kornelius Isaac, on furlough from mission work in 1956, used a year of study at the seminary to improve his ability in the Spanish language. After reaching a peak enrollment of about fifty students, the numbers of students declined until the seminary had to close in 1974. Factors in the decline included an extended political crisis in Uruguay, the absence of a professional ministry in colony churches to provide jobs for seminary graduates, and the increasing Mennonite mastery of the Spanish language which enabled young students to attend national schools and universities.[10] In November 1977 a new Mennonite seminary opened with six students at Asunción, Paraguay, with the hope of carrying on the tradition of the Montevideo seminary.

Location of Mennonite Colonies in Brazil and Uruguay

PARAGUAY

New Witmarsum

Curitiba

Curitiba Settlements

Blumenau

Old Witmarsum Settlement

BRAZIL

ARGENTINA

Colonia Novo
(Mennonite Settlement)

Brabancia

El Ombú

URUGUAY

Atlantic Ocean

Buenos Aires

Montevideo

From the Mennonite migration from Russia to Brazil there have grown three GC congregations, two in the Curitiba area and one fifty miles (eighty kilometers) northwest, with a total of about five hundred members. These congregations belong to a GC South American Conference of Mennonite Churches which includes churches from Uruguay and Paraguay and which holds triennial meetings. Mennonite mission activity in Brazil has resulted in Portuguese-speaking congregations around Curitiba and Witmarsum. The MC (Elkhart) mission board has carried on mission work in Brazil since 1954, and the GC churches have joined the MC churches and mission in an Association of Evangelical Mennonites of Brazil since 1964. The GC Commission on Overseas Mission sent its first missionaries to Brazil in December 1975 when Erwin and Angela Albrecht Rempel began working in Gama, near Brasilia. Mennonites of Brazil served as hosts to the Ninth Mennonite World Conference, held in Curitiba in 1972.

Bolivia and Costa Rica

In the 1970s General Conference Mennonite mission work was extended to the two additional countries of Bolivia and Costa Rica. MCC was engaged in development work in the Santa Cruz area of Bolivia since 1960, and evangelistic work began with Sunday school classes and prayer groups started by MCC volunteers. The GC Commission on Overseas Mission became involved in this work together with the MC (Elkhart) mission board and Mennonites from Argentina, who began church planting work. LaVerne and Harriet Fischbach Rutschman were the first GC missionaries to go to Bolivia in 1974. Rutschman reported in 1975 that four church nuclei had been established with a total of forty-two baptized believers. In 1976 an executive committee to coordinate the mission work was set up, with two missionaries, two Bolivians, and two MCC workers on the committee. There were eleven Mennonite settler colonies in Bolivia, made up of immigrants from Mexico, Canada, Paraguay, and Belize. MCC endeavored to establish relationships with the colony leaders, but with only limited success. The mission work in Bolivia did not grow out of, and was not directly related to, the Mennonite settler colonies.

In 1975 Rutschman accepted a new assignment as professor of Old Testament and Hebrew at Latin American Biblical Seminary in San José, Costa Rica. This seminary was a progressive and innovative institution which creatively sought new form and content for theological education in the Latin American context. It was hoped that a Mennonite professor could represent an Anabaptist point of view in the theological dialogue at the seminary. Evangelical theologians in Latin America in the 1970s were increasingly interested in Anabaptist understandings of the church and discipleship, influenced in part by John Howard Yoder's book, *The Politics of Jesus.*[11] It was also hoped that Latin American Biblical Seminary could attract Mennonite students from Colombia and Central America.

Mexico

From 1922 to 1926 there took place a great migration of Old Colony Mennonites from Canada to Mexico. These were conservative farming people who had come from Russia to Canada in the 1870s, but who left Canada in order to maintain their own cultural separateness, their schools, language, dress, and other customs.[12] Most of the five or six thousand Old Colonists who migrated to Mexico in the early 1920s settled in the state of Chihuahua in the area around the city of Cuauhtémoc; a few settled in the state of Durango and in other states. A smaller group of Sommerfelder Mennonites also moved to Mexico. Another small group from Russia who were not allowed to enter Canada for health reasons after World War I also found their way to the Cuauhtémoc area.

The Russian Mennonite group, which was far more modern in outlook and life-style than the Old Colonists, organized their own church congregation in 1935 with the help of H. P. Krehbiel of Newton, Kansas.[13] This Hoffnungsau congregation, which joined the GC Western District, suffered from the migration of members to Canada and to the United States, and from disagreements over relationships with ex-members of the Old Colony.

The Mennonite Central Committee began work in the Cuauhtémoc area in 1947, concentrating at first upon a health program, but moving into relief and agricultural development after a prolonged drought in 1951-53. MCC aid was available to Old Colony people as well as to Mexican nationals, but the Old Colonists were deeply suspicious that MCC's intention was to undermine their traditional way of life. In 1957, MCC services in Cuauhtémoc were handed over to the GC Board of Christian Service. Eventually the work in Mexico came under the Commission on Overseas Mission, as agreed at the time of the 1968 constitutional revision of the General Conference. GC church members, mostly from Canada, had supplied most of the workers for Mexico from the time of MCC's earliest involvement.

The Old Colony leaders successfully resisted the authority and spiritual influence of GC mission workers in Mexico. They exercised severe discipline against their members who associated with the missionaries. Old Colony members who sent their children to outside schools, for example, were excommunicated. While the mission work did not achieve the goal of progressive change and spiritual renewal within the Old Colony settlements themselves, there did emerge three General Conference church congregations (at Cuauhtémoc, Steinreich, and Burwalde) which formed the basis for the ongoing ministry. The membership of the congregations totalled 315 in 1977; they operated five day schools and a high school at Cuauhtémoc. [14] The achievement of strong institutions was hindered, however, by the tendency of young people and potential leaders to emigrate to Canada. Even though this area of northern Mexico had made great economic growth and progress since the Mennonites arrived in the 1920s, it was not felt to be an attractive and secure home by non-Old Colony Mennonites who lived there.

Although the story in Mexico has been primarily one of troubled inter-Mennonite relationships, there also have been efforts to evangelize and minister among national peoples. In the 1940s a missionary named Randall Groening, supported by the Bergthaler Mennonite Church in Manitoba, initiated evangelical and agricultural work among the Tarahuanara Indians to the west of Cuauhtémoc. MCC medical and agricultural services were designed to help Spanish-speaking nationals as well as the Mennonites. When the Mexican government adopted an agricultural experimentation program along lines started by MCC, the Mennonite workers took up employment in the government program. The mission has undertaken programs for Spanish-language religious radio broadcasting. The Mennonite congregations hold Sunday school classes for Mexicans on Sunday afternoons in the town of Anáhuac. There were no Spanish-speaking GC Mennonite congregations in Mexico in 1978, but the vision for moving in that direction was taking shape.

Members of the Spiritual Healing Church in Mochudi, Botswana, 1973.

Photo by James C. Juhnke

11 A New Model for Missions

African Independent Churches

Mokaleng Motswasele, a man of the Barolong tribe who lived in the village of Matsiloje on the Botswana (then Bechuanaland) side of the Shashi River, received the power of Christian healing and prophecy in 1952.[1] He separated from the church where he had been worshiping, the St. John's Apostolic Faith Mission, and founded his own church which he called the Apostolic Spiritual Healing Church. Prophet Mokaleng soon became widely known as a healer-prophet in central southern Africa. He healed in the name of Christ "by water alone," admonishing his followers to throw away their traditional fetishes. His church grew to become one of the larger churches in the small country of Botswana, gathering many who had been nominal members of older established missions churches.

The prophet's oldest son, Israel Motswasele, received a modern education including some study in a seminary in Lesotho, and eventually became the president of the Apostolic Spiritual Healing Church. The son was not a healer-prophet like his father, but did have the gifts of efficient administration and strong leadership. Although this church lacked the benefits of overseas missionary funds, personnel, schools, and hospitals, it was rich in the resources of authentic African rhythm, worship style, and spiritual vitality. When it was officially recognized and registered by the Botswana government in 1973 (and required to shorten its name to Spiritual Healing Church), the church was constructing new church buildings at a faster rate than any other group in the country. Mennonites first became acquainted with the church in 1972 when three of its members accepted an invitation to attend the annual MCC southern African retreat in Francistown, Botswana.

The rise of the Spiritual Healing Church in Botswana was part of a vast movement of separate independent churches in Africa which, according to a 1967 accounting, numbered over five thousand groups, had nearly seven million adherents, and increased at a rate of over three hundred thousand adherents per year.[2] There was great variety in this mass of proliferating groups. Some groups, often identified as "Ethiopian," became organizationally independent while retaining patterns of worship and church life similar to that in missions churches. Other groups, in southern Africa identified as a "Zionist" type, emphasized certain charismatic gifts of prophesy, healing, and religious expression rooted more directly in African tradition.

Mission churches typically viewed the separatists with alarm, sometimes condemning them as the Antichrist and conspiring with colonial governments to have the movements outlawed. In recent decades a great deal of literature has appeared in which the independent churches have been described and evaluated.[3] While on one hand the independent church movement has been seen as the result of a "failure in love" by Western-oriented missions, it has also been suggested that the movement represents a way to evangelize peoples of Africa through cultural forms which are more indigenous and authentic than those brought by missionaries.

The Kimbanguists

The largest independent church on the continent of Africa is the Church of Jesus Christ on Earth Through the Prophet Simon Kimbangu, or the "Kimbanguist" church, which has its "Jerusalem" at the former home of the prophet at the village on N'Kamba in lower Zaire.[4] Simon Kimbangu received his first vision during the worldwide influenza epidemic of 1918, and after a brief ministry was arrested and imprisoned in 1921 by Belgian colonial authorities on false charges of sedition. He died thirty years later in prison, but his movement survived decades of persecution and eventually gained acceptance in independent Zaire as the second largest church in the country.

Mennonites in Zaire had mixed reactions to the Kimbanguists. The Africa Inter-Mennonite Mission missionaries and the Mennonite church in Zaire, who were in a position of competition with this burgeoning denomination, tended to be suspicious. But some North American Mennonites, especially those associated through Mennonite Central Committee, were interested and enthusiastic about prospects for Mennonite-Kimbanguist contacts. The Kimbanguists maintained a spirit of nonviolence toward their opponents, based on Kimbangu's teaching and upon his submission as he reenacted the passion of Jesus in his own persecution, arrest, and imprisonment. Harold Fehderau and Clarence Hiebert, traveling for the MCC Peace Section in 1967, saw a parallel between the Mennonite doctrine of nonresistance and the

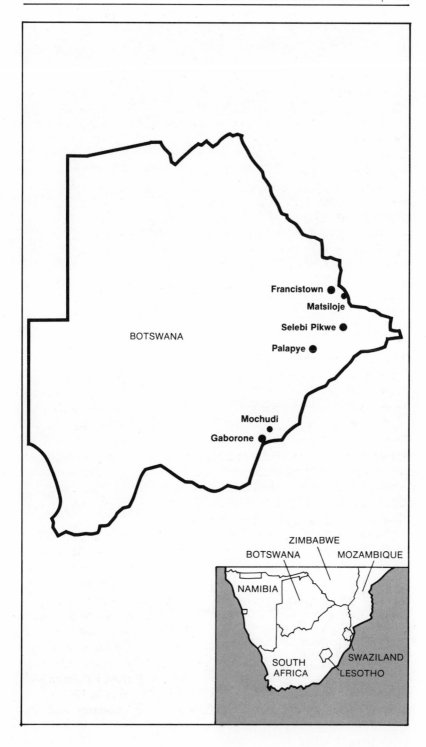

apparent Kimbanguist teaching. But Fehderau and Hiebert also reported, "In almost every instance of speaking with missionaries, I sensed real resistance to the idea of setting up contacts with Kimbanguists."[5]

James Bertsche was one AIMM missionary who was interested in pursuing relationships with the Kimbanguists. After some reading and research into the movement, Bertsche wrote an article entitled "Kimbanguism: A Challenge to Missionary Statesmanship," in which he called for mutually beneficial contacts and suggested that future developments would determine whether Kimbanguism would move in the direction of syncretism or of Christian orthodoxy.[6] Bertsche's interest and openness were important, because in 1974 he became executive secretary of AIMM.

The opening for mission work with independent churches (apart from limited MCC involvements in Zaire) was to come in southern Africa rather than in Zaire. There were no Mennonite missions or churches in Botswana, Lesotho, and Swaziland, so it was possible to establish contacts without complicating or straining relationships with an already existing national Mennonite church.

An Entirely New Direction

Edwin and Irene Lehman Weaver, two seasoned Mennonite missionaries who had experience both in India and in pioneer work with independent churches in West Africa, became the pathbreakers for AIMM work with independent churches in southern Africa.[7] The Weavers included southern Africa in a 1973 tour sponsored by two Mennonite church mission boards, and in 1974 they accepted an assignment under AIMM for one year in Botswana to make the contacts and lay the groundwork for mission work there. Mennonite Central Committee had been supplying teachers and development workers to Botswana since 1968. Some of these workers had been in touch with the Apostolic Spiritual Healing Church and with other independent churches since 1972. The Weavers were joined and followed by missionaries who began various kinds of ministries with and for independent churches in Gaborone, Francistown, Palapye, and Selebi-Pikwe.

AIMM also began work in Lesotho in 1973, first in youth work with the Lesotho Evangelical Church and then in pastoral work with a United Church of Maseru congregation in the capital city. A ministry among independent churches in Lesotho became possible through the help of Samuel Mohono, a pastor who was also secretary of the Lesotho Bible Society. Stan and Lorri Berends Nussbaum in 1977 became the first AIMM missionaries to Lesotho who were assigned specifically to work as Bible teachers to independent churches.

James Bertsche noted in a 1975 report to the COM that involvement with independent churches was taking AIMM in an "entirely new direction." The policy outlines for the new direction were suggested in a set of eight guidelines adopted in 1976.[8] AIMM's primary interest was in supplying Bible teachers, and the method was to be oriented to "grass roots, non-formal, TEE (theological education by extension), inductive type of Bible study." AIMM would not build institutions or provide budget monies for other organizations. The accent in this work was to be upon the services that persons could provide as teachers and as facilitators of communication between people and groups.

One guideline for the work was that AIMM missionaries would work with several independent churches in a given country, rather than focusing upon one particular church. In Botswana, where early contacts with Mokaleng's Spiritual Healing Church might have led to a special relationship with AIMM, care was taken to make contacts with other groups from the beginning. It was a goal of the work to foster dialogue among the leaders of these churches both within their own country and elsewhere in southern Africa, as well as to facilitate contacts between leaders of independent churches and mission churches. The multichurch approach was also designed to avoid the possibility of AIMM becoming an overseas sponsor of a particular church and thus reduplicating the problems of dependence experienced elsewhere.

To Learn as Well as Teach

Another guideline was that missionaries should, in Bertsche's words, "walk softly among the independent church folk." This was to be a low-profile ministry of servanthood. Missionaries were counseled to bear a nonjudgmental spirit, even when they found certain practices of the churches to be strange or distasteful. Missionaries were not to be policymakers for the church, nor were they on the front line of evangelism. They were rather to serve in various roles of Bible teaching and leadership training, and to let growth emerge out of mutually respectful dialogue. They were expected to learn as well as to teach. This task required missionaries liberally endowed with the virtues of maturity, tolerance, and patience.

AIMM was also clear that this work to and with independent churches had no hidden goal of the establishment of Mennonite churches in southern Africa. It might have been possible to "buy" one or more Mennonite churches in southern Africa by offering certain resources to a group that would add the name Mennonite to its title. But such a procedure would violate a central principle of the work—respect for the independence and integrity of the churches.

One characteristic of AIMM's involvement in southern Africa was a high degree of inter-Mennonite cooperation and communication. The central forum for exchange of information and for cooperative planning among the various Mennonite agencies interested in southern Africa was the Council on International Mission (CIM), earlier known as the Council of Mission Board Secretaries. The three agencies most deeply involved in southern Africa were Mennonite Central Committee, Africa Inter-Mennonite Mission, and the Eastern Mennonite Board of Missions and Charities. MCC placed workers in Botswana, Lesotho, and Swaziland, and assessed possibilities for work in South Africa or in the South African homelands. The Eastern Board, which had a major mission church in Tanzania, took up work with independent churches in Swaziland. The shadows of troubled race relations in South Africa and Rhodesia (Zimbabwe) were present for all who lived and worked in southern Africa. In regions dominated and ruled by a wealthy white minority, it was important for the Mennonite witness to incorporate concerns for human dignity, justice, and liberation.

In 1976 the Mennonite Brethren Church officially joined AIMM, placing a member on the AIMM board in order to follow through an interest in the work with independent churches. The first MB missionaries to work with AIMM in Botswana were Irvin and Lydia Gunther Friesen, who worked at Palapye and Selebi-Pikwe, and John and Ruth Fast Kliewer, who followed the Weavers as country coordinators in Gaborone.

The new frontier of mission work among independent churches in southern Africa generated much excitement among North American Mennonite church and mission leaders in the 1970s. As is perhaps true of all innovations, however, there was concern whether this new thrust would be understood and accepted by rank-and-file missions supporters in the churches. It was, after all, a much different model of mission work than had been known in the past. One would not be able to tally the results of this work by the traditional benchmarks—persons baptized, institutions built, or Mennonite congregations founded. The AIMM board approached a goals, priorities, and strategy meeting in the spring of 1979 without clear-cut criteria for assessing the success or failure of this new venture. In a new era of missions, however, when the accent was upon young churches, independent of missionary control, as well as upon cultural authenticity in worship and church life, the AIMM experiments with new strategies of mission in southern Africa deserved serious attention and consideration.

Foreign Mission Board, 1908: (back) J. W. Kliewer, C. H. A. van der Smissen, C. H. Wedel; (front) S. F. Sprunger, A. B. Shelly, Gustav Harder

Commission of Overseas Mission, 1978: (back) Peter J. Dyck, Milton Claassen, Paul Detwiler, Margaret Ewert, Henry T. Dueck, Arthur C. Waltner, Anne Warkentin Dyck, Larry Kehler, Harris Waltner; (front) Albert Bauman, Loretta Fast, Harold Schultz, Vern Preheim, Jeanne Pierson Zook, Jacob K. Klassen.

12 A People of Mission

There have been four major thrusts, or periods of expansion of mission work to new fields, in General Conference Mennonite missions history.

The first thrust began with the mission to the Native Americans in 1880; the second with the planting of missions in India (1900), China (1910), and Zaire (1912); the third with the beginning of mission work in Japan, Taiwan, and Colombia in the postwar era; and the fourth in the 1970s with expansion into new areas of Africa and Latin America.

First Thrust: To Native Americans

Although the first thrust began with the mission to the Arapaho and Cheyenne in 1880, momentum had been building since the founding of the General Conference in 1860 and the Mennonite seminary in Wadsworth, Ohio, in 1868. From the beginning there was a close connection between Mennonite higher education and missions. However, both higher education and missions in the early decades had to overcome the resistance to change of a conservative, German-speaking, religious-ethnic community.

Mennonites had a history of persecution and sanctuary. The missions movement was part of a coming out into the world, and it was fraught with the dangers of creeping worldliness. The mission movement came on the scene with a new vocabulary, new organizational structures, a new group of leaders, and new claims upon the resources of church members. Traditionalist Mennonites sensed that something of Mennonite simplicity, humility, and separateness was being lost in the rush toward the modern missions movement. They were probably right. It was the price of a new awakening to the biblical missionary responsibility of the church—an awakening received at the hands of a Protestant community which had once persecuted Mennonites with bitter violence.

207

Mission work among the Arapaho and Cheyenne Native Americans (and, after 1893, the Hopi in Arizona) fell far short of the first hopes. Native Americans resisted the gospel preached by white people who followed the wake of buffalo hunters and the United States cavalry. The Mennonites never fully appreciated how their mission work was handicapped by identification with whites who destroyed the very life sources of the Cheyenne and Arapaho people. The situation for Mennonite missionaries in India, China, and Congo was qualitatively different. In these overseas fields Mennonite missionaries worked for the most part with people who remained in control of their traditional means of economic production. It was easier for these people to receive the gospel as a message of liberation than it was for Native Americans whose world had been destroyed by whites.

Mennonites were undaunted by the meager results among Native Americans. The missionary movement at the turn of the century generated momentum quite independent of reports of people converted and churches founded. News of hindrances and failures only generated a redoubling of conviction and effort.

Second Thrust: To India, China, Congo

The second thrust was identified with the onset of the twentieth century, hailed in its time as the *Christian* century. Mission stations were planted in the rural interior of India (1900), China (1910), and Zaire (then Congo, 1912). Mennonites had arrived late on the field. They joined Protestant missionary efforts which had been under way for many decades. They accepted the counsel of others on where to find open areas for work, and they established imposing missionary stations with medical and educational institutions to minister to the needy. They evangelized with vigor and looked forward to the Christianization of the heathen social order.

This generation of mission station founders was made up of hardworking inner-directed pioneers who had made lifetime commitments. They worked up to nine years before the luxury of a furlough. They made their own policy decisions on the field. It was two decades before the first mission board representative visited the missionaries in the field. But the news was more encouraging from the far-off lands than it had been from the reservations close to home. Small congregations of new Christians emerged from the poor and outcaste people with whom Mennonite missionaries worked.

The similarities among these three overseas mission fields are striking. In each case Mennonites worked in villages of remote interior plains, and focused their efforts upon rural peoples who were poor and uneducated. In each case missionaries endeavored to address themselves to the broad range of human needs—emergency relief in times of drought, flood, and famine; clinics, hospitals, and asylums for people needing medical care; schools for boys and girls who would otherwise remain illiterate; a new spiritual center for those who decided to become Christians and join the church. In each case missionaries were identified, more than they realized, with the attitudes and life-styles of foreign colonial powers.

The differences among the fields were also notable. Events seemed to unfold most rapidly in China, where political instability led to repeated missionary evacuations and eventual exclusion. Christian missions in China eventually had to bear the stigma of failure, given the apparent collapse of the church after the Communist revolution. But the "failure" was deceptive. In 1940 Mennonites in China were better educated and had a stronger core of leadership than in GC missions in India, Congo, or Oklahoma. The Mennonite mission in China had been at least as successful as those in India and Congo in providing human services, initiating social change, and developing churches through the mission-station-based strategy. Mennonite missionaries in China were the first to face the difficult questions of transferring authority from the mission to the new church. The issue turned into an unhappy struggle for power. For twelve years (1923-35) the mission and church were unable to agree on a constitution which would define their respective prerogatives. Mission and church in their own way reflected the political and social upheavals of China in her troubled relationship with Western nations.

The church in India, made up of people from the lowest castes, could not rise to maturity as rapidly as in China. The pervasive caste system reinforced relationships of dominance and subordination between mission and church. Christians of low-caste origin in India might be able to overcome their former caste restrictions through education and wage-earning employment, but they somehow retained their culturally ingrained habits of deference to superior authority. In the new Christian communities, to exaggerate somewhat, the missionaries unwittingly displaced the Brahmans, the upper caste to which the lower people naturally deferred.[1] India benefited from greater political stability and continuity than China, but it was a Hindu-dominated political order in which Christians—particularly in the Central Provinces—remained on the defensive. The GC Mennonite mission remained dominant in relationship to the national church for a longer period of time than in Congo or China.

The Congo Inland Mission in its first decades lacked the stable leadership and identity which were provided by P. A. Penner in India and H. J. Brown in China. Resistance to the Christian gospel was apparently not as great in societies which lacked written Scriptures and a long heritage of "revealed religion." In the Congo, Christianity became the predominant religion of the independent nation. Because the Catholic and Protestant missions had a complete monopoly of education in the colonial period, all national leaders in the new Congo came out of Christian mission schools. But education in the colonial era was geared to educating people at elementary levels rather than choosing a few who would be prepared for leadership roles. There emerged in Congo a church which was vigorous and growing at the local level, but lacking in leaders to replace the missionaries in leadership positions in the 1950s and 1960s. Under the leadership of CIM executive secretary Harvey Driver in the 1950s, the mission expanded rapidly while preparing for transfer of authority to the national church. The path of church-mission "integration," with the national church eventually taking the dominant role, was fixed for Congo Inland Mission just prior to the upheavals which came with the Belgian departure in 1960.

A Thirty-Year Pause

In the three decades between the beginning of the First World War and the end of the Second World War—or between the GC decision in 1914 to take over the Brown mission in China and the 1945 arrival of Gerald and Mary Hope Stucky in Colombia—the General Conference did not open mission work in any new countries. There were a number of reasons for this extended pause. Even though North American Mennonite church giving for missions increased dramatically during and immediately after the First World War, the mission board preferred to use resources to develop the mission work already started among Native Americans and overseas. General Conference Mennonites cooperated with others in the postwar period through a new organizational structure—the Mennonite Central Committee—which provided relief for victims of war and famine in South Russia and elsewhere. The General Conference was a small denomination and the demands from missionaries in already established fields outstripped available funds and personnel. The economic depression of the 1930s eventually forced cutbacks in budget and programs, and made expansion to new countries unthinkable. Moreover, the church was afflicted by the fundamentalist-modernist conflicts in the interwar years.

Third Thrust: Japan, Taiwan, Colombia

A new missions expansion—a third outward thrust—occurred in the years after the Second World War. The General Conference had been strengthened with immigrants from Russia, primarily to Canada, who were now sufficiently settled to make a major contribution to missions. High agricultural productivity and favorable prices during the war had been good for North American Mennonite pocketbooks. As a nonresistant, pacifist people who were unable to identify with excessive nationalism and militarism of the war years, Mennonites were eager to engage in positive altruistic enterprises whose goals and methods they could affirm. In the postwar era, General Conference Mennonites started new mission work in Japan, Taiwan, Colombia, and, together with Mennonite settler communities, in the Latin American countries of Paraguay and Uruguay.

The new workers of this postwar thrust had to deal with a set of complex forces set loose by the war. Movements of anticolonialism and national independence in Asia, Africa, and Latin America fueled the desire of Mennonite leaders in national churches to become free from dependence upon missionary control and financing. In the new fields missionaries tried to apply the "lesson of China." Missions should be less oriented toward mission stations and institutions and more directed toward the development of churches which would survive in case missionaries had to leave.

The Second World War led to a burst of activity by Mennonite Central Committee not only for war relief in Europe but also for relief and development in other countries around the world. Executives of Mennonite mission boards increasingly responded to intitiatives from MCC programs and from the leadership of MCC executive secretaries Orie O. Miller and William T. Snyder. The patterns of relationships between mission board and MCC varied widely from country to country. In Taiwan the GC mission took over the MCC-initiated program intact. In Japan the MCC Peace Section established an office which attempted to activate and focus a Mennonite peace witness for Mennonites in the country. In Paraguay MCC assisted Mennonites migrating from Russia and provided major funding for the program of agricultural settlements for the Chaco Indians. In Colombia MCC sponsored a development program—Mencoldes—with a Colombian Mennonite director and board, including the cooperation of both the General Conference Mennonite and the Mennonite Brethren churches.

Cooperative planning among Mennonite agencies became increasingly important in the postwar era, not only between various mission boards and MCC, but also in new groupings of Mennonite overseas churches. An Asia Mennonite Fellowship emerged in the 1970s, with members from churches in India, Indonesia, Taiwan, and Japan, and felt its way toward a cooperative mission in Bangladesh. National Mennonite churches in Africa and in Latin America held regional meetings to share concerns and plans. It was widely felt in the 1970s that the splintered organizational structures of separated Mennonite mission boards in North America, and of separated newly independent Mennonite churches in other countries, were in need of reconsideration and reevaluation. A Council on International Mission in North America, made up of mission board and MCC representatives, took on new coordinating responsibilities. The Mennonite World Conference became an important forum for sharing among Mennonite churches around the world.

Fourth Thrust: Africa and Latin America

A fourth thrust of General Conference missions expansion into new fields took place in the 1970s, although it was still too early to judge whether this recent movement would have equivalent impact to the earlier three. The Africa Inter-Mennonite Mission expanded into Upper Volta and initiated a new form of mission work in cooperation with independent African churches in Botswana and Lesotho. COM sponsored workers in the new areas of Bolivia, Costa Rica, and Brazil. But the possibilities of expansion were restricted by the severe effects of worldwide inflation. Young people who were willing to make lifetime career commitments to missionary work did not seem to be as numerous as two decades earlier. As always, the future of the missionary enterprise depended upon the continuing commitments and sacrifices of people in the churches.

A Century of Change

In his spirited, one-hundred-page missions manifesto of 1877, Samuel S. Haury argued that a major reason Mennonites should begin a vigorous missions effort was to bring blessing and revival to the church at home. Mennonites should stop fighting and banning each other over matters of outward form, said Haury, and rather turn their attention to "the foundation essence of Christianity—the new birth and the spread of the kingdom of Christ."[2]

"The Kingdom of God in a Changing World" was the theme of the Tenth Mennonite World Conference a century later in Wichita, Kansas, in July 1978. Haury, had he still been alive, might have been gratified to see the extent to which his hope and his promise had been fulfilled. From a century ago when not a single Mennonite from North America was involved in overseas mission work, Mennonites of various groups had spread out to all the corners of the earth to preach the gospel. Petty bickering among Mennonite groups had not ended, to be sure, and the church had not really found the key to transcending its tribal-ethnic boundaries in North America. But the story of church planting and growth in foreign lands had been, by and large, a huge success, and the focus upon that effort through the decades had helped to give purpose and unity to the churches at home. By the 1970s, the number of Mennonites of non-European, non-American background was nearly as great as the number who claimed biological European roots.[3]

Haury surely would have been bewildered in Wichita by the cultural variety in the ways Mennonites around the world expressed their faith. There were Taiwanese Mennonite women doing traditional Chinese folk dances. There were Mennonite youth from India accompanying their singing with the strange rhythms and sounds of the tabla and sitar. There was a Cheyenne women's group singing with a high-pitched nasal sound that Haury in his own time had identified with heathenism.

Christianity had been indigenized. There had been a time when new converts in Africa and Asia expressed their new faith by learning to sing "Gott ist die Liebe" or "Jesus Loves Me, This I Know." Now American Mennonites struggled in their turn to learn the non-Western tunes which appeared in the international Mennonite World Conference songbook.

In 1877 Haury had called for missions programs which would engage in programs of social transformation—to root out the evils of cannibalism, child sacrifice, widow burning, polygamy, slavery, and the oppression of women and children.[4] A century later he would find much to rejoice over in the history of Mennonite missionary confrontation with injustice and oppression—the assault on caste in India, on foot binding in China, on baby killing in Paraguay, and much more. But Haury would also be surprised to discover how the years had revealed the paganism and the heathenism which were a part of the social, economic, and political structures of Western Christendom. Mennonite World Conference speakers in 1978 repeatedly decried the structural evils in the modern industrialized world which threatened destruction of civilization in nuclear holocaust, fostered a widening gap between rich and poor nations, and despoiled the earth's environment.[5]

A New Spirit

Perhaps the greatest shift that had taken place in Mennonite missions was the erosion of the confident wholeness which inspired the founders of missions around the turn of the century. The early missionaries were sure of the rightness of their message, their strategy, and their ultimate triumph. They did not doubt the essential goodness of their own national and Germanic culture. Haury, and those who followed him, were quite aware that missionaries had been accused of sallying forth with the sword in one hand and the Bible in the other. He conceded that "so-called Christians have committed countless crimes against the heathen peoples they have come in contact with."[6] But this was only added cause for the enlightened, modern missionary enterprise to make up for the sins of the past. Missionaries who sought no personal reward or profit would preach a transforming gospel to redeem and liberate peoples in bondage to fear, superstition, and injustice. God would give the victory.

Many forces combined to tarnish this vision of confidence and wholeness. One corrosive force was the impact of two great world wars in the allegedly "Christian" West. Visions of social and religious progress, whether in missions or in other endeavors, had trouble surviving in an era when the so-called civilized peoples so senselessly destroyed each other.

Another fragmenting force was the impact of the fundamentalist-modernist debate in Mennonite circles. Not only did this debate alienate Mennonites from each other, it also divided soul from body and evangelism from social action in Mennonite understandings. The General Conference lacked a clear and commanding center position. Too many Mennonites thought they had to make a choice: If they were not modernists, they must be fundamentalists, and vice versa.

Nevertheless, it must be said that a widespread General Conference Mennonite agreement on the validity and urgency of the missionary cause was one force which kept General Conference conservatives and liberals together in the twentieth century.

Finally, the early confidence was eroded when movements of anticolonialism and national independence revealed that missionaries and mission programs, to a much greater degree than they had intended or realized, had absorbed the attitudes and patterns of paternalism and condescension which were a part of their social-political environment. The transition from missionary control to national church independence and control was experienced with great frustration in nearly every country where missionaries worked. This was not because missionaries were uncommitted to the goal of independent national churches, for that goal had been repeatedly affirmed from the beginning. Everyone had simply underestimated the difficulties of this transition.

When the transition in fact took place—when national Mennonite churches overcame dependence and subservience and began to fashion their own destiny—a new era in missions took shape. In this new era, the needed missionary qualities were those of patience and servanthood, rather than those of initiative and mastery which were needed in an earlier era. Where the archetypal missionary had once been P. A. Penner, a distinguished pioneer and founder of institutions, the model missionary for contemporary times was found in such people as Earl Roth in Zaire, who successfully transferred his positions of authority to national leaders in schools at Nyanga and Mukedi, and served as "missionary counselor" in a time of difficult transition.

The GC mission board worked to establish a new sense of focus in the 1970s. The Chicago conference of "Goals, Priorities, and Strategies" in 1972 charted the purposes and direction of mission work more comprehensively than had ever been done before in the General Conference Mennonite Church. A series of annual retreats for missionaries on furlough brought workers together from various fields to learn from each other and from missions leaders.

The Overseas Missions Training Center in Elkhart became more widely recognized and accepted as a place for GC Mennonite missionary preparation than had any other school in the past. Never in Mennonite history had there been such an abundance of reflective literature, study conferences, and historical investigations on missions themes.

A People of Mission

Mennonite missions is a twice-born movement. It was born first in the radical wing of the sixteenth-century Reformation, and it was born again in the late nineteenth century as a belated child of the modern Protestant missionary movement. As Mennonites seek resources to renew and reshape their missionary enterprise in the last decades of the twentieth century, they need to tap the principles of both their first and their second births in missions.

The collapse of Christendom as a motivating force in the twentieth century has lent new relevance to the Anabaptist sixteenth-century view of the church. The church is not a political establishment but a voluntary body of believers committed to obedience to Christ. Christians face the world as a prophetic minority rather than as a dominant majority. Essential to the missionary message is an emphasis upon the costs of discipleship in a world which, on the whole, rejects salvation in Christ. Mennonites bear a heritage and speak a language which is particularly appropriate for the contemporary scene of Christian missions.

At the same time North American Mennonites cannot deny that they have taken on the institutional shape, and much of the theology, of Protestant denominationalism. That Mennonites went into all the world to preach the gospel was due to a movement of Protestant renewal, not of Anabaptist renewal. Mennonites should celebrate this renewal, for it not only led them into greater faithfulness to the Great Commission, but it also helped free them from the traps of ethnic sectarianism. To be true to the best of their peculiar missionary heritage, Mennonites need to be in touch with other Christians who are also endeavoring to be people of mission.

List of
Missionaries

According to available records, these are the General Conference missionaries who have served in the United States under the Board of Missions/Commission on Overseas Mission, 1880 to 1968 (when these areas came under the administration of Commission on Home Ministries).

NAME	STATE SERVED	DATES
Allebach H. G.	Oklahoma	1897-98
Baerg Anna	Arizona, Colorado	1945-
Bartel Norman Mary Giesbrecht	Mexico, Oklahoma	1954-56, 1958-65, 1966-68
Boehr Mary	Arizona	1952-54
Brookover June	Montana	1920-21
Buller Marie	Montana	1941-42
Burkhalter Caroline	Arizona	1915-22
Busenitz Willis Nadine Wiebe	Oklahoma, Montana	1965-
Claassen Albert H. Catherine Andreas	Oklahoma	1912-20

Dalke
  Herbert
  Bertha Penner
	Oklahoma	1947-60

Diller
  Donavin
  June Geiger
	Montana	1957-62

Dirks Erna	Arizona	1957-59

Dirks
  Walter
  Marie Epp
	Montana	1965-69

Dirksen
  P. K.
  Dorothy Jantzen
	Arizona	1949-59

Duerksen
  Ed
  Elsie Graber
	Arizona	1961-?

Duerksen
  John R.
  Susie Quiring
	Arizona	1912-26

Ediger
  Jacob B.
  Agatha Regier
	Oklahoma	1907-47

Epp
  Jacob B.
  Nettie Harms
	Oklahoma, Arizona	1900-01, 1901-13

Epp
  J. H.
  Helene Ratzlaff
	Oklahoma	1904-07

Epp
  Larry
  Lorna Rempel
	Arizona	1960-62

Fehr Helen	Arizona	1966-68

Flickinger
  Calvin
  Sidonnia Nickel
	Arizona	1955-56

Frey
  Cornelius J.
  Anna Balzer
	Arizona	1912-14

Frey
  J. B.
  Aganetha Balzer
	Arizona	1903-29

Friesen
  Arthur
  Viola Graber
	Oklahoma	1940-58

Friesen
  Karl
  Frieda Balzer
	Arizona	1919-26

Froese	Arizona	1957-60, 1963-67
Isaac		
Margaret Neufeld		
Funk	Oklahoma	
J. A.		1896-1920
Cornelia Schwake		1899-1920
Goosen	Arizona	1948-54
Walter		
Ethel Koehn		
Habegger	Montana	
Alfred		1918-56
Barbara Hirschy		1918-58
Habegger	Montana	1949-50
David		
Harder	Arizona	1945-46, 1960
Waldo		
Abby Claassen		
Hart	Oklahoma	1963-68
Lawrence		
Betty Bartel		
Haury	Oklahoma	1880-87
Samuel S.		
Susanna Hirschler		
Hiebert	Oklahoma	1968-69
Henry C.		
Linda		
Hirschler	Oklahoma	
D. B.		1885-90
(Mrs.)		1885-87
Hirschler	Oklahoma	1888-90
Katie		
Horsch	Oklahoma	1892-1902
M. M.		
Ottilie Dettweiler		
Jantzen	Arizona	1950-70
Albert		
Wilma Lichti		
Johnson	Arizona	1922-46
Fred A.		
Minnie Jenkins		
Johnson	Arizona	1968-
Karl		
Louise		
Kaufman	Mississippi	1957-
Orlo		
Edna Goering		
Kehler	Arizona	1957-60
Katie		

Kinsinger Bertha (see Petter, Rodolphe)	Oklahoma, Montana	1896-1949
Klassen Rita	Arizona	1962-65
Kliewer Henry A. Hannah	Arizona	1947-70
Kliewer H. J. Christina Horsch	Oklahoma	1893-95, 1899-1936 1899-1936
Kliewer J. J. Helena Schmidt	Oklahoma	1884-97
Kliewer P. A. Katherine Braun	Montana	1908-19
Koehn Clifford Anna Ruth	Oklahoma	1960-75
Krehbiel J. S. Katie Ringleman	Oklahoma	1891-97
Linscheid G. A. Anna Hirschler	Oklahoma, Montana	1895-98, 1900-04, 1920-38
Littlewolf Frank (Mrs.)	Montana	1945-50
Mouttet Paul (Mrs.)	Oklahoma	1890-92
Neufeld H. T. Anna Harder	Oklahoma, Montana	1912-13, 1916-27
Nickel Norma	Arizona	1963-65
Nussbaum Harold Marie Wiebe	Arizona	1959-64, 1965-72 1966-72
Pankratz Otto B. Eva Winsky	Montana	1923-26
Penner Aganetha	Arizona	1955-67
Penner Helen A.	Arizona	1960-?

Peters	Arizona	1953-69
Herbert		
Justina Wiens		
Peters	Arizona	1966-68
William		
Sara Hiebert		
Petter	Oklahoma, Montana	
Rodolphe		1891-1947
Marie Gerber		1891-1910
Bertha Kinsinger		1911-1949
(see Kinsinger)		
Petter	Montana	
Valdo		1924-35
Laura Rohrman		1924-64
Ratzloff	Arizona	1964-65
Vernon		
Bonnie Sommers		
Regier	Mississippi	1957-70
Harold		
Rosella Wiens		
Rohrman	Montana	1936-37
Edward		
Roth	Arizona	1960-61 (?)
Earl		
Ruth Jantzen		
Schirmer	Arizona, Montana	1934-49, 1964-75
Daniel		
Amy Talasnemptewa		
Schirmer	Arizona	1907-11, 1913-19, 1930-43
Mary		
Schlink	Montana	1926-27
H. A.		
(Mrs.)		
Schmidt	Oklahoma	1954-63
August		
Esther Schmidt		
Schmidt	Arizona	1911-39
Elizabeth		
Shoulderblade	Montana	1965-73
James Benedict		
Julia		
Sprunger	Oklahoma	1965-75
Lyman		
Adeline Ensz		
Suderman	Arizona	1930-47
John		
Mabel Wedel		
Thiessen	Arizona	1961-
Margaret		

Tieszen Wanda Isaac	Arizona	1959-61

Toews
  Benno
  Catherine Friesen
	Oklahoma, Arizona	1938-40, 1954-56

Voth
  A. S.
  Katie Nickel
	Oklahoma	1886-95

Voth
  Heinrich R.
  Barbara Baer
  Martha Moser
	Oklahoma, Arizona	1883-91, 1893-98
		1883-89
		1893-98

Walde
  Herman
  Alice Braun
	Oklahoma	1959-63

Wenger
  Malcolm
  Esther Boehr
	Montana	1944-66

Whiteman
  Milton
  Moheno
	Montana	1945-?

Wiebe
  Alfred
  Agnes Thiessen
	Arizona, Montana	1911-15, 1920-22, 1947-59

Wiebe
  Leonard
  Marguerite Sprunger
	Arizona	1945-52

Williams Agnes	Oklahoma, Montana	1898-27, 1905-06

Zacharias
  Arthur
  Edna
	Arizona	1964-66

According to available records, these are the General Conference missionaries who have served overseas and in Mexico under the Board of Missions/Commission on Overseas Mission for at least two years, 1900 to 1978.

NAME	COUNTRY SERVED	DATES
Andres Esther Mae (see MacDonald)	Taiwan	1957-62
Augsburger Samuel Mary Wyse	Colombia	1967-69
Bachert Alice	Colombia	1948-68
Bargen Eldon Helen Bartel	Colombia	1962-64
Baergen Rita	Mexico	1959-61?
Banman Hulda	Zaire	1956-64, 1967-71
Bartel George Hilda Loewen	Taiwan	1970-73
Bartel Larry	Zaire	1958-60
Bauman Albert Katherine Kaufman	India	1958-63
Bauman Harvey Ella Garber	India	1925-61
Bauman John Ruth Gilliom	India	1959-70
Bauman Kenneth Mary Gallagher	India	1954-73
Becker Frank Rachel Senner (see VanWingen)	Japan	1968-70
Becker Mary (see Valencia)	Colombia	1945-49
Becker Palmer Ardys Preheim	Taiwan	1958-63

Bergen Menno Esther Klassen	Mexico	1956-68
Bergmann Nettie	India	1964-69
Birkey Erma	Zaire	1923-60
Blackwood Loretta Lehman (see Lehman)		
Block Tina (see Ediger)	India	1961-63
Block William Dolores Friesen	India	1976-79

Boehr
  P. J.
  Jennie Gottschall
  Frieda Sprunger
    (see Sprunger)
	China	
		1915-51
		1915-35
		1921-51

Boehr
  Richard
  Lena Peters
	Taiwan	
		1962-71
		1955-71

Bohn
  John
  Tina Warkentin
    (see Warkentin)
	
	Lesotho
	Zaire, Lesotho
		
		1978-
		1964-75, **1978-**

Boldt Cornie	Mexico	1948-49
Boschman Paul Laverne Linscheid	Japan	1951-71
Brandt Kornelius Edwin Anne Peters	Mexico	1976-
Braun Anna P. (see Gerig)	India	1908-17
Braun Henry Sara Lehman	Zaire	1970-72
Braun Wesley Catherine Gerber	Taiwan	1976-78
Brown H. J. Maria Miller	China	1909-49
Brown Roland Sophie Schmidt	Taiwan	1956-

Buhr	Taiwan	1960-63
Martin		
Buller	Zaire	1966-
Herman		
Ruth Lehman		
Buller	Zaire	1951-
Peter		
Gladys Klassen		
Burkhalter	India	1947-
Ed		
Ramoth Lowe		
Burkhalter	India	1917-59
Martha		
Burkhalter	India	
Noah		1919-20
Adah Good		1919-52
(see Wenger, Paul)		
Burkhard	India	1924-31
Mary (see Yoder)		
Busenitz	Lesotho	1973-76
Allen		
Marabeth		
Butler	Japan	1977-
Stanley		
Claassen	India	1945-73
Curt		
Olga Schultz		
Claassen	Taiwan	1970-73
Elwin		
LaVonne Enns		
Claassen	Colombia	1969-71
Eugene		
Dorene Flaming		
Claassen	Zaire	1976-78
Gordon		
Claassen	Colombia	1971-76
Mark		
Lillian Jacobson		
Claassen	Uruguay	1964-72
Sara		
Claassen	Japan	1959-
Virginia		
Cressman	India	1947-
Leona		
Cummings		
Alida Schrag (see Schrag)		
Dahl	India	1964-67
Alfred		
Bertha		

Davis Etta	China	1938-41
Daza Leona Jean Schrag (see Schrag)		

Derksen
  Peter
  Mary Klaassen
	Japan	1954-

Derksen
  Richard
  Marilyn Carter
	Zaire	1976-

Dester
  Herbert
  Hilda Reusser
	India	1927-57

Dick
  Delbert
  Susan Mast
	Zaire	1975-78

Dick
  Elmer
  Esther Quiring
	Zaire	1946-

Dick LaVerna (see Stonina)	Zaire	1972-76

Dirks
  Henry
  Tina Weier
	Zaire	1963-72

Dirks
  Marvin
  Frieda Albrecht
	China	1939-45

Dirks
  Otto
  Elaine Ross
	Taiwan	1968-

Dueck Agnes	Japan	1964-67

Dueck
  Henry
  Helga Helen Driedger
	Paraguay	1956-68

Dueck
  Henry
  Alice Helen Redekop
	Uruguay	1969-

Dueck
  John
  Winnifred Pauls
	India	1964-66

Dueck Margaret	Mexico	1963-78

Duerksen
  Jacob
  Christina Harder
	India	1926-55

Duerksen
  Joseph
  Mary Lou Franz
	India	1956-69

Duerksen	India	1948-63
Marie (see Kleinsasser)		
Dyck	Japan	1953-
Anna		
Dyck	Botswana	1975-
B. Harry		
Lois Riechl		
Dyck		
Eleanore Schmidt (see Schmidt)		
Dyck	Mexico	1946-48
Frank		
Dyck	Paraguay	1953-67
Frank		
Anne Regehr		
Dyck	Thailand	1967-71
Gerald		
Edith Fagerbourg		
Dyck	Paraguay	1967-70
Hans		
Bertha Schmidt		
Dyck		
Margaret Helen	Taiwan	1968-71
	Mexico	1977-
Dyck	India	1956-68
Paul		
Lois Bartel		
Dyck	Mexico	1962-74
Philip		
Lora Klassen		
Dyck	Zaire	1956-58
Sara		
Ediger	Japan	1953-
Ferd		
Viola Duerksen		
Ediger	Colombia	1963-75
George		
Margaret Voght		
Ediger	Zaire	1971-74
Sam		
Betty Regehr		
Ediger		
Tina Block (see Block)		
Elizabeth		
Joann (see Martens, Larry)		
Enns	Colombia	1976-
Erdman		
Linda Rempel		

Enns	Zaire	
Frank		1926-61, 1966-69
Agnes Neufeld		1926-61
Enns	Taiwan	1970-73
Madeleine		
Ens	Mexico	1955-
Helen		
Ens		
Henry G.	Brazil	1964-66
	Mexico	1966-
Sara Zacharias	Brazil	1964-66
	Mexico	1966-
Entz	Upper Volta	1977-
Loren		
Donna Kampen		
Entz	Zaire	1949-76
Samuel		
Leona Enns		
Epp	Mexico	1975-
Aaron		
Betty Schmidt		
Epp		
Bruno	Paraguay	1954-64
	Brazil	1965-72
Elizabeth Jantzen	Paraguay	1954-64
	Brazil	1965-72
Epp	Taiwan	1972-
Carl		
Hilda Schroeder		
Epp	Japan	1973-76
Delvyn		
Lucille Kroeker		
Epp	Japan	1958-?
Dennis		
Epp	Paraguay	1956-58
Henry H.		
Mary Reimer		
Epp		
Henry P.	Paraguay	1956-57
	Uruguay	1957-58
Hilda Penner	Paraguay	1956-57
	Uruguay	1957-58
Epp	Zaire	1958-
Mary		
Ewert	China	1929-41
August		
Martha Wiens		

Ewert	Zaire	1962-72
Ralph		
Fern Bartsch		
Falk	Zaire	1952-74
Peter		
Annie Rempel		
Fast	China	1917-50
Aganetha		
Fast	Taiwan	1966-70
Frieda (see Jong)		
Fehr	Mexico	1955-
Tina		
Flickinger	Colombia	1958-62
Calvin		
Sidonnia Nickel		
Frank	India	
Edgar		1937-39
Johanna Schmidt		1929-39
Fransen	Mexico	1972-74
Nicholas		
Tina Martens		
Friesen	Taiwan	
Alvin		1957-76
Ruby Chin-lan		1965-76
Friesen	Paraguay	1948-50
A. W.		
Margaret Friesen		
Friesen	Paraguay	1959-64
B. Theodore		
Margaret Klassen		
Friesen	Mexico	
David		1967-68
Gertrude Peters		1965-68
(see Peters)		
Friesen	Mexico	1957-?
Helen		
Friesen		
Huldah Myers Weiss (see Myers)		
Friesen	Mexico	1950-?
John		
Mary Giesbrecht		
Friesen	Mexico	1976-
Tina		
Friesen	Japan	1950-68
Leonore		
Funk	India	1906-12
Annie		
Funk	India	1969-75
Irene		

Gaeddert
  Kathryn (see Teichroew)

Gerhart	Lesotho	1974-

  Robert
  Joyce Stradinger

Gerig
  Anna Braun (see Braun)

Gering	Taiwan	1961-64

  Gordon

Giesbrecht	India	
Jacob		1952-77
Dorothy Andres		1951-77
Gingerich	India	1976-78

  Kermit
  Clydene Jantz

Goering	China	1919-35

  Samuel J.
  Pauline Miller

Goertz	China	1921-51

  Elizabeth

Graber	Taiwan	1956-64

  Glen
  June Straite

Graber	Zaire	1951-64

  Harold
  Gladys Gjerdevis

Graber	Taiwan	1967-70

  Kenneth
  Ruth Buhler

Graber	Zaire	1957-59

  Larry

Graber	India	1962-65

  Richard
  Melita Goerzen

Groff	Colombia	1968-70

  Lynn

Guengerich	Zaire	1946-60, 1968-74

  Frieda

Habegger	China	1918-21

  Christine

Habegger	Colombia	1962-68

  Howard
  Marlene Short

Harder	Zaire	1968-

  Arnold
  Grace Hiebner

Harder	Taiwan	1973-76

  Eloise

Harder
  Ernst
  Ruth Ewert
	Uruguay	1956-75

Harder
  Peter
  Claire Landis
	Colombia	1966-69

Harder
  Waldo E.
  Abbie Claassen
	Zaire	1951-61, 1971-73

Heese John	Zaire	1959-60

Heinrichs
  Jake
  Gertrude Loewen
	Mexico	1960-78

Hiebert Elda	Zaire	1963-

Hildebrandt
  Dietrich
  Margaret Spenst
	Taiwan	1968-75

Hildebrand Shirley	Taiwan	1962-
Hirschler Richard	Zaire Taiwan	1971-75 1977-79
Jean Simpson	Zaire Taiwan	1971-75 1977-79
Hostetler Elizabeth Rumer (see Rumer)		
Huebert Roderick	Mexico	1958-60

Hunsberger
  Merrill
  Mabel Metzger
	Taiwan	1970-72

Isaac Anna	Paraguay	1958-61 (?)

Isaac
  Ferdinand J.
  Anna Penner
	India	1921-46
		1921-47

Jansen
  Arlin
  Ruth Whittaker
	Japan	1965-68

Jantzen
  Albert
  Wilma Lichti
	China	1938-45

Jantzen
  Aron J.
  Kathryn Louthan
	India	1938-63, 1969-74

Jantzen
  Lubin W.
  Mathilda Mueller
	India	1947-68, 1974-

Jantzen
  John B.
  Ann Dyck
	Zaire	1949-59

Janzen Anita	Zaire	1967-70, 1976-

Janzen
  George
  Martha Giesbrecht
	Japan	
		1959-
		1953-

Janzen
  Homer
  Margaret Janzen
	India	1960-74

Janzen John	Zaire	1957-59
Janzen Marie J. Regier Frantz (see Regier)		
Jimenez Julia Schutz (see Schutz)		
Jong Frieda Fast (see Fast)		

Kageie
  Jerry
  Judy Friesen
	Colombia	1967-69

Kampers Gladys Klassen (see Klassen)		

Kauffman
  Lloyd
  Esther Nickel
	Taiwan	1970-79

Kaufman
  Edmund G.
  Hazel Dester
	China	1918-31

Kaufman Larry	Zaire	1955-56
Keeney Lois	Taiwan	1977-79

Kehler
  Peter
  Lydia Pankratz
	Taiwan	1959-75

Keidel
  Levi
  Eudene King
	Zaire	1951-66, 1971-

Keiser
  Arthur
  Helen Morrow
	Colombia	1948-61

Klaassen
  Glendon
  Reitha Kaufman
	Colombia	1959-77

Klaassen	Zaire	1964-76
John		
Olga Unruh		
Klassen	India	1947-50
Gladys (see Kampers)		
Kleinsasser		
Marie Duerksen (see Duerksen)		
Kliewer	Japan	1976-
Henry		
Nellie Krause		
Kliewer	Japan	1967-70
Ray		
Loralee Weinbrenner		
Kornelsen	India	1948-
Helen		
Krehbiel	Zaire	1976-78
Jean		
Krehbiel	Taiwan	1973-75
Beth Anne		
Kroeker	India	1900-1909
John F.		
Susie Hirschler		
Kuehny	India	1921-37
Clara		
Kuyf	China	1936-51
Wilhelmina		
Lehman	Taiwan	1975-77
Cynthia Ann		
Lehman	India	1960-63, 1977-79
Jim		
Hilda Hirschler		
Lehman	India	1921-37
Loretta (see Blackwood)		
Lehman		
Melva	India	1947-67
	Taiwan	1977-79
Lehman	China	1918-21
Metta		
Lehman	Japan	1968-71
Terry		
Louise Clemens		
Lehman	Zaire	1977-79
Vernon		
Phyllis Lehman		
Letkemann	Bolivia	1975-
Henry David		
Sara Schroeder		
Liechty	Zaire	1946-
Anna V.		

Liechty
  Carl
  Sandra Cook
	Japan	1963-74; 1978-

Liechty
  Irena
    (see Sprunger, Vernon)
	Zaire	1952-72

Linscheid
  Marvin
  Elma Friesen
	Japan	1969-72

Loepp
  Franzie
  Dorothy Harms
	Japan	1961-64

Loewen
  Eleanor Marie Peters
    (see Peters)		

Loewen
  Henry
  Betty Schroeder
	Zaire	1972-75, 1978-

Loewen
  Robert
  Anne Konrad
	Japan	1969-72

Lohrentz
  Abraham M.
  Marie Wollmann
	China	1921-29

MacDonald
  Esther Mae Andres
    (see Andres)		

Mann
  Darrel
  Diane Crane
	Zaire	1967-69

Marshall
  Thomas
  Judy Ford
	Taiwan	1977-79

Martens
  Larry
  Joann Schrag
    (see Elizabeth)
	Colombia	1966-68

Martens
  Rudolph
  Elvina Neufeld
	Zaire	1952-60, 1970-

Martens Susan	Taiwan	1957-
Mathies Eleanor	Paraguay	1958-

Moyer
  Samuel T.
  Metta Habegger
	India	1920-56

Myers
  Huldah
    (see Friesen)
	Colombia	1957-62

Neuenschwander
  Bertha Reiff
    (see Reiff)		

Neufeld
  Anne
    (see Rupp)
	Mexico	1960-63

Neufeld
  George
  Justina Wiens
	Zaire	1944-60

Neufeld
  Jacob
  Ella Klassen
	Mexico	1975-78

Neufeld Mary	Mexico	1957-59
Neufeld Talitha	China	1915-28
Nickel Helen	India	1929-57

Nickel
  Jake W.
  Frieda Unger
	Paraguay	1948-50

Nickel
  Richard
  Bonnie Schmidt
	Colombia	1966-68

Nussbaum
  Elizabeth Janet Soldner
    (see Soldner)		

Nussbaum Karen	Taiwan	1968-72

Osborne
  Philip
  Lorna Hostetler
	Taiwan	1966-68

Pankratz
  Peter J.
  Theodora Marshchke
	Taiwan	1956-59

Pankratz
  Steven
  Elizabeth Raid
	Colombia	1967-69

Pannabecker
  C. L.
  Lelia Roth
	China	1926-41

Pannabecker
  S. F.
  Sylvia Tschantz
	China	1923-41

Patkau Esther	Japan	1951-74

Pauls Eva	India	1937-59

Pauls
  John
  Mary Schrag
	India	
		1958-77
		1952-77

Pauls Mary	Taiwan	1969-73
Penner Anne	India	1946-

Penner
  Melvin
  Anita Koslowsky
	Taiwan	1975-

Penner
  Peter A.
  Elizabeth Dickman
  Martha Richert
	India	
		1900-1941
		1900-1906
		1909-41

Penner
  Peter W.
  Mathilde Ensz
	India	1908-49

Peters
  Daniel
  Elma Tiessen
	Mexico	1950-51, 1956-

Peters
  Eleanor Marie
    (see Loewen)
	Mexico	1973-75

Peters
  Gertrude
    (see Friesen, David)
	Mexico	1965-68

Peters James	Zaire	1959-60
Peters Mary	Taiwan	1964-67

Peters
  Virgil
  Jennie Schmidt
	Taiwan	1964-71

Preheim
  Doyle
  LaDona Thomas
	Japan	1966-69

Quiring Anna	Zaire	1936-58
Quiring Betty	Zaire	1954-
Quiring Tina	Zaire	1949-77

Ramseyer
  Robert
  Alice Ruth Pannabecker
	Japan	1954-68, 1978-

Ratzlaff
  Harold
  Ruth Regier
	India	1940-76

Regier
  Arnold
  Elaine Waltner
	Zaire	1957-60

Regier Fremont	Zaire Mexico	1955-57, 1964-76 1961-63
Sara Janzen	Zaire Mexico	1964-76 1961-63

Regier
  Ivan
  Anna Preheim
	Japan	1962-64

Regier
  Marie J.
    (see Janzen)
	China
	Paraguay
	Taiwan
		1926-32, 1940-48
		1950-53
		1954-62

Regier
  Willard
  Elma Frey
	Mexico	1975-77

Reiff
  Bertha
    (see Neuenschwander)
	Colombia	1966-68

Reimer
  Raymond
  Phyllis Mueller
	Japan	1957-69

Reimer
  Victor
  Mary Thiessen
	India	1972-75

Rempel
  Abram
  Johanna Vogt
	Mexico	1961-63

Rempel Elfrieda	Mexico	1957-59

Rempel
  Erwin
  Angela Albrecht
	Brazil	1975-

Reusser
  Loren
  Peggy Stout
	Taiwan	1966-69

Ries
  Dennis
  Shirley Epp
	Zaire	1975-

Roth
  Earl
  Ruth Jantzen
	Zaire	1954-

Roth Paul	Zaire	1958-60

Rumer
  Elizabeth
    (see Hostetler)
	Taiwan	1968-70

Rupp
  Anne Neufeld
    (see Neufeld)		

Rutschman LaVerne	Colombia	1947-55
	Uruguay	1959-73
	Bolivia	1974-76
	Costa Rica	1977-
Harriet Fischbach	Colombia	1947-55
	Uruguay	1959-73
	Bolivia	1974-76
	Costa Rica	1977-

Sawatzky
  Benjamin
  Leona Friesen
	India	1953-71

Sawatzky
  Sheldon
  Marietta Landis
	Taiwan	1965-68; 1971-

Sawatzky Ronald	Botswana	1977-
Schmidt Augusta	India	1927-57

Schmidt
  Edward
  Waldtraut Regier
	India	1964-69

Schmidt Donald	Mexico	1960-62

Schmidt
  Eleanore
    (see Dyck)
	India	1945-51

Schmidt
  Jacob
  Lydia Buhler
	Mexico	1966-71

Schmidt
  Olin
  Tillie Nachtigal
	Zaire	1972-74

Schmidt
  Robert
  Joyce Williams
	Zaire	1969-72

Schnell
  Russell
  Helen Yoder
	Zaire	1932-64

Schrag
  Alida
    (see Cummings)
	India	1944-46

Schrag
  Erwin India 1948-53
    Mexico 1955-75
  Vera Clocksen Mexico 1955-75
Schrag Zaire 1968-
  Leona May
Schrag Colombia 1968-70
  Leona Jean
    (see Daza)
Schrag India 1973-76
  Myron
  Ericka Koop
Schroeder India 1952-63, 1968-75
  Lorraine
Schutz Colombia 1965-70
  Julia
    (see Jimenez)
Schwartz Zaire 1941-77
  Merle
  Dorothy Bowman
Senner Taiwan 1961-66
  Ed
  Barbara Beavers
Senner Taiwan 1966-75
  Raynold
  Shirley Leland
Shelly Zaire 1968-77
  Walter
  Elizabeth Bauman
Siebert Taiwan 1964-
  Gladys
Siemens Taiwan
  William 1963-68, 1970-73
  Elsie Hiebert 1970-73
Soldner
  Elizabeth Janet Colombia 1945-70
    (see Nussbaum) Mexico 1972-75
Sommer Japan 1970-73
  John
  Sharon Wiebe
Souder Colombia 1963-66
  Daniel
  Dale Myers
Sprunger Colombia 1968-70
  Barton
  Judith Beitler
Sprunger Zaire 1958-72
  Charles
  Geraldine Reiff

Sprunger
  Frieda
    (see Boehr, P. J.)
	China	1921-51

Sprunger
  Hugh
  Janet Frost
	Taiwan	1954-

Sprunger
  Lewis
  Judy Stucky
	Colombia	1971-74

Sprunger Marsha	Mexico	1977-78

Sprunger
  Vernon
  Lilly Bachman
  Irena Liechty
	Zaire	1931-72
		1931-59
		1952-72

Sprunger
  Wilmer
  Kenlyn Augsburger
	Zaire	1964-73

Sprunger
  Walter Frederic
  Sara Hostetler
	Japan	1964-

Steider Kenneth	Taiwan	1966-69; 1974-

Steiner
  Ezra
  Elizabeth Geiger
	India	1913-24

Steury
  Clinton
  Nedra Brookmeyer
	Colombia	1970-72

Stolifer
  Albert
  Lois Unruh
	Taiwan	1969-74

Stonina
  LaVerna Dick
    (see Dick)		

Stucky
  Gerald
  Mary Hope Wood
	Colombia	1945-65, 1973-

Stucky
  Willard
  Marjorie Olsen
	Mexico	1958-61

Suckau
  Cornelius H.
  Lulu Johnson
	India	1909-28

Teichroeb
  Abram
  Tina Olfert
	Paraguay	1964-66

Teichroew
  Allen
  Kathryn Gaeddert
  (see Gaeddert)
	Japan	1969-71

Thiessen
  Arthur D.
  Jeannette Martig
	India	1952-74

Thiessen
  Bernard
  Ruby Seibert
	Japan	1952-

Thiessen
  John
  Elizabeth Wiens
	India	1921-49

Toews
  Henry
  Mary Wiens
	Zaire	1936-54

Toews
  Richard
  Betty Janzen
	Mexico	1966-71

Tschetter
  Larry
  Edith Hofer
	Colombia	1971-73

Unrau
  Walter D.
  Ruth Baughman
	India	1965-66, 1970-73

Unruh
  Donovan
  Naomi Reimer
	Zaire	1968-

Unruh Esther	Mexico	1958-60
Unruh Larry	Zaire	1958-60?
Unruh Selma	Zaire	1946-60, 1963-64
Unruh Verney	Japan Taiwan	1951-66 1979-
Belva Waltner	Japan Taiwan	1951-66 1979-

Unruh
  Willard
  Selma Dick
	India	1948-53

Unruh
  William F.
  Pauline Schmidt
	India	1928-38

Valencia
  Mary Becker
  (see Becker)		

Vandenberg	Taiwan	
Johan		1957-
Martha Boschman		1955-
Van Wingen		
Rachel Senner		
(see Becker, Frank)		
Voran	Japan	1951-71, 1978-
Peter		
Lois Geiger		
Voth		
William	China	1919-50
	Japan, Taiwan	1951-55, 1955-58
Matilda Kliewer	China	1919-50
	Japan, Taiwan	1951-55, 1955-58
Waltner	India	1939-56
Orlando		
Vernelle Schroeder		
Waltner	India	1966-69
Robert		
Barbara Burdette		
Warkentin	Mexico	1969-72
Dietrich		
Katie Janzen		
Warkentin	Paraguay	1957-?
Mary		
Warkentin		
Tina	Zaire	1964-75
(see Bohn, John)	Lesotho	1978-
Wenger	India	
Paul		1923-52
Adah Good Burkhalter		1919-52
(see Burkhalter, Noah)		
Wiebe	Colombia	1969-77
John		
Elma Giesbrecht		
Wiens	India	1965-73
J. Wendell		
Norma Bachman		
Wiens	India	1906-37
Peter J.		
Agnes Harder		
Willms	Taiwan	1957-
Helen		
Wilson	Colombia	1975-77
Larry		
L. Jane Krabill		
Wuethrich	China	1940-50
Lester		
Agnes Harder		

Wyse
  Rosemary | Colombia | 1963-64
   | Uruguay | 1964, 1967-69
Yoder | Zaire | 1935-50
  Roy
  Bessie
Yoder
  Mary Burkhard
  (see Burkhard)
Yoder | Colombia | 1953-
  Vernelle
Zacharias | Paraguay | 1968-70
  Frank
  Mary Anne Ens
Zerger | Colombia | 1967-69
  John
  Sandra Dee Schrag
Zook | Zaire | 1955-77
  John
  Jeanne Pierson
Zweiacher | Mexico | 1957-58
  Clifton

List of Members of Board of Missions/ Commission on Overseas Mission

List of COM Administrative Staff

Executive Secretaries		Dates
Habegger, Howard J.		1971-
Shelly, Andrew R.		1960-71
Waltner, Orlando		1958-60
Thiessen, John		1954-58
Nyce, Howard G.		1948-54
(No Executive Secretary during this time)		1917-48
M. M. Horsch		1915-17

Others		
Ediger, Tina Block	Administrative Assistant	1963-71
	Director of Mission Services	1971-
Jantzen, Aron E.	Personnel Secretary	1964-68
Jantzen, Lubin W.	Personnel Secretary	1969-74
Kehler, Peter	Secretary for Asia	1978-
Kuyf, Wilhelmina	Administrative Assistant	1951-63
Sommer, John	Personnel Secretary	1974-
Unruh, Verney	Secretary for Asia	1966-78
Valencia, Hector G.	Secretary for Latin America	1975-
Wenger, Malcolm	Home Missions and Evangelism	1966-68

Members of the Board of Missions/Commission on Overseas Mission

Aeschliman, Paul R.	1899-1908
Amstutz, J. E.	1917-44
Baer, John B.	1908-17

Balzer, Jacob J.	1890-1914
Balzer, Peter	1896-1904
Bauman, Albert S.	1974-
Baumgartner, S. S.	1917-41
Claassen, Milton	1971-
Detweiler, Paul N.	1969-
Dueck, Henry T.	1971-74; 1977-
Dyck, Anne Warkentin	1972-
Dyck, Peter J.	1968-
Dyck, Walter H.	1953-71
Ediger, Peter J.	1965-68
Eicher, Benjamin	1893
Epp, Arnold A.	1971-74
Epp, G. G.	1947-58
Epp, Henry H.	1959-68
Esch, Ben	1947-53
Ewert, Margaret	1973-
Fast, Henry A.	1929-35
Fast, Loretta Janzen	1977-
Fast, Peter	1969-77
Fretz, Allen M.	1887-90
Funk, A. E.	1881-84
Gaeddert, Dietrich	1887-95
Gering, Walter	1968-71
Goering, Samuel J.	1947-59
Goerz, David	1884-90 & 1893
Gottshall, William S.	1893-1938
Groening, George	1959-68
Harder, Gustav	1890-1923
Harder, Leland	1959-68
Haury, Gustav A.	1914-17
Hirschy, Noah C.	1896-1911
Horsch, Michael M.	1908-41
Kehler, Larry	1977-
King, Harley	1941-62
Klassen, J. K.	1969-
Kleinsasser, Marie Duerksen	1971-77
Kliewer, J. W.	1908-35
Krehbiel, C. E.	1945-47
Krehbiel, Christian	1872-96
Krehbiel, Dorothy Kaufman	1968-77
Krehbiel, H. P.	1914-23
Kreider, Amos E.	1935-53
Kreider, Robert S.	1969-71
Mehl, J. C.	1905-14
Moyer, J. S.	1884-1905
Moyer, Manasses S.	1887-1903
Musselman, Samuel M.	1911-32
Neuenschwander, A. J.	1935-53

Neufeld, Abe	1974-77
Neufeld, D. P.	1965-69
Neufeld, Elmer	1959-74
Nyce, Howard G.	1935-47
Oberholtzer, John H.	1872-81
Pannabecker, S. F.	1947-65
Penner, G.	1902-8
Penner, Heinrich D.	1917-26
Penner, J. K.	1902-5
Penner, John	1896
Plenert, John J.	1938-56
Preheim, Vern	1969-71; 1974-
Regier, J. G.	1923-32
Regier, J. M.	1923-50
Richert, H.	1876-81 & 1895
Richert, Peter H.	1911-47
Schantz, J. W.	1914-23
Schantz, Peter	1907-16
Schmidt, Herbert R.	1962-75
Schowalter, Christian	1872-95
Schultz, Harold	1974-
Shelly, Andrew B.	1872-1911
Shelly, Andrew R.	1950-59
Shelly, Anthony S.	1890-93; 1911-20; 1926-28
Shelly, Ward W.	1956-74
Shelly, Wilmer	1953-56
Snyder, Jakob	1917-26
Soldner, Grover T.	1926-35
Sprunger, Samuel F.	1884-87; 1893-1917
Stucky, Gerald	1968-72
Suderman, John P.	1950-68
Suderman, Leonhard	1887-90
Thiessen, J. J.	1947-57
Toews, David	1911-47
Toews, Jacob	1887-90
Troyer, Lotus E.	1956-64
Unruh, Daniel J.	1941-53
Van der Smissen, C. J.	1872-90
Van der Smissen, C. H. A.	1890-96; 1902-11
Waltner, A. P.	1932-50
Waltner, Arthur C.	1975-
Waltner, Erland	1962-68
Waltner, Harris	1971-
Wedel, C. H.	1902-10
Wedel, P. P.	1933-50
Wedel, Philip A.	1943-59
Wiebe, Willard	1953-67
Wiens, Esther	1959-65
Zook, Jeanne Pierson	1977-

Notes and Acknowledgments

CHAPTER 1

1. Mariam Schmidt, "Peter A. Penner, 1871-1949," in *General Conference Mennonite Pioneers,* comp. Edmund G. Kaufman (North Newton, Kans.: Bethel College, 1973), p. 345.

2. S. F. Pannabecker, "Missions, Foreign Mennonite," *Mennonite Encyclopedia,* vol. 3 (Scottdale, Pa.: Mennonite Publishing House; Newton, Kans.: Mennonite Publication Office; Hillsboro, Kans.: Mennonite Brethren Publishing House, 1959), pp. 712-17. (*Mennonite Encyclopedia* hereafter cited as *ME.*)

3. On Anabaptist and Protestant missions, see John H. Yoder, "Reformation and Missions: A Literature Review," *Occasional Bulletin from the Missionary Research Library* 22 (June 1971): 1-9; and Cornelius J. Dyck, "Early Anabaptist *Sendungsbewusstsein*" (Unpublished paper, University of Chicago, 1957).

4. Pannabecker, "Missions, Foreign Mennonite," p. 713.

5. Dietrich Gaeddert, "Das Entstehen der Missionsthaetigkeit in Suedrussland unter uns Mennoniten," *Christlicher Bundesbote* (1 July 1886), p. 2.

6. Leo Laurense, *125 Jahre Zusammenarbeit in der mennonitischen Mission 1847 bis 1972* (Europaeischen Mennonitischen Evangelisations-Kommittee, 1972), p. 16.

7. Oberholtzer's publication, the *Religioser Botschafter,* founded in 1853, did not have a great emphasis on missions. The first missions article, a piece about missions activity among the Methodists, did not appear until issue no. 12 of that periodical.

8. Quoted in Samuel Floyd Pannabecker, *Open Doors: A History of the General Conference Mennonite Church* (Newton, Kans.: Faith and Life Press, 1975), p. 52.

9. Eva F. Sprunger, *The First Hundred Years* (Berne, Ind., 1938), p. 26. S. F. Sprunger later served on the foreign mission board for twenty-four years and led the Berne church to a stance of strong missions support.

10. S. S. Haury, *Briefe ueber die Ausbreitung des Evangeliums in der Heidenwelt* (Halstead, Kans.: Westlichen Publikations Gesellschaft, 1877), p. 92. This book appeared first in serial form in 1876 in *Der Mennonitische Friedensbote,* beginning 24 January 1876.

11. The name "New" Mennonites is no longer in popular use. Members of the General Conference Mennonite Church, the branch which is the subject of this book, are often referred to as "GCs." The name "Old" Mennonites, however, is still widely used, although this group prefers to be known as the Mennonite Church. Because it is necessary to distinguish the Mennonite Church from Mennonites generally, we will use "MC" to indicate reference to this branch of Mennonites.

12. For the minutes of this Halstead meeting, see *Der Mennonitische Friedensbote,* 1 December 1876, p. 181.

13. *Nachrichten aus der Heidenwelt,* October 1877, p. 75.

14. Mrs. G. A. Linscheid, "Historical Sketch of the General Conference Mennonite Mission Enterprise in Oklahoma," *Missions Quarterly* (June 1930), p. 21.

15. Haury, *Briefe.*

16. *The Mennonite*, September 1892, p. 90.
17. *Christlicher Bundesbote*, 1 December 1884, p. 183.
18. *The Mennonite*, September 1892, p. 94.
19. *Christlicher Bundesbote*, 1 June 1884, p. 87.
20. Three of the most prominent leaders of Mennonite colleges had earlier experience on the mission field: C. H. Wedel, president of Bethel College (North Newton, Kansas 1893-1910); H. H. Ewert, founder and principal of Mennonite Collegiate Institute (Gretna, Manitoba, 1891-1943); and S. K. Mosiman, president of Bluffton College (Bluffton, Ohio, 1909-35).
21. *The Mennonite*, July 1896, p. 78.

CHAPTER 2

1. "Mennonitische Mission in Indien," *Christlicher Bundesbote*, 14 April 1898, p. 5.
2. John A. Lapp, *The Mennonite Church in India, 1897-1962* (Scottdale, Pa.: Herald Press, 1972), pp. 27-35; George Lambert, *Around the Globe and Through Bible Lands* (Elkhart, Ind.: Mennonite Publishing Company, 1896); and George Lambert, *India, the Horror-Stricken Empire* (Elkhart, Ind.: Mennonite Publishing Company, 1898).
3. Lambert, *India, the Horror-Stricken Empire*, author's preface.
4. "A Mission to India," *The Mennonite*, March 1898, p. 55.
5. P. A. Penner, "The Beginnings," in *Twenty-Five Years with God in India* (Berne, Ind.: Mennonite Book Concern, 1929), p. 13.
6. *School and College Journal*, April 1902, p. 25.
7. Penner switched from German to English in his diary with the beginning of 1909, "because," he said, "in a few years hence, all of those for whose eyes these books are intended will be able to read English." Penner preached his first sermon in Hindi after a year and a half in India.
8. Paul Irvin Dyck, "Emergence of New Castes in India" (M.A. thesis, University of Manitoba, 1970), pp. 7-11; Lawrence A. Babb, *The Divine Hierarchy: Popular Hinduism in Central India* (New York: Columbia University Press, 1975), pp. 15-19.
9. Reported by P. A. Penner, *School and College Journal*, April 1902, p. 26.
10. Babb, *Divine Hierarchy*, p. 17.
11. Penner, *School and College Journal*, p. 26.
12. *The Mennonite*, December 1901, p. 21.
13. *The Mennonite*, 10 April 1902, p. 6.
14. *The Mennonite*, 19 June 1905, p. 2.
15. *Ibid.*
16. *The Mennonite*, 18 May 1902, p. 5. For a description and analysis of the *holi* festival, see Babb, *Divine Hierarchy*, pp. 168-75.
17. *Ibid.*
18. *The Mennonite*, 14 May 1903, p. 5.
19. *Ibid.*
20. *The Mennonite*, 2 October 1902, p. 2.
21. Diary of P. A. Penner, 21 December 1901.
22. *The Mennonite*, 17 November 1904, p. 2.
23. 16 December 1901.
24. Report by Martha Burkhalter, quoted in Tina Block, "P. A. Penner, the Champa Sahib-Ji" (Research paper, Bethel College, North Newton, Kans., 1965), p. 51; quoted in Linda Schmidt, "A Seventy-Seven Year Transition" (Research paper, Bethel College, North Newton, Kans., 1977), p. 5.
25. *The Mennonite*, 6 February 1902.
26. *Twenty-Five Years*, p. 14.
27. P. A. Penner to A. B. Shelly, 17 April 1906, Board of Missions Correspondence, folder 54, Mennonite Library and Archives, Bethel College, North Newton, Kans. (cited hereafter as MLA).
28. *The Mennonite*, 28 February 1907.
29. Lapp, *The Mennonite Church in India*, pp. 140-41.
30. Penner to C. van der Smissen, 18 April 1907, Board of Missions Correspondence, folder 58, MLA.
31. *Twenty-Five Years*, p. 125.

32. Orlando Waltner, "The General Conference Mennonite Church of India" (Unpublished manuscript, Institute of Church Growth, Eugene, Oregon, 1962), Board of Missions Correspondence, 1962, folder 76, MLA.

33. Penner tells the story of the work with victims of Hansen's disease in *Twenty-Five Years,* pp. 107-26. See also Harold R. Ratzlaff, "Planting a Church in India" (M.Th. thesis, Mennonite Biblical Seminary, Chicago, 1950), pp. 123-27.

34. Waltner, "General Conference Mennonite Church of India."

35. Harihar Mahapatra, interview with the author, Saraipali, Madhya Pradesh, 28 January 1978.

36. Kroeker's energies were burned out by eight years of pioneering work, by severe health problems with eczema, and by frustration over lack of adequate support from the mission board. A. B. Shelly, mission board secretary, thought part of the problem was Kroeker's jealousy that Penner had such good connections for North American moral and financial support. Kroeker had been a popular missionary in Janjgir. After his departure some Janjgir citizens circulated a petition to the mission board requesting his return. (Letter, 4 June 1909. Board of Missions Correspondence, folder 70, MLA) The Kroeker family, which included five children by 1909, moved to Borisowka, Siberia, where they disappeared after the Russian Revolution. One story holds that they eventually died on the flight eastward to escape Russia via China. Another story is that they were betrayed by their daughter who had married a Russian military officer. (Mariam Penner Schmidt, interview, 31 October 1977.) For another account, see Samuel T. Moyer, *They Heard the Call* (Newton, Kans.: Faith and Life Press, 1970), p. 40. Their fate symbolized the sad ending of the cooperation between Russian and North American Mennonites which had been so important in the early years of the General Conference Mennonite mission to India.

37. Ratzlaff, "Planting a Church in India," p. 51.

38. *The Mennonite,* 24 September 1903, p. 1; quoted in Ratzlaff, "Planting a Church in India," p. 35.

39. *The Mennonite,* 10 September 1903, p. 1; 5 November 1903, p. 1.

40. "To the President of the Chhattisgarh Missionary Association," undated document, Board of Missions Correspondence, folder 57, MLA.

41. P. A. Penner to A. B. Shelly, 19 January 1910. Board of Missions Correspondence, folder 74, MLA.

42. *The Mennonite,* 6 June 1915, p. 2.

43. *The Mennonite,* 10 March 1910, p. 2.

44. The GC mission board did not have an official delegate at the Edinburgh conference, although Alfred Wiebe, missionary candidate for work among the Native Americans, was in attendance.

45. *Twenty-Five Years,* p. 70.

46. Ratzlaff, "Planting a Church in India," p. 109.

47. Leah Sonwani, interview with the author, Champa, 21 January 1978.

48. Mrs. Harold Ratzlaff, comp. and ed., *Fellowship in the Gospel* (Newton, Kans., The Mennonite Publication Office, 1950), p. 52.

49. *Ibid.,* p. 53.

50. Dyck, "Emergence of New Castes in India," pp. 90-102.

51. Samuel T. Moyer, *With Christ on the Edge of the Jungles* (Jubbulpore: F. E. Livengood, 1941), pp. iii, 7-11.

52. Ratzlaff, "Planting a Church in India," pp. 64-65.

53. Moyer, *They Heard the Call,* pp. 82-86.

54. For a brief biography of Mathuria "Bai," see Helen Kornelsen, "A Mother to Phuljhar: Mathuria Bai (1885-1964)" in *Full Circle: Stories of Mennonite Women,* ed. Mary Lou Cummings (Newton, Kans.: Faith and Life Press, 1978), pp. 12-27.

55. Ratzlaff, "Planting a Church in India," p. 67.

56. Moyer, *With Christ,* p. iii.

57. Helen Kornelson to the author, 5 and 6 April 1978, Board of Missions Correspondence, folder 178, MLA.

58. Moyer, *They Heard the Call,* pp. 117-18.

59. *Christlicher Bundesbote,* 17 November 1931, 24 November 1931, pp. 2-3.

60. Moyer, *They Heard the Call,* p. 124.

61. J. W. Pickett, *Christian Mass Movements in India* (New York: Abingdon Press,

1933). The Pickett survey included an unflattering portrayal of some of the Mennonite mission work in India. W. F. Unruh was another Mennonite missionary reader of Pickett's book, which he said "had inspired the missionaries very much to work for large ingatherings. We hope the day will soon be here when our people here in Chhattisgarh will come to be baptized [sic] in crowds." (W. F. Unruh to P. H. Richert, 8 April 1936, Board of Missions Correspondence, folder 348, MLA). In a later book, Pickett sharply critiqued Mennonite missionary strategy among the Garas. See *Church Growth and Group Conversion* (Lucknow: Lucknow Publishing House, 1956), pp. 21-35. The Gara revival was arrested after 1923, Pickett said, because of Mennonite ignorance of the social principles of church growth and because Mennonites adopted the mission station approach at Jagdeeshpur.

62. Moyer, *They Heard the Call,* p. 153.

63. Basna was the village 5.5 miles (8.8 kilometers) from the Mennonite mission station. "C. P." stands for Central Provinces. Moyer's appreciative correspondents in relation to the article included M. J. Shaw, G. H. Singh, R. A. Wilson, and D. A. McGavran. (Board of Missions Correspondence, folder 353, MLA.)

64. The number of inpatients treated at the hospitals at Jagdeeshpur and Champa, where Drs. Harvey and Ella Bauman worked, rose from 900 in 1933 to 2,900 in 1949. Ratzlaff, "Planting a Church in India," p. 121.

65. For a survey of the various stages of this development, see Schmidt, "A Seventy-Seven Year Transition."

66. The mission conference invited six Indian leaders for the discussion of amalgamation. These were G. M. Roberts, M. R. Asna, H. C. Samaya, John Walters, John Asna, and P. P. Asna. See "Report of the Forty-Second Missionary Conference," 1933, Board of Missions Correspondence, folder 516, MLA.

67. *Christlicher Bundesbote,* 21 January 1936, pp. 36-37.

CHAPTER 3

1. Henry J. Brown, *Chips of Experience* (n.p., 1929), p. 165.

2. *Ibid.,* p. 31. Maria Miller had heard of the mission field from one "Missionary Duerkson from Sumatra" and from Peter A. and Elizabeth Penner just before Penners left for India in 1900. Mrs. H. J. Brown, *Praise the Lord* (Freeman, S. Dak.: Pine Hill Printery, 1963), pp. 8-9.

3. A. B. Shelly to the foreign mission board, 28 June 1909, Board of Missions Correspondence, folder 70, MLA. Shelly at first wanted to send the Browns to work with the Cheyenne in Montana. (Shelly to board, 24 August 1907, folder 59.)

4. Brown, *Chips of Experience,* p. 33.

5. See *The Mennonite,* September 1890, p. 186; January 1893; October 1893, p. 6.

6. For H. C. Bartel's biography, including his relationship with the Houlding mission, see Margaret Epp, *This Mountain Is Mine* (Chicago: Moody Press, 1969). H. C. Bartel was originally from the Krimmer Mennonite Brethren Church; Nellie Schmidt Bartel was from the Evangelical Mennonite Brethren.

7. For a broad comparison of China and India, see Kenneth Scott Latourette, *A History of the Expansion of Christianity,* vol. 6, *The Great Century in Northern Africa and Asia* (New York: Harper, 1944), pp. 253-56.

8. Brown, *Chips of Experience,* p. 195.

9. John K. Fairbank, "The Many Faces of Protestant Missions in China and the United States," introductory chapter in *The Missionary Enterprise in China and America* (Cambridge, Harvard University Press, 1974), p. 2.

10. Aganetha Fast and La Vernae J. Dick, "Missionary Fast Goes to China" (Unpublished manuscript, MLA, 1968), p. 14.

11. Matilda Voth, "Clear Shining After Rain" (Manuscript in possession of Mrs. Voth), p. 12.

12. Brown was hardly a demonstrative or self-revealing person, but his autobiographical notes in *Chips of Experience* suggest genuine turmoil beneath his austere exterior. See particularly the chapter in which he characterizes himself as "The Odd One," pp. 90-96.

13. Fast and Dick, "Missionary Fast Goes to China," pp. 11-12.

14. Aganetha Helen Fast, *Out of My Attic* (Freeman, S. Dak.: Pine Hill Printery, 1970), pp. 21-22. After 1919 the missionaries took language study in Peking.

15. Marie Regier, "Cultural Interpretation in a Local Community in China" (Draft copy of M.A. thesis, University of Chicago Divinity School, 1936), p. 31.

16. E. G. Kaufman, interview with the author, 9 November 1977.

17. Voth, "Clear Shining After Rain," chap. 6, p. 21.

18. Marie Regier, "Mennonite Teaching and Practice in a Chinese Community" (B.D. thesis, Chicago Theological Seminary, 1950), pp. 80, 76-77.

19. E. G. Kaufman, Schowalter Oral History Interview Transcript, MLA, p. 99.

20. Reports and Resolutions of the Foreign Mission Board 1901-1924, p. 11.

21. Kaufman, Schowalter Interview Transcript, pp. 95-97.

22. Edmund G. Kaufman, *The Development of the Missionary and Philanthropic Interest Among the Mennonites of North America* (Berne, Ind.: Mennonite Book Concern, 1931), p. 361.

23. W. C. Voth, "Development of the Native Churches," *The Mennonite*, 21 April 1936, p. 3.

24. Kaufman, *Missionary Interest Among Mennonites*, p. 363.

25. Quoted in *Ibid.*, p. 364.

26. Missionaries Sam and Pauline Goering and William C. and Matilda Voth happened to be on the same ship to China in 1919 as the disappointed Chinese delegation to the Versailles Conference. The Chinese had been greatly encouraged by Woodrow Wilson's Fourteen Points and were embittered when the European powers accepted Japanese demands for an imperial stake in China. Matilda Voth, interview with the author, 6 December 1977. For a survey of the rise of Chinese nationalism, see John K. Fairbank, *The United States and China*, 3rd ed. (Cambridge: Harvard University Press, 1971), pp. 195-239.

27. E. G. Kaufman, *The Present Situation in China and the Student Movement* (Bluffton, Ohio: Women's Missionary Society, 1925), p. 2.

28. For H. J. Brown's account of these incidents, see Brown, *Chips of Experience*, pp. 132-58.

29. Kaufman, *Missionary Interest Among Mennonites*, pp. 371-72.

30. Kaufman, "The War and Kai Chow," *Mennonite Weekly Review*, 27 January 1925, p. 1. Kaufman's positive attitude toward Feng would appear to be an anomaly for a pacifist Mennonite. On one hand, it may show how deep was the desire for political order in a situation threatened by anarchy. On the other hand, it may show how Protestant notions of Christianization through political authority influenced Mennonite perceptions of their mission work.

31. Kaufman, *The Present Situation*, p. 13.

32. Kaufman, *Missionary Interest Among Mennonites*, p. 372.

33. H. J. Brown, "The Bible School," *The Mennonite*, 21 April 1936, pp. 20-21.

34. *Ibid.*

35. Kaufman, *Missionary Interest Among Mennonites*, p. 355. In 1925 a total of 1,641 Chinese students were in Mennonite mission schools.

36. Regier, "Mennonite Teaching," p. 94.

37. Stephen Wang, "The Chinese Christians and Their Environment," *The Mennonite*, 21 April 1936, p. 17.

38. Maria Brown, "Woman's Work," *The Mennonite*, 21 April 1936, p. 7.

39. Matilda Voth, interview with the author, 6 December 1977. Voth, "Clear Shining After Rain."

40. W. C. Voth, "Development of the Native Churches," *The Mennonite*, 21 April 1936, pp. 3-4.

41. *Twenty-Five Years*, pp. 246-47.

42. *The Mennonite*, 24 April 1936, pp. 4, 7. S. F. Pannabecker's report in *Christlicher Bundesbote*, 11 May 1937, pp. 291-92, was somewhat more optimistic, but he declined to claim "maturity" for the Chinese congregations: ". . . in 25 years a congregation is hardly capable of arriving at maturity."

43. *China-Home Bond*, April 1941, p. 2. The remaining missionaries at Taming Fu were H. J. and Maria Brown, Marie Regier, and Wilhelmina Kuyf; remaining at Kai Chow were Elizabeth Goertz, August Ewert, C. L. Pannabecker, and S. F. Pannabecker. Kuyf and Regier were critical of the evacuation. Mission board secretary P. H. Richert published their critique: "Is Danger God's Call to Leave a Place of Duty?" *The Mennonite*, 28 October 1941, pp. 3, 7.

44. For a fascinating account of concentration camp life, see Langdon Gilkey, *Shantung Compound* (New York: Harper and Row, 1966). The couples interned in the Philippines were Marvin and Frieda Albrecht Dirks, Albert and Wilma Lichti Jantzen, and Lester and Agnes Harder Wuethrich.

45. *China-Home Bond,* June-July 1941, p. 8.

46. *Ibid.*

47. S. F. Pannabecker, interview with the author, Goshen, Indiana, 22 July 1977.

48. Tim E. Schrag, "The Mennonites Confront the Revolution, the Rise and Fall of MCC in China, 1945-50," (Research paper, Bethel College, North Newton, Kans., 1976), pp. 2, 26.

49. Regier, "Mennonite Teaching," p. 176.

50. After reading judgments that China missions had failed because of excessive institution building, GC Mennonite missionaries in India declared a moratorium on new mission compound buildings in the early 1950s. The moratorium proved to be short-lived. Edward Burkhalter, interview with the author, Jagdeeshpur, 28 January 1978.

51. *The Mennonite,* 27 January 1910, p. 4.

52. For three stimulating essays on the meaning of the China experience, see J. Lawrence Burkholder, "Notes on the Theological Meaning of China," *Mission-Focus,* January 1976, pp. 1-5; Donald E. MacInnis, "The People's Republic of China: Challenges to Contemporary Missiology," *Review and Expositor,* Spring 1977, pp. 159-71; "China and the Churches in the Making of One World," *Pro Mundi Vita* Bulletin 55 (1975): 1-39.

53. Brown, *Chips of Experience,* p. 181.

54. The Mennonite missionaries did not involve themselves in Chinese politics or comment extensively upon the political scene in reports to the North American constituency. But their identification with Chiang Kai-shek's Nationalist movement was very strong. Aganetha Fast, for example, listed "Generalissimo Chiang and Madame Chiang" as among those used by God to prepare "the people of His love for the persecution to come." Fast, *The Power of Christ's Love in China* (Newton, Kans: Faith and Life Press, 1972), p. 119.

55. *The Mennonite,* 21 April 1936, p. 17.

CHAPTER 4

1. The official name of the Congo has changed a number of times. Until 1908 it was known as Congo Free State. It then became the Belgian Congo until independence in 1960, when it became the Congo Republic. In 1971 President Mobutu changed the name to the Republic of Zaire. This chapter, which tells the story until 1960, will use the name Congo. In chapter 9 the name Zaire will be used.

2. Ralph Winter, "The Deadly Dozen," *AIMM Messenger,* Spring 1978, p. 9.

3. The founder and principal of the Union Missionary Training Institute was Mrs. L. D. Osborn. See James S. Dennis, *Centennial Survey of Foreign Missions* (Revell, 1902), p. 251.

4. Although men dominated CIM administrative positions at home and on the field, it should be mentioned that Sara Kroeker, a CIM missionary from the Evangelical Mennonite Brethren Church, was appointed "superintendent, secretary, and official representative on the field" during the furlough of L. B. Haigh in 1915. *CIM Minute Book,* pp. 41-42, AIMM archives, Bluffton, Ohio.

5. On the Defenseless Mennonites, who adopted the name Evangelical Mennonite Church in 1948, see the article in *ME,* vol. 2, pp. 164-66. On the Central Conference, see Samuel Floyd Pannabecker, *Faith in Ferment: A History of the Central District Conference* (Newton, Kans.: Faith and Life Press, 1968).

6. *The Mennonite,* 5 October 1905, p. 5.

7. Elizabeth Schlanzky and Alma Doering, *Die Kongo-Inland-Mission—Ihre Entstehung und ihre Richtlinien,* AIMM archives, Bluffton, Ohio.

8. *Ibid.,* p. 13.

9. Congo Field Minutes, 19 March 1924, AIMM archives, Bluffton, Ohio.

10. Congo Field Minutes, 16-21 February 1925, p. 117, AIMM archives.

11. Melvin Loewen, *Three Score: The Story of an Emerging Church in Central Africa* (Elkhart, Ind.: Congo Inland Mission, 1972), pp. 96-97. *Three Score* is based on Loewen's doctoral dissertation, "The Congo Inland Mission, 1911-1961" (Free University of

Brussels, 1961). The dissertation includes more complete documentation and statistics.

12. Louise Howard (D & D Missionary Homes, St. Petersburg, Florida), to Mrs. A. Stahly, 14 November 1977; Nancy Osgood, "Alma Doering—Missionary Heroine," *St. Petersburg Times,* 4 January 1959, p. 5-E (copies in the author's possession).

13. For a brief description of the people and the geography of the CIM field, see the first chapter of Loewen, *Three Score.* Two additional historical accounts of the mission are William B. Weaver, *Thirty-Five Years in the Congo* (Chicago: Congo Inland Mission, 1945); and Pannabecker, *Faith in Ferment,* pp. 158-64, 285-303.

14. David B. Barrett, "AD 2000: 350 Million Christians in Africa," *International Review of Mission* 59 (January 1970): 39-40.

15. *Christian Evangel,* October 1911, p. 441.

16. Mrs. Oskar Anderson (Sarah Kroeker Anderson), "History of Djoko Punda," AIMM files, Elkhart, Indiana. Another account of the same event alleges that Chief Kalamba was being punished for participating in the slave trade.

17. Diary of L. B. Haigh, 11 March 1913, AIMM archives, Bluffton, Ohio.

18. Haigh diary, 3 April 1912.

19. Donald L. Wiedner, *A History of Africa South of the Sahara* (New York: Vintage Book, 1962), pp. 432-33.

20. Mukedi Station Report, Congo Field Minutes, 5-11 December 1933, AIMM archives, Bluffton, Ohio.

21. Loewen, *Three Score,* p. 27.

22. Banga Station Report, Congo Field Minutes, 1954, AIMM archives, Bluffton, Ohio.

23. Congo Field Minutes, 16-21 February 1925, p. 120, AIMM archives, Bluffton, Ohio.

24. Congo Protestant Council, 1958-59, AIMM archives, Bluffton, Ohio.

25. Records of the Congo Inland Mission Board, 22 March 1911, p. 2, AIMM archives, Bluffton, Ohio.

26. "Our Policy," *The Congo Missionary Messenger,* August 1929, p. 3. The new magazine bore the subtitle, "A Mennonite Missionary Magazine."

27. Congo Field Minutes, 22-29 September 1919, AIMM archives, Bluffton, Ohio.

28. Congo Field Minutes, December 1936. AIMM archives, Bluffton, Ohio.

29. CIM Board Minutes, October 1959. AIMM archives, Bluffton, Ohio.

30. Congo Field Minutes, 16-21 February 1925, p. 115, AIMM archives, Bluffton, Ohio.

31. F. J. Enns, "Customs of the Bampende in Nyanga Territory," *The Congo Missionary Messenger,* May 1930, p. 149.

32. Congo Field Minutes, 7-9 November 1918, AIMM archives, Bluffton, Ohio.

33. Kornelia Unrau, "My Years in Congo," manuscript in AIMM files, Elkhart, Ind.

34. Levi Keidel, *Footsteps to Freedom* (Chicago: Moody Press, 1969).

35. Kabangu Lubadi, interview with the author, 18 July 1977.

36. John P. and Matilda Barkman, "How God Led Us to Serve Him Under CIM," AIMM archives, Bluffton, Ohio; Congo Field Minutes, December 1933, Kalumba Station Annual Report for 1933, AIMM archives.

37. Congo Field Minutes, 1940, AIMM archives, Bluffton, Ohio.

38. *Congo Missionary Messenger,* June 1930, p. 167. This story was taken from a Presbyterian mission publication.

39. Congo Field Minutes, December 1934, AIMM archives, Bluffton, Ohio.

40. Sara Regier, conversation with the author, 22 April 1978.

41. Congo Field Minutes, 7 December 1934, AIMM archives, Bluffton, Ohio.

42. Congo Field Minutes, 8-11 December 1941, AIMM archives, Bluffton, Ohio.

43. CIM Board Minutes of Annual Meeting, 27 February 1934, AIMM archives, Bluffton, Ohio; Raymond L. Hartzler, interview with the author, 4 August 1977.

44. See the mission statistics in *Congo Missionary Messenger,* May-June 1931, p. 161; and June 1936, pp. 44-45.

45. Vernon Sprunger, interview with the author, 10 October 1977.

46. Congo Field Minutes, Kalamba, 1 October 1930, AIMM archives, Bluffton, Ohio.

47. Merle and Dorothy Schwartz, interview with the author, 25 June 1977. The story of this ship, the *Zamzam,* was covered in an article in *Life* magazine, 23 June 1941, pp. 21-27 ff.

48. Harvey Driver interview with the author, 29 November 1977, Schowalter Collection, MLA. For Driver's personal assessment of CIM work in the 1950s, see *Zaire Missionary Messenger,* Spring 1972, pp. 15-19.

49. Harvey Driver, 7 March 1952, "Trip to the Field," Reports 1951-52, AIMM files, Elkhart, Ind.

50. Driver interview, 1977; Pannabecker, *Faith in Ferment,* p. 296.

51. "Memo of Understanding Between H. A. Driver and Field Committee," 31 January and 1 February 1952, Nyanga Station, AIMM archives, Bluffton, Ohio.

52. Driver, "Trip to the Field," Reports 1951-52, AIMM files, Elkhart, Ind.

53. *Ibid.*

54. Pannabecker, *Faith in Ferment,* p. 301.

55. Loewen, *Three Score,* pp. 102-6.

56. *Ibid.,* pp. 93-97.

57. Harvey Driver to F. J. Enns, 15 January 1953, AIMM files, Elkhart, Ind.

58. Pannabecker, *Faith in Ferment,* p. 298.

59. Enns to Driver, 15 July 1952, Personnel File, Enns 1952-54, AIMM archives, Bluffton, Ohio.

60. Kazadi Matthew, interview with the author, 30 July 1977.

61. Driver to Enns, 16 August 1956, Personnel File, Enns 1955-56, AIMM archives, Bluffton, Ohio.

62. *Ibid.*

63. Driver to CIM board members, 17 March 1960, AIMM files, Elkhart, Ind.

64. James Bertsche, interview with the author, 1 December 1977.

CHAPTER 5

1. Leland Harder, *General Conference Mennonite Church Fact Book of Congregational Membership* (n.p., 1971), p. 3.

2. H. P. Krehbiel, *The History of the General Conference of the Mennonites of North America* (Published by the author, 1898), p. 25.

3. *The Mennonite,* September 1900, p. 4.

4. "Rueckblick ueber die Missionsthaetigkeit des letzten Jahrhunderts und Ausblick in das 20. Jahrhundert," *Christlicher Bundesbote,* 18 July 1901, p. 1. The article was continued in the July 25 and August issues.

5. *The Mennonite,* 31 August 1905, p. 4.

6. See "The Untroubled Generation," chapter 6 in James C. Juhnke, *A People of Two Kingdoms* (Newton, Kans.: Faith and Life Press, 1975), pp. 65-82.

7. Samuel Floyd Pannabecker, *Open Doors: A History of the General Conference Mennonite Church* (Newton, Kans.: Faith and Life Press, 1975), p. 280.

8. Richert to C. C. Regier, 1 February 1919, cited in Mark Stucky, "Bethel Meets the Modernist Challenge" (Research paper, Bethel College, North Newton, Kans., 1969), p. 13.

9. The impact of "modernism" upon the GC church has never been thoroughly studied. For one helpful discussion of the context, see Samuel Floyd Pannabecker, *Faith in Ferment: A History of the Central District Conference* (Newton, Kans.: Faith and Life Press, 1968), pp. 221-27.

10. Application Form for General Conference missionaries, Board of Missions Correspondence, n.d., folder 76, MLA.

11. A. B. Shelly to Balzer and Harder, 20 July 1907, Board of Missions Correspondence, folder 58, MLA.

12. Report of the mission board meeting, 12 June 1918, supplement to the *Bundesbote,* 15 August 1918.

13. Letter from "The Missionary Body Assembled in Korba," 27 November 1928, P. H. Richert Collection, folder 119, MLA.

14. The correspondence relating to Suckau's dispute with the India missionaries is in the P. H. Richert Collection, folder 132.

15. E. G. Kaufman, Schowalter Oral History Interview Transcript, pp. 126-27, MLA.

16. (Berne: Mennonite Book Concern, 1931).

17. See the reviews by H. P. Krehbiel in *Der Herold,* 26 November 1931; and by John

Horsch in the *Gospel Herald,* 9 October, 5 November, and 12 November 1931.

18. Copy of the book in MLA.

19. Conversation with John Sommer of the COM staff, 6 September 1978.

20. Penner to H. D. and Lizzie Epp, 15 November 1916, P. A. Penner Collection, unnumbered folder, MLA.

21. Delbert Wiens, "From the Village to the City," *Direction* 2, no. 4 (October 1973, January 1974): 98-149.

22. J. Howard Kauffman and Leland Harder, *Anabaptists Four Centuries Later* (Scottdale, Pa.: Herald Press, 1975).

23. Gladys Goering has compiled a card file on General Conference Mennonite missionaries, including information on family relationships of missionaries. The data in the file remains to be quantified and analyzed, but a cursory investigation gives an overwhelming impression of the extensive web of family relationships among those involved in the missionary enterprise.

24. Matilda Voth, "Clear Shining After Rain" (Manuscript in possession of Mrs. Voth), chap. 6, pp. 9-10.

25. C. H. A. van der Smissen, "Entstehen und Fortgang der Missions-naehvereine unter den Mennoniten," *Christlicher Bundesbote,* 19 October 1899, p. 1.

26. Pannabecker, *Open Doors,* p. 291.

27. Interview with the author, 17 June 1977.

28. Report by Waldo Harder, Board of Missions Correspondence, 1961, folder 119, MLA.

29. J. W. Kliewer, *Letters on a Trip Around the World* (North Newton, Kans.: Bethel College, 1936).

30. *Ibid.,* p. 121.

31. *Ibid.,* p. 137.

32. Andrew R. Shelly, interview with the author, 17 June 1977.

33. Kaufman, *Missionary Interest Among Mennonites,* p. 46.

34. C. H. A. van der Smissen, *Kurzgefaszte Geschichte und Glaubenslehre der Altevangelischen Taufgessinten oder Mennoniten* (Summerfield: 1895); C. H. Wedel, *Abriss der Geschichte der Mennoniten* (Newton, Kans.: 1900-1904); C. Henry Smith, *The Mennonites* (Berne, Ind.: 1920).

35. Bender's essay was published together with other essays on Anabaptist history in Guy F. Hershberger, ed., *The Recovery of the Anabaptist Vision* (Scottdale, Pa.: Herald Press, 1957).

36. (Waterloo, Ontario: Conrad Press, 1973).

CHAPTER 6

1. This account of the Kobe Garage Group is based upon conversations with Masami Homma in Tokyo, 29 December 1977; Torao Abe in Kobe, 2 January 1978; Hiroshi Yanada in Miyazaki, 9 January 1978; and Takashi Yamada in North Newton, Kansas, 31 July 1978.

2. Takashi Yamada, "The Biblical Understanding of the Good News" (Address to the First Asia Mennonite Conference, 13 October 1971), p. 12.

3. W. C. Voth and Verney Unruh, "Kyushu Report," 25 July - 7 August 1951, Missions files at Miyakonojo.

4. Thiessen to Voth, 12 December 1952, Mission files at Miyakonojo.

5. Interview with Peter and Lois Voran, 28 June 1977.

6. Mission files, Miyakonojo.

7. Peter and Lois Voran, interview with the author, 28 June 1977.

8. Hiroshi Yanada, interview with the author, 9 January 1978.

9. Hiroshi Isobe, interview with the author, 10 January 1978.

10. Masami Homma, interview with the author, 28 December 1977.

11. Gan Sakakibara, "My Pilgrimage to Anabaptism," *Mennonite Life,* March 1973, p. 13.

12. Paul W. Boschman, Neil Braun, and Takashi Yamada, *Experiments in Church Growth: Japan* (Kobayashi City: Japan Church Growth Research Association, 1968).

13. Takashi Yamada, "The Anabaptist Vision and Our World Mission," *Mission Focus,* March 1976, pp. 7-14. Yamada read this paper to the Mennonite World Conference Presidium in San Juan, Puerto Rico, July 1975.

14. Paul Boschman, interview with the author, 26 July 1978.

15. Hiroshi Hidaka, interview with the author, 30 December 1977.

16. Gan Sakakibara, interview with the author, 31 December 1977.

17. Hiroshi Yanada, interview with the author, 10 January 1978.

18. Peter Voran, "A Missionary Looks at the Peace Witness" (Paper presented in Osaka, 5 July 1959).

19. Robert Ramseyer, "The Christian Peace Witness and Our Missionary Task: Are Mennonites Evangelical Protestants with a Peace Witness?" Mimeographed paper, June 1976, MLA.

20. *Ibid.,* p. 7.

21. Hiroshi Yanada, interview with the author, 9 January 1978.

22. Takashi Yamada, "The Good News for Asia Today," 12 June 1970, p. 4, COM archives, Newton, Kans.

23. E. Frederick Sprunger, "TEE in Japan: The Feasibility of a Theological Education by Extension Program for the Kyushu Mennonite Christian Church Conference in Japan," (M.A. thesis draft, 1976), p. 79.

24. *Ibid.,* p. 58.

25. See the article on the Tokyo Conference by Carl Beck in *Mennonite World Handbook,* ed. Paul N. Kraybill (Lombard, Ill: Mennonite World Conference, 1978), pp. 157-60.

26. For a brief survey of the statistics, background, and current conditions of the Japan Mennonite Christian Church Conference, see the article by Hiroshi Yanada, *Mennonite World Handbook,* pp. 168-72.

27. Frederick Sprunger's master's thesis thoroughly examines the problems of leadership training and proposes a program of theological education by extension. See Sprunger, "TEE in Japan."

CHAPTER 7

1. Interview with the author, Taipei, 12 January 1978. Dickson has a short description of Mennonite work with mountain people in her book, *These My People* (Grand Rapids: Zondervan Publishing House, 1958), pp. 45-48.

2. For further information regarding the name and the origins of the Taiwanese see Robert J. Bolton, *Treasure Island, Church Growth Among Taiwan's Urban Minnan Chinese* (South Pasadena: William Carey Library, 1976), pp. 4-24.

3. David Wurfel, "Taiwanese Nationalism: Problem for United States Policy," *Studies on Asia* (Lincoln: University of Nebraska Press, 1963), pp. 101-19.

4. For the most thorough history and analysis of the Mennonite mission and church in Taiwan, see Sheldon Sawatzky, "The Gateway of Promise: A Study of the Taiwan Mennonite Church and the Factors Affecting Its Growth" (M.A. thesis, Fuller Theological Seminary, Pasadena, Calif., 1970).

5. *Taiwan-Home Bond,* October 1956. Dr. and Mrs. Liu later joined the Mandarin-speaking church of the Taiwan Gospel Mission in Taipei.

6. The film project was never completed. The text is untitled and is identified as being written by "M. J. Regier and others." Board of Missions Correspondence, 1950-60, folder 200, MLA.

7. Lu Chhun-Tiong, interview with the author, Taichung, 16 January 1978.

8. "Fifteenth Annual Report of the Mennonite Christian Hospital, 1968," p. 18, MLA.

9. Andrew Shelly, "Report of Study Trip to Taiwan, April 1965," p. 40, MLA.

10. "Investigating Committee Report, October 25, 1955," Board of Missions Correspondence, 1950-60, folder 194, MLA.

11. Bolton, *Treasure Island,* pp. 89-109.

12. Andrew K. C. Lu, ed., *The Twentieth Anniversary of the Founding of the Mennonite Church in Taiwan* (Taichung: Fellowship of the Mennonite Church in Taiwan, 1975), p. 3.

13. "Introducing Our Pastors," *Taiwan-Home Bond,* Summer 1966; Martha Vandenberg, "A Celebration of Marriage and Ministry," *The Mennonite,* 21 September 1976, p. 550.

14. Wung Tien-Min, interview with the author, 12 January 1978.

15. Simon H. H. Wung, "The Mennonite Church and Mission in Taiwan" (Research paper, Mennonite Biblical Seminary, Elkhart, Ind., 1973), p. 13; Sawatzky, "Gateway of Promise," pp. 89, 202.

16. Andrew Lu, "FOMCIT Chairman's Report," Commission on Overseas Mission Report to Council of Commissions for 1977, p. B-24.

17. Paul Lin, interview with the author, 15 January 1978.

18. J. Winfield Fretz, "Taroko Community Development Program Evaluation," April 1972, COM archives, Newton, Kans.

19. Commission on Overseas Mission Report to Council of Commissions for 1977, pp. B-31-32.

20. Otto Dirks, "School for Retarded Begins in Taiwan," *The Mennonite,* 3 May 1977, p. 296.

21. For a review of the nursing school story see Verney Unruh, "The Peace Position and Decision in Taiwan," *The Mennonite,* 5 September 1972, pp. 505-6.

22. Roland Brown to Mr. Chuan-Kai Teng, Deputy Secretary of the Kuomintang Party, 4 February 1956, Board of Missions Correspondence, 1950-60, folder 196, MLA.

23. Bessie Plant to W. C. Voth, 24 February 1956, Board of Missions Correspondence, 1950-60, folder 196, MLA.

24. Roland Brown to "Mission Workers," 15 February 1971, unprocessed Taiwan files, folder "Mission Correspondence 1972," COM archives, Newton, Kans.

25. *Taiwan-Home Bond,* Spring 1963, p. 2.

26. (North Newton: Mennonite Press, 1955).

27. Evangelistic Committee Annual Report, August 1960, Board of Missions Correspondence, 1950-60, folder 200, MLA.

28. Quoted in Unruh, "The Peace Position," p. 506.

CHAPTER 8

1. "Historia de Cachipay," annotated photo album, entries for 1947. The Halloween party was dropped after the first year.

2. Andrew R. Shelly, "Colombia Report," 19 May 1960, MLA.

3. For a recent account of "La Violencia," see Suzanne Dailey, "Religious Aspects of Colombia's *La Violencia:* Explanations and Implications," *Journal of Church and State,* Autumn 1973, pp. 381-405. An account which gives less emphasis to the role of religion in The Violence is Robert H. Dix, *Colombia: The Political Dimensions of Change* (New Haven: Yale University Press, 1967), pp. 360-86.

4. James Goff, "The Persecution of Protestant Christians in Colombia, 1948 to 1958;" (Th.D. dissertation, San Francisco Theological Seminary, 1965), quoted in Dailey, "Religious Aspects," p. 396.

5. Figures on Protestant membership from Ruperto Velez, interview with the author, Bogota, 1 June 1978.

6. Gerald and Mary Hope Stucky, interview with the author, Bogota, 6 June 1978.

7. Reports of the incident by Arthur Keiser dated 8 December and 25 December 1950, Board of Missions Correspondence, 1950-60, folder 518, MLA.

8. *Colombian News,* 1 April 1954.

9. Letter from Art Keiser, 4 July 1955, Board of Missions Correspondence, 1950-60, folder 523, MLA.

10. See correspondence from Art Keiser in Board of Missions Correspondence, 1950-60, folders 520, 523, MLA.

11. Arthur Keiser to Wilhelmina Kuyf and Gerald Stucky, 2 August 1955, Board of Missions Correspondence, 1950-60, folder 523, MLA.

12. *Colombian News,* 1 November 1953.

13. *Colombian News,* 1 January 1953, p. 4.

14. *Colombian News,* 1 August 1954, p. 4.

15. *Colombian News,* 1 July 1953, p. 3.

16. Howard J. Habegger, "A Comparative Study of the Peace Corps and the Mennonite Mission as Change Agents in Rural Community Development in Colombia, South America" (Research paper, School of Theology at Claremont, Calif., 1969), p. 8.

17. "Progress Seen on All Sides in Colombia," *The Mennonite,* 22 April 1969, p. 268.

18. Luis Correa to Jerry Shank, 11 July 1977, Mencoldes files in Bogota.

CHAPTER 9

1. John Thiessen, Board of Missions Correspondence, 1950-60, folder 545, MLA.

2. *Report of the Christian Missionary Activities Inquiry Committee, Madhya Pradesh* (Nagpur: Government Printing, 1956).

3. Bishop Gurbachan Singh, interview with the author, Raipur, 26 January 1978.

4. *Report of Inquiry Committee,* vol. 1, p. 132.

5. John A. Lapp, *The Mennonite Church in India, 1897-1962* (Scottdale, Pa.: Herald Press, 1972), pp. 180-88.

6. Ruth Ratzlaff, "Steps in Partnership," *Missions Today,* November 1970, pp. 7-12.

7. Interview with the author, Janjgir, 24 January 1977.

8. Verney Unruh to Ruth Ratzlaff, mission secretary, 7 December 1971.

9. Unruh to "Dear Co-workers," author's file, 18 October 1971.

10. For a more complete description of this visit and its results, see Linda Schmidt, "A Seventy-Seven Year Transition" (Research paper, Bethel College, North Newton, Kans., 1977).

11. Linda Schmidt, "The Irene Funk Incident" (Research paper, Bethel College, North Newton, Kans., 1977). See also "Missionary's Body Reburied in India," *The Mennonite,* 15 June 1976, p. 404.

12. In addition, there were three missionaries on the staff at UBS in Yavatmal—Helen Kornelsen and Lubin and Tillie Jantzen.

13. Grand Rapids: Zondervan, 1977.

14. James Bertsche, *Profile of a Communist Offensive* (Elkhart, Ind.: Congo Inland Mission, n.d.).

15. Loewen, *Three Score,* p. 129.

16. There had been some consideration given to starting Congo Inland Mission work in the Dominican Republic in the 1940s, and the CIM executive committee in 1944 actually did decide to initiate work there "as resources of personnel and finances are available, without becoming any handicap to the furthering of our work in Congo." (Congo Inland Mission Executive Committee Meeting Minutes, 18 July 1944, Bluffton.) It was later decided, however, that the Defenseless Conference (Evangelical Mennonite Conference) would begin the work in the Dominican Republic separate from Congo Inland Mission.

17. Report from James Bertsche to Reuben Short, 7 September 1970, Commission on Overseas Mission Correspondence, CIM Executive, 1970, MLA.

18. Vern Preheim, "MCC at Work in Zaire," *Women's Activity Letter,* July-August 1972.

19. Ngulubi Mazemba, "New Life for All," *AIMM Messenger,* Fall 1976, p. 10.

20. *Ibid.,* p. 8. For a description and analysis of SEDA as a development program, see Fremont Regier, "Ownership: Participation in Planning, Administration, and Operation of a Rural Development Project, Nyanga, Zaire" (Ph.D. thesis, University of Wisconsin-Madison, 1977).

21. Reuben Short, "The Structure of Mission-Church Relationships in the Republic of Zaire," 1972, AIMM files, Elkhart, Ind.

CHAPTER 10

1. Joseph Winfield Fretz, *Pilgrims in Paraguay, The Story of Mennonite Colonization in South America* (Scottdale, Pa.: Herald Press, 1953); Pannabecker, *Open Doors,* pp. 238-47. The most comprehensive and up-to-date study of Mennonites and their mission work in Paraguay has been written by Calvin Redekop and is scheduled to be published soon by Herald Press in the Anabaptist History Series. Redekop made available to the author an early draft of the book manuscript. For a recent brief assessment, see Ron

Ratzlaff, "Our Complex Presence in Paraguay," *Christian Leader,* (12 September 1978), pp. 8-11.

2. Redekop manuscript, chapter 1.

3. "Statut für den Missionsbund 'Licht den Indianern!'" From Calvin Redekop personal collection.

4. *Mennonite Weekly Review,* 25 September and 9 October 1958; A. E. Janzen, *The Moro's Spear* (Hillsboro, Kans.: Board of Missions of the Mennonite Brethren Church, 1962).

5. Jacob A. Loewen, "Research Report on the Question of Settling Lengua and Chulupi Indians in the Paraguayan Chaco" (Hillsboro, Kans., 1 February 1964).

6. Jacob A. Loewen, "Chaco Missionaries and an Anthropologist Cooperate in Mission Research" (Hillsboro, Kans., 1964), pp. 23-24.

7. Miguel Chase Sardi, "The Present Situation of the Indians in Paraguay" in *The Situation of the Indian in South America,* ed. W. Dostal (Geneva: World Council of Churches, 1972), pp. 173-217.

8. See "Declaration of Barbados for the Liberation of the Indians," *International Review of Missions,* July 1973, pp. 268-74.

9. Calvin Redekop, "Mennonite Mission in the Paraguayan Chaco," *International Review of Missions,* July 1973, p. 316.

10. Ernst Harder, interview with the author, 13 September 1978.

11. John Howard Yoder, *The Politics of Jesus* (Grand Rapids: Eerdmans, 1972).

12. The most complete description of the Old Colony Mennonites is Calvin Redekop, *The Old Colony Mennonites, Dilemmas of Ethnic Minority Life* (Baltimore: Johns Hopkins Press, 1969).

13. J. Winfield Fretz, "Report on My Trip to Mexico, 10 August 1944," p. 35, COM archives, Newton, Kans.

14. See the profile of this church by Aaron J Epp in the *Mennonite World Handbook,* ed. Paul N. Kraybill (Lombard, Ill.: Mennonite World Conference, 1978), pp. 230-32.

CHAPTER 11

1. The history of Prophet Mokaleng and the Spiritual Healing Church has not been researched and chronicled. The church gives the year 1923 as its date of origin. This is the year of the prophet's first dream that he was to be a healer. The first church building was constructed at Matsiloje in 1955. The author had some personal contact with this church in Botswana in 1972-73, but even the few details recorded here must be treated as tentative until more complete research is done. There is some information in a report by a Botswana MCC worker: Margaret Gingrich, "Gingrich Report on Independent Churches" (September 1973). See also the 14 June 1973 letter Edwin and Irene Weaver in "Letters from Southern Africa" (Elkhart, Ind.: MCC Southern Africa Task Force, 1974), pp. 21-31. For information on the South African origins of the St. John's Apostolic Church see Bengt Sundkler, *Zulu Zion and Some Swazi Zionists* (London: Oxford University Press, 1976), pp. 79-84.

2. David B. Barrett, *Schism and Renewal in Africa, An Analysis of Six Thousand Contemporary Religious Movements* (Nairobi: Oxford University Press, 1968), pp. 71, 78-79.

3. See Robert C. Mitchell and Harold W. Turner, *A Comprehensive Bibliography of Modern African Religious Movements* (Chicago, Ill.: Northwestern University Press, 1966).

4. Marie-Louise Martin, *Kimbangu, an African Prophet and His Church* (Grand Rapids: Eerdmans, 1975).

5. Harold Fehderau and Clarence Hiebert, "A Visit to Some Kimbanguists in the Congo, 29 January - 5 February 1967," pp. 20, 22, AIMM files, Elkhart, Ind.

6. *Practical Anthropology,* January-February 1966, pp. 13-33.

7. Edwin and Irene Weaver have written two books about their experiences with independent churches in Nigeria and Ghana in West Africa: *The Uyo Story* (Elkhart, Ind.: Mennonite Board of Missions, 1970), and *From Kuku Hill* (Elkhart, Ind.: Institute of Mennonite Studies, 1975).

8. "General Guide Lines/Philosophy of AIMM Work with AIC's," attached to minutes of 18-19 June 1977 meeting of AIMM administrators with staff in Gaborone, Botswana, AIMM files, Elkhart, Ind.

CHAPTER 12

1. Paul I. Dyck, interview with the author, 12 February 1978.

2. S. S. Haury, *Briefe ueber die Ausbreitung des Evangeliums in der Heidenwelt* (Halstead, Kans.: Westlichen Publikations Gesellschaft, 1977), p. 92.

3. Paul N. Kraybill, ed., *Mennonite World Handbook* (Lombard, Ill.: Mennonite World Conference, 1978), pp. 385-86.

4. Haury, *Briefe,* p. 68.

5. See the lectures by David Schroeder, Paul G. Hiebert, Hank B. Kossen, and Albert Widjaja in the Mennonite World Conference *Program and Information* book, pp. 70-95.

6. Haury, *Briefe,* p. 38.

Brief Note on Selected Historical Sources

A starting point for the study of General Conference missions is S. F. Pannabecker's history of the conference, *Open Doors* (1975), which includes three chapters on overseas missions. Pannabecker's volume superceded H. P. Krehbiel's two-volume *History of the Mennonite General Conference* (1898, 1938). E. G. Kaufman covered the developments of North American Mennonite missions in *The Development of the Missionary and Philanthropic Interest Among the Mennonites of North America* (1931). A wealth of statistical information on the conference is in Leland Harder's *General Conference Mennonite Fact Book of Congregational Membership* (1971), and in the sociological study by Harder and J. Howard Kauffman, *Anabaptists Four Centuries Later*. The *Mennonite World Handbook* (1978), edited by Paul Kraybill, is the most recent and most complete compilation of statistical information and historical sketches of Mennonite groups throughout the world.

The standard reference work for Anabaptism-Mennonitism is *The Mennonite Encyclopedia* (4 vols., 1955-59). An invaluable bibliographic tool is the two-volume *Mennonite Bibliography 1631-1961,* compiled by Nelson P. Springer and A. J. Klassen (1977). Two one-volume general histories of Mennonites are C. Henry Smith's *The Story of the Mennonites* (3rd ed., 1950), and C. J. Dyck, ed., *An Introduction to Mennonite History* (1967).

The official depository for historical records of the General Conference Mennonite Church, including the mission board, is the Mennonite Library and Archives at Bethel College, North Newton, Kansas. The MLA documents include valuable personal collections of missionaries and church workers as well as photographs and published materials. The official records of the Congo Inland Mission before 1960, and personnel records of CIM missionaries no longer living, are kept at the library of Bluffton College, Bluffton, Ohio. Current records of the Africa Inter-Mennonite Mission are at the AIMM office in Elkhart, Indiana.

GC Mennonite periodicals are a rich source of missionary reports from overseas as well as material designed to foster the missions spirit in home congregations. The record for the nineteenth century is in a sequence of

German-language periodicals: *Religioser Botschafter* (1852-56), *Christliche Volksblatt* (1856-67), *Mennonitische Friedensbote* (1867-82), and *Christlicher Bundesbote* (1882-1947). The first Mennonite periodical dedicated exclusively to missions was *Nachrichten aus der Heidenwelt* (1885-87), edited by C. J. van der Smissen. An English language publication, *The Mennonite* (1885-   ) eventually became the official English language organ of the conference. Retired missionary P. J. Wiens compiled an extremely valuable card index for articles on missions themes in the *Bundesbote* and other periodicals from the beginnings into the 1930s. This index is kept in the MLA.

Early reports on Congo Inland Mission developments can be found in the Central Conference periodical, *Christian Evangel* (1911-57), and in the Defenseless Mennonite periodicals, *Heilsbote* (Zion's Call), (1897-1921). The official CIM publication was the *Congo Missionary Messenger* (1929-   ), changed to *AIMM Messenger* in 1973. P. H. Richert edited a General Conference *Mission Quarterly* (1924-31). The Women's Missionary Association put out the *Missionary News and Notes* (1926-65), which became *Missions Today* in 1965 and *Window to Mission* in 1974. At various times missionaries on overseas fields have issued their separate newsletters or other publications which are an additional source of information.

Much of the writing about Mennonite missions history has been done by the missionaries themselves. Harold Ratzlaff's master's thesis, "Planting a Church in India" (1950) is the basic secondary source on the history and development of mission and church in India. Missionaries supplied the material for mission anniversary publications, *Twenty-Five Years with God in India* (1929) and *Fellowship in the Gospel* (1950), the latter edited by Ruth Regier Ratzlaff. Samuel T. Moyer was one of the more prolific missionary writers from India. He wrote *With Christ on the Edge of the Jungle* (1941) and *They Heard the Call* (1970). P. A. Penner did not write books, but he left a daily diary for the entire time of his missions service and wrote extensively for periodicals, for personal friends, and for the mission board.

H. J. Brown, founder of the GC China mission, told of his experiences in three books: *Chips of Experience* (1929), *The General Conference China Mennonite Mission* (1940), and *In Japanese Hands* (1943). E. G. Kaufman's view of the China mission, covered in a 55-page appendix to his 1931 book, has a more critical perspective. Two single missionaries, Aganetha Fast and Marie J. Regier, wrote accounts rich in detail and insight. Two of Fast's publications are *Out of My Attic* (1970) and *The Power of Christ's Love in China* (1972). Regier's master's thesis was "Cultural Interpretation in a Local Community in China" (1936), and her B.D. thesis was "Mennonite Teaching and Practice in a Chinese Community" (1950). The last years of *China-Home Bond*, edited by S. F. Pannabecker, tell the story of the final stages of the mission in an exceptionally objective and insightful way. It is most unfortunate that Pannabecker did not finish a history of the China mission before he died in 1977. That task remains to be done.

Two secondary accounts chronicle the development of Congo Inland Mission: William B. Weaver's *Twenty-Five Years of Mission Work in Belgian Congo* (1938), and Melvin J. Loewen's *Three Score, The Story of an Emerging Mennonite Church in Central Africa* (1972). Loewen's book is an abridgement of his Ph.D. dissertation, "The Congo Inland Mission 1911-1961" (1961). The dissertation has a vast amount of information, including statistics on church growth on the various mission stations, which was left out of the book. Levi Keidel's books, *Footsteps to Freedom* (1969) and *War to Be One* (1977), are more successful than most missionary writing in portraying the drama inherent in the encounter of missionaries and nationals.

None of the overseas mission programs started since World War II have become the subject for research and writing to match the scope of Loewen's dissertation and book on Congo Inland Mission. There have been a number of shorter publications to celebrate ten- or twenty-year anniversaries in Japan, Taiwan, and Colombia. Two master's theses which have a wealth of information on the work in Taiwan and Japan are by Sheldon Sawatzky, "The Gateway of Promise: A Study of the Taiwan Mennonite Church and the Factors Affecting its Growth" (1970), and E. Frederick Sprunger, "TEE in Japan: The Feasibility of a Theological Education by Extension Program for the Kyushu Mennonite Church Conference in Japan" (1978). An important volume for understanding the mission in Kyushu is Paul W. Boschman, ed., *Experiments in Church Growth: Japan* (1968). Gerald Stucky described the early work in Colombia in *Colombia's Challenge* (1951).

A valuable tool for finding writings on Mennonites in Latin America is "Mennonites in Latin America, An Annotated Bibliography, 1912-1971," ed. by R. Herbert Minnich, Willard H. Smith, and Wilmar Stahl (1972). The Latin America Mennonite story has benefited from thorough sociological and anthropological investigation, especially in the works of Jacob A. Loewen, "Research Report on the Question of Settling Lengua and Chulupi Indians in the Paraguayan Chaco" (1964); Herb Minnich, *The Mennonite Immigrant Communities in Parana, Brazil* (1970); Calvin Redekop, *The Old Colony Mennonites: Dilemmas of Ethnic Minority Life* (1969); and J. Winfield Fretz, *Pilgrims in Paraguay* (1953). There is much more literature, however, on German Mennonites than on non-German Mennonites in Latin America.

Mennonite missions is a wide open field for historical investigation. A list of potential topics, many barely mentioned or hinted at in this book, could be extended indefinitely. We need up-to-date missionary biographies. We need to evaluate the role of women on the mission fields, in the new churches abroad, and in congregations of North America. It would be helpful to have current church growth studies of all of the mission fields. What were the patterns of financial giving for missions in the churches? the patterns of recruitment of missionaries? What did the missions movement mean for the psychological and social consciousness of North American Mennonites? There is also a need for studies of the dynamics of relationships between missionaries and nationals in the long and often painful transition to local autonomy. The question of Mennonite identity on the mission field should be explored at greater depth. The impact of missions on Mennonite ecumenical involvements has hardly been touched. What was the real meaning of the fundamentalist-modernist division for Mennonite missions? And what does missions history look like when written from the point of view of the receiving peoples?

Another source which needs to be mentioned, if these and other topics are to be addressed adequately, is oral interviews with living participants in the missions movement. The Schowalter Oral History collection at Bethel College has made a small beginning in collecting interviews, but the major work remains to be done, and it should be done soon while older people with rich memories are living. There are in the AIMM archives transcripts of interviews with Africans who experienced the Kwilu rebellion of 1964. These interviews, conducted in the native language and translated into English for transcription, may be a model for what could be done in all countries where Mennonite churches have been planted. In coming decades the writing of the history of Mennonite missions, church plantings, and church growth will, more than ever, need to be undertaken in cooperation and partnership with the newer churches.

List of Acronyms
Used in the Text

AID	Agency for International Development
AIMM	Africa Inter-Mennonite Mission
BIOLA	Bible Institute of Los Angeles
CEDEC	Evangelical Confederation of Colombia
CIM	Congo Inland Mission
CIM	Council on International Mission
CMZA	Zaire Mennonite Church
COM	Commission on Overseas Mission
CPC	Congo Protestant Council
EMB	Evangelical Mennonite Brethren
EMC	Evangelical Mennonite Church
FCC	Federal Council of Churches
FOMCIT	Fellowship of Mennonite Churches in Taiwan
GC	General Conference
GPS	Goals, Priorities, Strategies
KDK	Keihin Dendo Kyoryokukai (Tokyo Area Mennonite Evangelism Cooperative Conference)
KGG	Kobe Garage Group
MB	Mennonite Brethren
MC	(Old) Mennonite Church
MCC	Mennonite Central Committee
ME	Mennonite Encyclopedia
MEDA	Mennonite Economic Development Associates
MELARC	Mennonite Literature and Radio Council
MENCOLDES	Mennonite Colombian Foundation for Development
MENNO	Mennonites Encountering New Neighbors Overseas
MLA	Mennonite Library and Archives, Bethel College, North Newton, Kans.
MMKFP	Mennonite Missions Committee for Paraguay
OMTC	Overseas Missionary Training Center
REACH	Rural Economic Development and Community Health Association
SEDA	Service for Development of Agriculture
TELARC	The Economic Life and Relief Council
UBS	Union Biblical Seminary
UMTI	Union Missionary Training Institute
UTM	Unevangelized Tribes Mission

Index